TRACING YOUR HOUSE HISTORY

A Guide for Family Historians

Gill Blanchard

Pen & Sword
FAMILY HISTORY

First published in Great Britain in 2013 by
PEN & SWORD FAMILY HISTORY
an imprint of
Pen & Sword Books Ltd
47 Church Street
Barnsley
South Yorkshire
S70 2AS

ISBN 978 1 84884 254 0

A CIP catalogue record for this book is available from the British Library.

Typeset in Palatino and Optima by
Phoenix Typesetting, Auldgirth, Dumfriesshire

Printed and bound in England by
CPI Group (UK) Ltd, Croydon, CR0 4YY

Pen & Sword Books Ltd incorporates the imprints of
Pen & Sword Aviation, Pen & Sword Family History, Pen & Sword Maritime, Pen & Sword Military, Pen & Sword Discovery, Wharncliffe Local History, Wharncliffe True Crime, Wharncliffe Transport, Pen & Sword Select, Pen & Sword Military Classics, Leo Cooper, The Praetorian Press, Remember When, Seaforth Publishing and Frontline Publishing

For a complete list of Pen & Sword titles please contact
PEN & SWORD BOOKS LIMITED
47 Church Street, Barnsley, South Yorkshire, S70 2AS, England
E-mail: enquiries@pen-and-sword.co.uk
Website: www.pen-and-sword.co.uk

TRACING YOUR HOUSE HISTORY

FAMILY HISTORY FROM PEN & SWORD

Birth, Marriage and Death Records
David Annal and Audrey Collins

Tracing Your Channel Islands Ancestors
Marie-Louise Backhurst

Tracing Your Yorkshire Ancestors
Rachel Bellerby

Tracing Your East Anglian Ancestors
Gill Blanchard

Tracing Your Royal Marine Ancestors
Richard Brooks and Matthew Little

Tracing Your Pauper Ancestors
Robert Burlison

Tracing Your Huguenot Ancestors
Kathy Chater

Tracing Your Labour Movement Ancestors
Mark Crail

Tracing Your Army Ancestors
Simon Fowler

A Guide to Military History on the Internet
Simon Fowler

Tracing Your Northern Ancestors
Keith Gregson

Tracing Your Ancestors Through Death Records
Celia Heritage

Your Irish Ancestors
Ian Maxwell

Tracing Your Scottish Ancestors
Ian Maxwell

Tracing Your London Ancestors
Jonathan Oates

Tracing Your Tank Ancestors
Janice Tait and David Fletcher

Tracing Your Air Force Ancestors
Phil Tomaselli

Tracing Your Secret Service Ancestors
Phil Tomaselli

Tracing Your Criminal Ancestors
Stephen Wade

Tracing Your Police Ancestors
Stephen Wade

Tracing Your Jewish Ancestors
Rosemary Wenzerul

Fishing and Fishermen
Martin Wilcox

Tracing Your Canal Ancestors
Sue Wilkes

Tracing Your Lancashire Ancestors
Sue Wilkes

CONTENTS

PREFACE

The place we call home is more than just a structure. Its style and design reflect the personality and personal interests of the owners, designers and builders. It is also affected by fashion, architectural and artistic influences, the geology of area it was built in, and even politics and religion.

This book will help you to trace the history of your home, the people who lived in it and its local and social history whatever its age, size and origins. The term 'house' is used throughout as a generic term for any type of building that people live in, although the sources and resources explored can be used for researching other types of building or places associated with your ancestors.

This guide focuses on English and Welsh research as there are some major differences in resources available for Ireland and Scotland and, in the case of Scotland, how land was held. Northern Ireland is included because it does have some records in common with England and Wales.

Whilst no guide should ignore national resources the vast majority of your research will be conducted at your local library or record office. This guide explores those local resources in depth as well as directing the researcher to what can be found at The National Archives and online. It also makes the research process understandable, and in the process demystifies some of the language and documents you will come across.

As a result this is a holistic guide on how to gather evidence from buildings; understand the important of architectural changes and influences of local craftspeople; explore the local area in order to place modern buildings in their historical landscape and find and use documentary sources. Discovering who lived in your property and how and why a building has changed use over time are also absolutely crucial to investigating its history.

Each section within this book has a 'finding' section, which lists useful addresses, websites and recommended publications. The introductory section provides details of where to go and complementary websites.

A major step is to physically date your building and place it within a time period. This is why a chapter on dating your home, which looks at architecture and how houses have developed over time, comes first. Within this are some tips on what to look for when 'reading' a building and other resources for developing this skill.

Another major section is 'Building up Knowledge of Your Local Area'. I have deliberately not called this just 'local history', as tracing the history of a house is more than just looking at how it has evolved physically over time. Whether new or old, it is all about the place a building stands in, and the people who built it, made changes and shaped its personality. This is an organic process which helps create a building's character or 'feel'. This chapter encourages you to put your home in its local context and in doing so you may uncover relevant information and expand your research in all sorts of directions.

Researching the history of your house will take you on a journey through a huge range of documents and other resources locally, nationally and online. Whilst some types of records are complex and difficult to understand or read, even the most seemingly straightforward can throw up problems and questions. The documents and resources section introduces you to each of the main types of records you may use. It starts with a brief overview of the variety of records that can be used to discover your home's history and then looks at each resource in more depth alphabetically. There is also a timeline of key historical events and the creation of documents relevant to researching the history of your home.

Before beginning your research it is vitally important to identify your house on a modern map and take it with you when visiting archives, as the landscape is likely to have changed over time. Note on the map where it is in relation to prominent landmarks such as a church or pub that has stood there for some time. When comparing it with old maps look at how roads may have changed shape, size and direction, and whether the street on which it was built corresponds with old field boundaries.

People are what make a house a home, and it is by tracing the men, women and children who lived in them that we find out the most. Investigating the history of your house therefore involves a certain amount of genealogical and local history research. For instance, census returns will give you details of who these people were, when and where they were born, and their occupations. This in turn may lead you to other resources such as wills, which may give you more detail about the property and bring the people who once lived or worked in it to life.

Genealogical research is a huge topic in itself. If you have not done much research yourself, you will find it helpful to invest in a good beginner's guide and guides that relate specifically to your own geographical area, such as the Pen and Sword series *Tracing Your East Anglian Ancestors* et al. These will explore sources in your area that go beyond the basics, many of which will be directly relevant to your house history research as well as the people connected with it.

Following the sections on different resources is a segment on presentation and writing. The Resource Directory at the end includes contact details for all major archives, local history libraries, museums and organizations, websites and places of interest mentioned in the text.

Throughout the book I have used examples from my own research to illustrate the types of information that can be found and how to use different documents. Because I am based in Norfolk and work primarily in the eastern region, there is a bias towards this area. Nevertheless, once you know what to look for and what to expect from a source you can apply that knowledge anywhere in the country.

Unless mentioned otherwise, all the examples referred to throughout this book are taken from documents, indexes, transcripts and catalogues from The National Archives, local record offices, and Access to Archives. Most of the work in this book has been gathered through extensive work in East Anglian archives. Some research was conducted further afield, with examples from Surrey, Sussex, Buckinghamshire, Lincolnshire, Kent, Wiltshire, Yorkshire and County Durham, amongst other places.

ACKNOWLEDGEMENTS

To my family, in every sense of the word. In memory of my brother Séan Blanchard, 1958–2008, political activist and writer; my father Bryan Edwin Blanchard, 1931–2011, who always stopped to look at buildings as 'wonderful pieces of engineering'; and my mother Bridget Christina (Chris) Blanchard (née Naughton), 1928–2012, who stressed the importance of always working hard and helping others.

INTRODUCTION

The commonest questions people ask are 'Where do I start?' and 'How do I go about researching the history of my home?' In some ways these are one and the same thing, as the steps you need to take cannot be neatly parcelled up into defined or rigid blocks. You will look at one set of documents, move on to another, talk to people and go back to the documents you have already looked at. Whilst it is advisable to start in the present and work back step-by-step from what you know, you may find that in practice your research doesn't always follow such a neat line. You may dip sideways or come forwards because a character amongst the owners and occupiers catches your interest, or you want to know more about how the building was used in a particular time period.

You may find you get stuck with your research and cannot find out anything beyond a certain point. In this case you may find that changing the emphasis of your research into the background of particular owners or occupiers, the local and social history of the area, or the factors which influenced its building style gives you a different perspective and allows the hunt to continue. This was the case with a house in Boxford in Suffolk which developed into a community history through investigation of nearby properties.

Another example is an Elizabethan house in Norfolk that could only be traced back to the early nineteenth century due to a lack of documentary resources. The house and its immediate neighbours were built on freehold land so ownership could not be established through manorial records. When the house was sold in 1888 the deeds included the names of the current tenant and a previous one. They stated the house was being sold by the widow of a man who had bought it in 1849, but did not say whom he bought it from. The owner's will was written a month after its purchase and in it he mentions he had just bought property in this village, and that it was being leased out.

These small scraps of information were enough to find out more about the owners and occupiers from the nineteenth century onwards through census returns; electoral registers; wills; trade directories; sales particulars and births, deaths and marriages. These sources revealed that the house had been lived in by a vicar, a grocer and a dealer in fancy goods, as well as being used as a school and an antique shop at different times.

Whilst some of the occupants could be identified on the census returns, it was not possible to find out who owned it before 1849. This was because there was a clerical error on a tithe apportionment of 1840. This would normally list owners and occupiers, but had omitted most of the people on this street even though their plot numbers are shown on the accompanying map. Casting our search wider also failed despite there being an estate survey from 1803 which listed many other owners and occupiers on the same street, but merely listed this plot as belonging to *'sundry owners'*.

In this case an architectural assessment established that the house was built in the 1500s. The quality of the building materials, size and its design clearly indicates it was built for wealthy residents. As a result the history has two distinct strands. The first is the physical history of the building. The second is the people who lived in it from the 1840s onwards. Investigating the social and local history indicated that the early owners were probably tradesmen of high social status who benefitted from being at the heart of an important trade route from King's Lynn to towns and villages inland.

Chapter 1

WHERE TO FIND INFORMATION AND RESOURCES

Knowing where to go to find information is just as important as reading and understanding documents. Information on the history of your house will come from a range of historical documents; indexes; transcripts; online resources and records. Before you start looking at documents you need to find out where these are likely to be kept and what to expect when you visit a record office or use an online resource.

Some of the terminology used to refer to places and the collections of documents they hold can be confusing. An archive can either be a collection of documents, usually referred to as 'records', or the place (repository) where those records are kept. The terms 'archives' and 'record offices' tend to be used interchangeably. This is partly because most places where records are stored were traditionally known as record offices. There has been a gradual move towards renaming them archive centres because most hold more than just paper records. Nevertheless, within this book I generally use the term 'record offices' as this is what the majority are still called.

You may wonder why you can only find certain items in one place and not another. That is because there is no centralized location for records. Every county has at least one record office where they take care of documents from that area, and a local studies or history library (sometimes combined), whilst The National Archives holds national collections. Record offices holding church (diocesan) records have a wider spread as church jurisdictions did not follow county lines. Only a small percentage of record office resources can be found online. This means the majority of your research will be conducted locally using original records or microfilm and microfiche copies. Most record offices require proof of identity, operate a strict 'no bags' policy in the search room and have limited space, so it is essential to check opening times and whether you need to book in advance.

The growth of the internet has made it an extremely useful tool for research. The main groups of original records that can be found online are census returns; indexes to births, marriages and deaths; some parish registers; wills and their indexes; directories and some maps. One example is London Lives **www.londonlives.org**, which has a free searchable collection of manuscripts from eight archives, including parish and taxation records. Other sites enable you to check for documentary references in advance of a visit to a record office. Most of these websites are aimed at family or local historians, but there is an obvious overlap. Some of the most useful are listed in the 'Finding' section below.

Indexes, Transcripts and Catalogues

Every record office and archives centre has catalogues and indexes of the records they hold in a variety of formats. Very few record offices have one single list of everything they hold. The most traditional format is individual reference cards, usually arranged alphabetically under surnames, place names and subjects such as maps. Some have separate printed or electronic catalogues listing specific collections such as the business records of a local organization, or particular types of records such as brewery records. Many of these will cross-reference to each other. The National Archives has its own system based on 'class lists'. Catalogues for each class have to be checked and there are a number of helpful leaflets and guides to these as well as online guidance.

Indexes do not necessarily list everything and the amount of detail involved varies from record office to office. Some will summarize information contained within documents, whilst others simply cross-reference to other lists or collections of documents. These in turn can be anything from a single sheet of paper or parchment to hundreds of bundles or volumes. All archives will have a backlog of collections which are waiting to be listed (known as 'accessions'), and it is worth checking whether there are any for your area.

Finding Archives, Record Offices, Local History Libraries, Heritage, Local and Family History Organizations and Online Resources

The National Archives, Ruskin Avenue, Kew, Richmond, Surrey, TW9 4DU
www.nationalarchives.gov.uk

National Library of Wales, Aberystwyth, Ceredigion, Wales, SY23 3BU
www.lgc.org.uk

The Public Record Office for Northern Ireland (PRONI), 2 Titanic Boulevard, Belfast, BT3 9HQ

www.proni.gov.uk

Access to Archives (A2A) **www.nationalarchives.gov.uk/a2a** is a database of catalogues contributed by hundreds of record offices, searchable by name, place and topic. For example, when looking for details of a property in Dorset, a search for the occupier's name provided a reference to two messuages, a tenement, field names, deeds, plans from 1870 and 1871 and copies of various wills from the eighteenth and nineteenth centuries.

Although primarily a family history website the links and resources found on GENUKI **www.genuki.org.uk** are equally relevant to house history research. It is an umbrella site to information across the country arranged by county.

There are still vast numbers of references which can only be found by searching indexes and catalogues within a particular record office. The National Register of Archives contains information on the location of archives across the country.

www.nationalarchives.gov.uk/nra

The National Monuments Record Centre (NMR) has a huge collection of material relevant to property research. The Royal Commission on Historical Monuments (RCHME) and English Heritage archives can also been found at the NMR Centre, Great Western Village, Kemble Drive, Swindon, SN2 2GZ **www.english-heritage.org.uk/professional/archives-and-collections/nmr**

Cyndi's List has thousands of worldwide family and local history links and useful information.

www.cyndislist.com

Archives Wales has a very good introductory guide to tracing house histories in Wales.

www.archiveswales.org.uk/index

Chapter 2

DATING YOUR HOME AND HOUSE STYLES

It is perfectly possible to trace the history of a house without looking at its architecture in any great depth. This, to my mind, means missing out on an essential part of its history. How and why your home was built and what materials were used in its construction all intermingle with local and national influences to play a part in how your building's personality developed. Dating a building therefore allows you to physically step back in time and put your home into its historical context as well as inform which direction you take with your research.

When looking at your home you should ask yourself questions. What shaped its architecture? What effect did various art, design and craft movements have? Were there particular local factors, or political, social or religious influences? How do you know if a building has been recycled from a former use, such as a pub, shop, factory, farm building, mill, workhouse, hospital, rectory or chapel? What stood there before?

It might seem obvious, but note what type of house or home it is – terraced, detached, semi-detached, a flat or maisonette – as even this may have changed over time. Take photographs of the house and close-ups of any interesting, intriguing or significant features so you can look at them closely and compare with other buildings and against illustrations.

My own method of working is to create timelines in a table or spreadsheet on which I plot when alterations and additions have occurred, include details about the people who lived in the house and add local and national events to give context. I add brief notes about what has been done and found, what still needs to be done and questions I want to follow up on. This means I have a working crib sheet with me at all times which highlights gaps in knowledge, problematic areas of research and anomalies, and acts as a check list.

Houses change according to the needs of the people who live and work in them. For instance, what many people consider the archetypal English cottage is often a subdivision of a bigger farmhouse. Old houses may have had their interiors radically remodelled so that no original features are visible, whilst reproductions are often used in older houses to replace something damaged or removed. Newer houses may have older fireplaces or doors that originally belonged elsewhere. This can be seen in many Victorian houses which had their fireplaces blocked up when electric or gas heating was installed, only for more recent owners to unblock them and install Victorian fireplaces they have bought from elsewhere.

If yours is a listed building then you will already know something about its structure. The first law passed to preserve old or interesting buildings was in 1882. Following a number of other Acts, the 1944 Town and Country Planning Act enabled buildings to be graded by importance. These are: Grade 1 – preserved from demolition under all circumstances; Grade 2 – can only be demolished under exceptional circumstances and

Grade 3 – less important. All buildings built before 1700 are listed, as are most up to 1840 if in any kind of original condition. Those built after 1840 are only listed if they are especially interesting. Even if your home is not listed, other listed buildings in your area may be useful for comparative purposes and local history.

A significant percentage of all British houses are over fifty years old and housing styles and building techniques have changed enormously over the last five hundred years. Many buildings have been altered, added to and extended so their original details remain hidden. To date a building therefore involves detective work looking at brick styles, the type of doorway or stairs, rooflines and other features. Features to check on the front of a building are the overall style of the façade; any contradictory features; what material it is built of; roof shape, style and materials; window size, shape and style; window panes; the style of door and fanlight if there is one; size of chimney stack and number of pots and any other features.

Building alterations and the repositioning of windows or doors can disguise an older building, but the ground plan – the way in which a building is laid out – can still give an indication of the time period in which it was built. Other clues might lie in the name or initials carved into brick, stone or lintels. Even though roofs are likely to have been replaced more than once, if you are fortunate then some original timbers will survive. Alternatively, their shape may provide pointers, such as a steep pitch being an indication it may have once been thatched. It is, however, important to be aware of possible exceptions such as toll houses. These were generally built with four sides to allow a clear view of the junctions where they were placed. As a result they typically had very steep pitched roofs to make it easier to cut and hang tiles to fit.

Bricks tell their own story. Look at the way the bricks are laid. Their size, shape and colour can provide clues to their geographical origin and age. If, for example, a house is built from stone, a narrow course of stone above the ground-floor lintels could mean additional floors were added later. Another clue is an interruption or change in a decorative pattern. Stone can also be dated by size, shape, colour and quality.

You may find that recycled materials have been used in parts of your building or that remnants from earlier eras remain. A Victorian house I used to live in had an old gas light fitting and a telephone junction box that had probably not been used for over thirty years. Whilst some of the floorboards in the same house appeared original, the shape and colour of others indicated that they were added later, even though they were roughly the same age. You may even find physical reminders of much earlier buildings, such as rubble infill or bricks, stone and tiles from a nearby church, priory, abbey or Roman camp that fell out of use hundreds of years ago.

An example of recycling materials from different periods and other

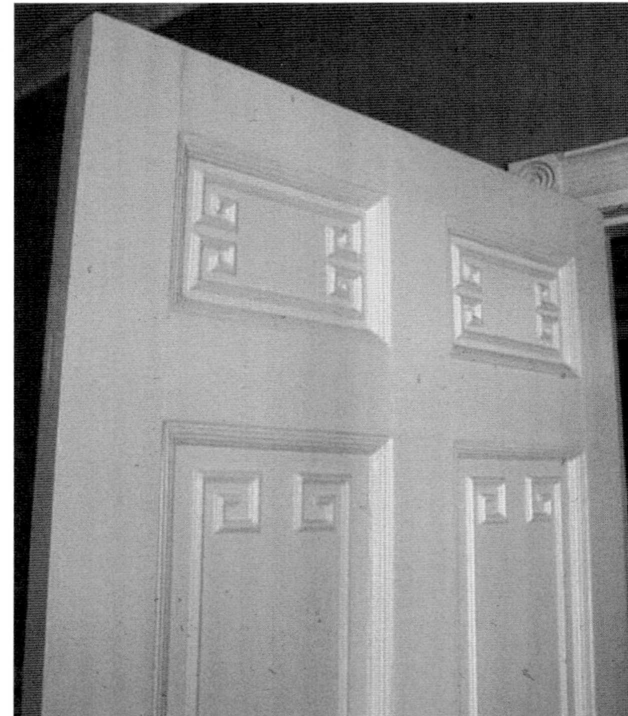

Modern door replicating a Georgian style and an original Georgian door.

buildings was discovered on an eighteenth-century house in North Norfolk. An architectural assessment identified cornerstone, a plinth and infill of reused ashlar limestone. Given the shelly nature of this particular stone it was probably quarried at Barnac near Stamford, a quarry that was exhausted by the end of the sixteenth century. It is very rare to find stone of this quality and workmanship in a domestic building and it was certainly reused, with the most likely source a nearby abbey easily reached by river.

Renovation work inside the same house had uncovered a Gothic-style sixteenth-century brick arch leading from the front part of the house to the rear. The arch has a molded groove on the front face and the remains of the door hinges which can still be seen to the rear of the arch. This suggests that the door opened into a rear extension no longer there and that this room was of some importance. The style and quality of the arch indicate that it probably also came from the remains of the nearby abbey.

It is important to remember that with older buildings it is the well-built ones that survive and they almost certainly once belonged to someone reasonably prosperous. As poor-quality housing tends not to last, the simple fact that a building does survive can in itself be a clue to age and status.

Investigating what a building has been used for in the past and the occupations of those who lived in it can lead you to records which will tell you more. Whilst it may be obvious if it was a former factory, other uses are not always so clear. For instance, purpose-built parsonages did not become the norm until the nineteenth century and many a schoolteacher ran a small school from their home, whilst a house occupied by a blacksmith or dressmaker could have doubled as their workplace.

Size, shape, status and condition can change over time. One property investigated was provisionally dated by estate agents as built in the late 1790s to early 1800s. The deeds, which began in 1808, appeared to support this. An architectural assessment revealed that whilst the most recent section did date from this period, another section behind a Georgian façade was much older. This can be seen in the lack of symmetry and thickness of walls, an exterior wall and window which had become part of the interior and some brickwork on the rear of the building dating from the early to mid–1700s. There was evidence of much older structures having once stood against the garden wall. With this knowledge more documentary research was conducted into manorial records and wills, which took its ownership back to 1740.

Many buildings are modelled on earlier styles, or use a mix of features from different eras. In some areas certain styles remained fashionable long after they were superseded elsewhere due to economic and practical factors. In the Cotswolds, for instance, economic decline meant Tudor features such as mullioned windows and gabled dormers were still in use

(Pages 10 and 11)
Older wall and original exterior window behind a Georgian façade. Brickwork dating from early to mid–1700s on rear of building.

into the eighteenth century when other areas had stopped using them. Another example is the widespread use of pargetting on timber buildings from at least the Tudor period in East Anglia. Pargetting occurred when the timber and wattle and daub panels were covered in plaster which was then combed into decorative patterns. East Anglia had enormous wealth built on the wool trade, but little stone, so pargetting was a way of showing off wealth and status. This technique survived many generations after the collapse of the wool trade as there was little money to replace it with new materials.

Sometimes it is the small details which provide clues. In *A Lust for Window Sills* Harry Mount describes how in London, if a window sill is over four inches deep the building must have been built after 1709, when anti-fire legislation was passed. You may be fortunate enough to find items left behind by previous occupants that help with dating and establishing what a building was used for. Eighteenth-century tools uncovered in a house in Biddenden in Kent indicated that at least one person who lived there was a shoemaker. In contrast, the naturist magazines, rent book, children's books given as Sunday school prizes and instruction books for railway employees found in the loft of a former council house in Norwich perhaps reflect the occupier's personal life.

Windows are equally important. You need to look at their overall shape and the size and shape of panes and how they open. Whether windows and doors are in proportion to each other or in odd places may indicate that the building has been modernized or built in different stages. Other physical features to look out for include blind windows, where there is a window shape bricked up. This can mean it was filled in following the introduction of window tax in 1696. In contrast, projecting bay windows became popular after the repeal of the window tax in 1851. However, keep in mind other factors such as rooms being extended or their use being changed.

Finding out what regional styles and building materials were used in your area is extremely important, particularly with houses built before the mid-nineteenth century when building practices and materials became more homogenized. For example, flint was widely used in buildings in counties such as Suffolk and Norfolk as it is hard, durable and

'Jacob's Tenement' on Swan Street in Boxford in Suffolk.

adaptable, whilst its irregular shape made it very suitable as a mass walling material when laid in a lime mortar. Once knapped, its glossy black silica proved immensely popular as an external decoration, particularly when set against lighter coloured stones.

Distinctive regional variations still play a part in modern developments, such as in Adderbury in Oxfordshire, where local materials and traditional building styles have been used so that the modern houses blend with the old. Nearby features such as roads and rivers can also be significant. One pub in Edgefield in Norfolk was built at the main crossroads into the village, presumably to catch passing trade.

The ages of some buildings are easily identifiable as they include a date plaque, or one which refers to an earlier building on the same site. In Boxford in Suffolk, a seventeenth-century house in Swan Street has the following words on the door: *'Jacob's Tenement stood here in the year of Our Lord 1454'*. Others have coats of arms or fire insurance plaques which can be dated.

Other plaques commemorate people who lived in a place. The English Heritage Blue Plaques can only be put up on the building a person lived in. Many local history societies have their own schemes to honour notable people and events, many of which are actively supported by local councils. Some note details about a building's history, as in numbers 23 to 25 King Street in King's Lynn, which describes how a seventeenth-century house was built on the site of two medieval hall house plots, then later remodelled. The English Heritage website **www.english-heritage.org.uk/blueplaques** has details of the Blue Plaque scheme. Or contact the Blue Plaques Team at English Heritage, 23 Savile Row, London W1S 2ET.

Some buildings can be dated by their names or the names of the street or area they were built on. Names such as Balaclava, Nelson, or Pitt Street, Victoria Close, Garibaldi Row or Nightingale Terrace often reflected patriotic feelings or made reference to historical figures and events. Others have links to local people or industries such as Iron Row in Ebbw Vale in Wales, which takes its name from the ironworks founded in the village in the eighteenth century. However, it is important to check whether or not the road was already there and simply renamed.

It is important not to underestimate the influence of religion on domestic architecture and building styles. The design, building techniques, shapes and carvings on cathedrals and churches shaped every other building well into the 1900s, either directly or indirectly. The building of cathedrals and churches required a vast investment of money, resources and skills, with many taking decades to be completed. The people working on them refined their skills and tried out new materials and techniques (not always successfully, if the number of church and cathedral towers falling down is anything to go by). In turn, these skills,

The last of the nineteenth-century houses that stood on Iron Row in Ebbw Vale.

designs and influences filtered down into domestic buildings.

The placement of other buildings in relation to the church was highly significant up to around the late 1700s. The manor house was almost always opposite or very close by. Other wealthy and socially prominent parishioners built their houses near to the church and manor house as a reflection of their status. This in turn influenced the location of pubs and market places.

Most building designs were created by master masons and builders. Some men built on an interest in architecture gained through studying the classics when travelling on their grand tours. The Royal Institute of Architects was founded in 1834, but there were few professionally trained architects before the late nineteenth century, after it began to be taught in universities.

I've dedicated a whole section of this book to learning about your neighbourhood, but it is also worth mentioning here. Discovering who might have built your home, what influenced them and whether it is part of a city suburb or a growing industrial village can assist with dating it. Other buildings in an area can also provide insights. A merchant's house in Lincoln not only gives you a glimpse of how people lived at that time, but its style will also reflect their practical needs. That stately home a couple of miles away may seem far distant in terms of size and status, but the features its architects and builders tried out will have filtered down to other buildings nearby. The influence of incomers can be seen in different styles, whilst people who travelled on the Continent and elsewhere brought back artifacts, art and architectural styles.

Even if your home is modern, or no remains exist of the place your ancestors lived, other buildings in the area will give you insights into how yours has developed and what might have been there in the past. Modern buildings still have a story to tell through their design and construction. Your investigation will take you into the history of the site, why particular styles are popular, the general landscape, or even just the building's name or the name of the street on which it stands. Questions to ask include why it was built; what influenced its construction; was there a reason why those particular materials were used and is there any significance in its shape, location, the way it faces or the colour of bricks? This was the case with a 1970s house on a street called Orchard Way, whose owner wanted to know why it was given that name, whether there had ever been an orchard there and who owned it.

Finding out more about Architects

Colvin is the biographical dictionary of architects and can be found in reference libraries. See also the *Dictionary of National Biography* for information on the best known. Even if the architect of your home is not identifiable you will discover likely influences as the architects of prominent houses are well documented.

Some records relating to locally-based architects are held in local archives and local history libraries. These often include plans and drawings of buildings they worked on. This was the case with Sidney French, a small-scale building developer and architect who built houses in the Cambridge area in the late nineteenth and early twentieth centuries. A profile of his career in the *Cambridge Independent Press* on 24 October 1930 was located at Cambridge library. This described French as 'tall, grey-haired and slim of build'. Sidney's interests in housing and rating problems were noted, as were details of his hobbies, wife and children. This information was supplemented by research into census returns, local trade directories and telephone books, which provided further details of where he lived and worked.

Finding out More about Dating a Building

There are a number of useful books and internet guides to architecture and dating buildings. I am particularly fond of the books by Trevor Yorke on the interior and exterior architectural features of houses in different eras. His excellent introductory guide is *British Architectural Styles: An Easy Reference Guide* (Countryside Books, 2008) which includes detailed drawings.

Tracing the History of Houses by Bill Breckton and Jeffrey Palmer (Countryside Books, 2nd Ed., 2000) is very strong on architectural styles and how houses have developed over time. It is well illustrated.

For more information on the development of towns and town planning see *The Making of English Towns. 2000 years of evolution* by David W. Lloyd (Victor Gollancz Ltd, 1992).

Architecture for Dummies by Deborah K. Dietsch (John Wiley & Sons, 2007) provides an excellent overview in a simple and easy-to-follow manner.

Pevsner architectural guides are the 'bible' for architectural historians, both amateur and professional. Started in 1951 by Sir Nikolaus Pevsner, they provide a guide to the most significant buildings in Britain and are still being published today. Their descriptions of places and buildings of interest give insights into the architectural history of all areas. A joint venture by the Pevsner guides and Buildings Books Trust describes regional variations, a glossary of terms and pictures of architectural features at **www.lookingatbuildings.org**.

County guides such as the Shell series published between 1933 and 1984, which were aimed at holiday-makers, provide an easily accessible introduction to places and buildings. Some local history libraries have copies, and second-hand copies can often be found in bookshops and at auctions.

A Lust for Window Sills by Harry Mount is an entertaining guide to architectural history which includes useful dating tips.

A very helpful book is *How To Read Buildings: A crash course in architecture* by Carol Davidson Cragoe (Herbert Press, 2008)

There are many books, websites, television shows and museums which illustrate the way in which people lived in the past, right down to furnishings and fixtures.

Listings of architectural historians can be found in the *Institution of Historic Building Conservation Yearbook* (copies in most reference libraries or from IHBS, Jubilee House, High Street, Tisbury, Wiltshire, SP3 6HA). Some record offices have contact details of local experts or historic buildings groups whose volunteers investigate the history of local buildings.

There are a growing number of websites which can help with dating buildings and understanding architectural developments. The Images of England website **www.imagesofengland.org.uk** lists all listed structures and includes many pictures. This gives the century in which they were built, their construction, and sometimes their previous owners, especially if they were involved in the construction or significant alterations in any way.

Building History has masses of information on architectural and building history of all kinds: **www.buildinghistory.org**.

The Builder is a journal published from 1842 to 1966. This includes much contemporary material on building materials, styles, debates, projects and wider influences. The first ten volumes can be found online **www.bodley.ox.ac.uk.ilej**.

There are several major organizations and local groups and societies that will be able to help you with dating and understanding how your building has evolved over time and putting it in its environmental context.

The National Monuments Record Centre, Great Western Village, Kemble Drive, Swindon, SN2 2G2, has much information on older buildings of all kinds. For Wales see also the Comisiwn Brenhinol Henebion Cymru – the Royal Commission on the Ancient and Historical Monuments of Wales, Plas Crug, Aberystwyth, Ceredigion, SY23 1NJ.

The BBC's *Concise History of British Architecture* provides helpful background information **www.bbc.co.uk/history/society_culture/architecture_01.shtml**.

Hidden House History has a useful historical timeline and a list of resources for researching its history, case studies and archived questions and answers **www.hiddenhousehistory.co.uk**.

The National Trust has lots of information about different historical periods in relation to building styles **www.nationaltrust.org.uk**.

Period Property has sections on different types of buildings and information on architectural features **www.periodproperty.co.uk/information.shtml**.

The Society for the Protection of Ancient Buildings has a series of technical Question and Answer pages which provide a lot of general historical information on buildings **www.spab.org.uk**.

The Bricks and Brass website includes a useful dating tool which can help with establishing the date of a building **www.bricksandbrass.co.uk/desroom/bedroom/bedsochist.htm**.

Chapter 3

ARCHITECTURAL STYLES IN ENGLAND

What follows is an overview of how buildings in England and Wales have developed and the key changes which have affected their design, building styles and interiors. Thanks go to Norfolk architectural historian and tutor, Dr Sarah Pearson, who provided the original outline and much guidance and tuition on architectural history generally.

One confusing element in any discussion of architectural style is that historians and architectural historians often describe the same period differently. Whilst the British and French custom is to name architectural styles after a reigning monarch (Elizabethan, Jacobean etc.) these do not always correspond exactly with the period those monarchs reigned. There might also be more than one architectural style within one time period, or overlaps with others, as styles obviously did not just stop being used, or being popular, when a new monarch came to the throne. Other styles are more fluid in relation to dates so can only be approximated. For example, the Georgian period runs from 1720 to 1840, during which time there were four kings called George. However, between 1790 and 1830 a distinct style known as Regency also developed, associated with the Prince Regent who went on to become King George IV. To confuse matters the Queen Anne style did not develop during the reign of Queen Anne, who died in 1714, but between 1870 and 1910. The reason for this is that the architecture and furniture in this later period was heavily influenced by the earlier genre.

Before industrialization, fashions took time to spread, so new styles adopted in London might not reach country areas for several decades. Very few people could afford to totally replace a home, so fashionable changes tended to be adaptations of existing buildings, involving changing the frontage or adding an extension. A common example is the Georgian façades found on many houses that pre-date that era.

Prehistoric to Norman Buildings

The earliest buildings were usually made of timber. Most such houses were circular, with thatched roofs with openings to let out smoke from a fire, and grouped within defensive stockades. Under the Romans brick and stone became more widely used, at least for the rich. This also influenced the shape of buildings, with locals copying their rectangular-shaped buildings.

Once the Romans withdrew from Britain, an Anglo-Saxon style emerged. The Anglo-Saxons were skilled in working with timber and their great hall designs for the rich continued to be used well into the Middle Ages. The Anglo-Saxon hall house was a series of bays – rectangular spaces – leading out from an entrance in a line with supporting roof rafters laid on top. Gradually, upper sections for the owner and family were added on to a raised platform or dais at the opposite end to the entrance. By the eleventh and twelfth centuries many halls were adapted and extended to provide storerooms and a separate kitchen. The way in which these homes were built influenced what came for hundreds of years afterwards. Some of the best reconstructions of these early buildings are at the Anglo-Saxon village at West Stow in Suffolk, the Chiltern Open Air Museum in Buckinghamshire and the Weald and Downland Open Air Museum at Singleton near Chichester in Sussex.

Medieval Homes, 1154–1485

Towards the end of the twelfth century a few stone houses began to be built, often called 'King John's Houses' as many originated during his reign. Living accommodation was usually on the upper floor, known as the hall or solar, supported on stone columns from the floor below and accessed by outside stone stairs. Examples are Boothby Pagnell Manor House in Lincolnshire and the Jew's House in Lincoln, both dating from the twelfth century.

The simplest homes in the medieval period had just one room with a central hearth, no windows and smoke escaping through a hole in the roof or gable. Walls might be built in timber, turf, stone or clay. This type of dwelling was common well into the Tudor period, with some still appearing up until the 1700s.

Cruck buildings became popular from the twelfth century. They take their name from the crucks used in their construction. These are pairs of curved or angled oak timbers set around twelve to sixteen feet apart and jointed to form an arch, which support the roof. Each pair was usually formed by halving a tree, so they are often symmetrical and were strengthened with jointed beams. The smallest cottages had two pairs of crucks, one at each end. Larger cottages repeated these pairs roughly every sixteen feet. This span was called a bay.

This design meant that the interior was opened up as aisle posts were no longer needed to support the roof. The walls of cruck houses were often made of wattle and daub panels – a net made of hazel wands woven

A timber-framed building.

with reeds and branches then matted (daubed) with horsehair, clay and dung. When the crucks were painted black and the wattle and daub in white the finished house took on a magpie look (also seen on later box-framed houses). Some wattle and daub panels were replaced later by lines of bricks set at decorative angles, known as brick noggin. The introduction of brick or stone chimney stacks in the fifteenth and sixteenth centuries allowed an extra storey to be added to the upper part of the building.

Box frames (also called timber frames) from this period are more common in the south and east of England. They are essentially a rectangular open box made of timbers. The rafters are prevented from splaying by cross beams which make a triangle with the rafter. Its advantage over the cruck frame was that it was easy to add extra storeys before the roof went on. The disadvantage was the need for a tie beam to counteract

Jettied house with decorative carvings.

outward pressure, which created an obstruction. One solution was to tie the roof at a higher level by using a collar beam with braces and struts to reduce the pressure.

An H-plan cross-wing design gradually developed, in which the hall formed the bar of the letter H. These houses usually had two storeys, with a chamber over the pantry and buttery and a main room or solar over the 'high' end room. A variation on this, which emerged in the fourteenth century, is the Wealden house, mainly associated with Kent, Surrey and Sussex. The Wealden house had a central hall open to the roof and flanked by end rooms on two floors. The top floor extended outward on jetties and many of the jetties had decorative carvings on the exposed ends.

Tudor Housing, 1485–1603

The Tudor period saw two major influences on housing styles and building techniques, mainly due to increased wealth and a big increase in population after the decimation caused by the plagues of the fourteenth and fifteenth centuries. The large open medieval hall buildings gradually died out as people wanted homes with more space and privacy, and Renaissance architecture reached Britain when Henry VIII employed the sculptor Pietro Torrigino to design his father's tomb. The first home-grown classical architect was Inigo Jones, born in 1573.

This period is known as the 'Great Rebuilding'. Although it is generally associated with the sixteenth century, it covered a much wider time span and there are regional variations. Stylistically, turrets, gatehouse towers, corkscrew shaped chimneys, pepperpot domes and gables became commonplace. Many traditional buildings were pulled down or adapted whilst new houses were built using oak and stone. Houses gradually got taller as storeys were added to provide more space, especially in towns, where building behind or to the side was often not an option. These upper rooms generally became bedrooms.

A radical change was the replacing of open fireplaces with enclosed chimney stacks. Some brick chimneys were added to outside walls. Others simply replaced timber smoke hoods and flues over older open hearths in the middle of the house. Some put the chimney stack between the parlour and hall with back to back fireplaces to heat both main rooms. Such changes often created a space in which a staircase or lobby could be built between the stack and an outside wall. Chimneys became symbolic of status and wealth, and some houses had more chimney flues built than they had fireplaces for.

Windows changed in shape and size with narrow unglazed mullions being replaced by larger glazed windows. Internally, the use of wood as a decorative feature became common, with studs on walls or geometrical

The irregular size and shape of the herringbone bricks on this fireplace reveals that they were handmade.

designs (known as 'magpie' work) created by using panels and diagonal wooden strips. The timber was blacked on these and the plaster infill whitened.

Another change was the building of farmhouses away from the centre of villages, where they had traditionally stood. This began with the enclosure movement of the sixteenth century. As the fields containing strips of common land were enclosed farmers were able to build farmhouses in the centre of their newly enclosed fields.

The sixteenth century is often described as heralding the birth of the big country house. Many were built for visits by Queen Elizabeth as she toured the country, with the E-plan shape being very popular from 1590 to 1620, helped by the fact that it was also the first letter of the queen's name. Tudor twists and turns were gradually replaced by rectangular classical columns grouped in twos and threes, but chimneys proliferated, partly due to increased use of coal in fires. Ornamentation filled rooms with wood panelling, plasterwork and black and white marble chessboard floors, typifying the period.

Stuart, 1603–1714

The seventeenth and eighteenth centuries also saw major changes. The Great Fire of London in 1666 and other large fires elsewhere led to a range of Building Acts that fundamentally shaped how urban areas developed. For instance, the 1667 Rebuilding Act enabled building inspectors to examine work in progress and make sure minimum standards were met.

Subsequent acts introduced specifications as to how houses should be built. Even the thickness of walls was regulated and there were rules on overall size in relation to the width of streets. Although only compulsory in London, other cities and towns copied these changes and became more uniform in style. Older houses were gradually modernized to conform to a more rectangular and compact plan. Developments in printing and publishing techniques in the eighteenth century meant the designs of leading architects began to appear in pattern books, which were copied by builders and other architects.

The seventeenth century saw the beginnings of a 'build to let' culture. Some of these buildings were of good quality, but many simply exacerbated the problems of overcrowding in cities and towns. People living in the countryside were also affected by the Enclosure Acts, which transformed how they worked and lived. Many new country houses for the gentry, wealthy farmers and prosperous people in trade sprang up. Another significant building programme occurred when Queen Anne's Bounty was set up in 1704 to augment the incomes of the poorer clergy. Part of this scheme provided loans for the purchase of new parsonage houses, which were used by clergymen of all backgrounds. This scheme was extended under the Gilbert Act of 1776, which allowed incumbents to mortgage glebe land for the purpose of building new parsonages or outbuildings or to improve existing ones.

Stylistically, the early 1700s saw the beginning of a revival and adaptation of Palladian classical and Baroque classical styles. Both had their own political symbolism, with Palladianism seen as representative of English rationalism, whilst Baroque was more florid, symbolizing its continental Roman Catholic roots. The Baroque influence was less widespread, and by about 1720 a severe, almost plain, classicism had become immensely popular.

Georgian, 1720–1840

The early eighteenth century saw the spread of what became known as Georgian architecture. Improvements in agriculture and industry in the eighteenth century brought many benefits, mainly to the aristocracy, wealthy farmers and the new middle classes, who lavished their wealth upon their houses. London and other cities grew rapidly, while ports, industrial towns and fashionable resorts like Bath and Brighton also expanded dramatically, typified by refined elegant terraces and squares. More information about Georgian homes can be found at **www.georgiangroup.org.uk**.

Tighter regulations, increased wealth and a booming population resulted in an increasing standardization of styles. Improved road networks and new canals meant building materials such as bricks could be transported across the country instead of made locally, thereby lowering costs. Vernacular (local) housing styles were gradually replaced by uniform brick and stone structures, with the latest fashion in decoration applied to the exterior.

Architectural designs were influenced by classical ideas from Europe. Houses were influenced by buildings such as Chiswick House (built in the 1720s by the third Earl of Burlington), which introduced the Palladian style based on the concept of the Roman temple with rusticated bases, rows of columns and a strict ratio of size, proportion and arrangement of parts.

Home-grown architects such as Inigo Jones and Christopher Wren used classical styles in domestic architecture. These designs filtered down from the grand mansions, churches and public buildings springing up. Inigo Jones refined the art of creating plans, so that his clients could see exactly what their house would look like before it was built. As plans were disseminated more quickly and freely, the new styles of building spread across the country, with the rich importing the necessary building materials.

Lord Leicester of Holkham Hall in Norfolk is an example of a landowner who helped the career of English architects. He employed Samuel Wyatt (1737–1807), who made a speciality of designing model farm buildings, including nearly fifty on the Holkham Estate. For these, Wyatt experimented with cast iron, and made extensive use of Coade stone and slate, the latter from the Penrhyn quarries managed by his brother Benjamin.

In towns and cities Georgian houses were typically large four-storey terraces, sometimes with a basement. Local stone was used if available, but bricks were still more common. Roofs tended to have a shallow pitch construction, be covered in slate and hidden behind a parapet or low wall around the top of the building. Some parapets displayed elaborate masonry detail such as a balustrade or carvings. A huge number of older buildings were simply remodelled to fit with the new fashion. As a result many a Georgian façade hides a less well proportioned room or thick walls.

Chimneys and doors were a very important feature on Georgian buildings of all sizes. A detached building such as Caistor Hall in Norfolk would have one chimney at either end, whereas terraces had chimneys supported by the thick walls in between properties which provided structural stability and prevented fires spreading. Front doors tended to be set within attractive door cases with decorative pilasters or pillars and a horizontal decorative piece of stone called an entablature over the door. Arches or pediments can often be seen above the entablature, whilst the doors were made of timber panelling and often featured coloured or patterned glass upper panels, usually recessed rather than flush against the wall.

During this period the ornate Dutch shaped gables disappeared and were replaced by the hipped roof, with the roof often hidden behind a parapet. The hall became part of the entrance area and staircases became a prominent feature. Even small houses imitated the idea of having more than one reception room. Service rooms such as the kitchen and scullery moved to the back of the house or the older part of the building. Roof styles adapted to meet the depth such houses required. Improved transportation saw the use of lighter Welsh slates spread, and the pitch of roofs become lower. Some Georgian houses had attics and cellars, which were used as servants' quarters, kitchens and children's nurseries.

The enclosure movement, which had begun in the sixteenth century, gained pace in the eighteenth and early nineteenth centuries. In general, the whole look and feel of the countryside was radically altered as large open fields farmed in common were replaced. Farmers began to build new houses on their land outside villages. Many former farmhouses within villages were sub-divided into cottages for their farm workers. These can be identified by the long communal roof on such rows, with one major original chimney stack and several minor ones added to heat

Typical Georgian features on Caistor Hall in Norfolk, built in the early 1800s.

the separate quarters. A more recent trend has been for such rows to be converted back again into one or two larger houses. Many small farmers and farm workers did not profit from enclosure, and some adapted to new financial circumstances by adapting part of their homes to new uses such as alehouses and shops.

As industrialization spread Georgian features were used by speculative builders on the rows of terraced homes springing up in cities, towns and suburbs across the country. The emerging middle classes were able to create interiors in the latest classical styles thanks to a growing number of decorators with pattern books. There also marked the beginning of the massive growth of smaller houses built for the working classes. Nevertheless, traditional buildings were still being constructed, particularly in rural areas. This can mean that a house might appear older than it really was because the building materials and styles were old-fashioned.

Regency architecture is a movement which fell within the Georgian period, taking its name from the Prince Regent (later George IV). Regency combined classical influences with those from Egypt, India, China and other parts of the Far East. It coincided with the expansion of the British Empire into those areas, and the general expansion of trade across the world. Brighton Pavilion, which was built between 1815 and 1820 for the Prince Regent, is the most famous Regency building.

Seaside resorts began to develop for the wealthy in this period. Straight roads and squares leading to the seafront were filled with tall terraces coated in stucco. This was a coloured render which imitated the fashionable beige and grey stone of the time, but was also useful for covering up poor-quality buildings. The terraces had balconies and bay windows from which people promenading could be seen. Symmetry was also very important.

Napoleon's expeditions to Egypt, and Britain's growing trade interests abroad produced a taste for Egyptian, Chinese and Oriental products which appear in interiors, and occasionally on exteriors. A key feature is decorative ironwork, which became more available as iron foundries spread, especially as the larger foundries published catalogues of designs. The main structural influence was the bow window on houses.

Victorian, 1837–1901

Victorian architecture is very strongly associated with industrialization. The population of England and Wales grew from nine million in 1801 to thirty-two and a half million in 1901. The growth of population, development of easy means of travel, scientific discoveries and new building techniques affected all areas of building and design. In terms of change and modernization, it was perhaps the most radical period in British history. When Queen Victoria came to the throne in 1837, Britain was an agrarian, rural society. By the time she died in 1901 Britain was a highly industrialized world power with a sophisticated travel system and an expanding communications system.

The transport revolution had a profound influence on housing, making the separation of city centres and living quarters possible and thereby fundamentally changing the nature of large cities in the second half of the nineteenth century. Until this point dwelling houses, commercial premises and civic buildings were mixed together. In London, for instance, 123,000 people lived within the boundaries of the ancient city in 1841. However, as the number of people engaged or employed in business in the city increased, residential accommodation decreased.

The Industrial Revolution, which really took off during this era, made possible the use of new materials and methods. One of the best examples of their use was the Crystal Palace built by Joseph Paxton (1803–1865) for the Great Exhibition in 1851. Paxton pioneered the use of prefabrication in the construction of large span glasshouses in the Great Conservatory and Lily House at Chatsworth House in Derbyshire. He achieved this by using steam-powered woodworking machines to make standardized components such as arches, glazing bars and gutters built up from timber sections. The Great Conservatory could therefore be described as the first building in Britain to have an industrial aesthetic, the direct result of the use of batch-produced components.

These industrial influences begin to show in domestic buildings. Emerging Victorian philosophical concepts converged to produce a number of contradictory building styles reflecting many of the new values and aspirations, such as Tudor, Gothic Revival, Queen Anne, Tudorbethan and the Arts and Crafts Movement.

Suburban semi-detached and detached houses (villas) benefitted from cheaper land costs and were now set back from the road and hidden behind walls and gardens where possible, as Victorians sought privacy. They were built in a variety of styles, although many had a distinctive shallow-pitched hipped roof, which had become possible with the availability of lightweight Welsh slate. The vast amount of money flowing from the British colonies and the emergent industrialization saw massive amounts of building work undertaken, with spare money often poured into frivolous ornamentation.

The debate surrounding national style became intense due to the many changes taking place. Britain's increasingly international role was often perceived as a threat to traditional ways of life. Many Victorian architects felt it was important to develop a national style reflecting both the values being lost to industrialization, and those which, with Imperial expansion, the British were trying to export around the world.

The exterior of houses therefore became more influenced by England's

House and pub in Shoreditch featuring ornate window decoration and glazed tile decoration across the lower section.

own past rather than the 'Ancient World', with the Gothic style beginning to shape all sizes of houses from the 1850s. The change came through the influence of architect Augustus Pugin (1812–1852), who argued that honesty was an integral part of building design and the most convenient layout of the interior should be reflected on the outside. Pugin also despised the use of render to imitate stone and was a staunch medievalist. This style was loosely based on medieval castles, abbeys and churches. Upon the successful commissioning of the new Houses of Parliament in the Gothic style, it became a national trend.

As a result, homes were frequently ornamented like churches with pointed arches, stained-glass windows, heraldic and biblical emblems and cusping – projections of gargoyles' heads or elements of nature. On domestic houses it saw the use of pointed arched windows, battlements, hood moulds and 'Y'-shaped tracery on standard symmetrical houses. The Napoleonic Wars also encouraged the building of large mock castles for the very rich as a patriotic gesture. Horace Walpole was at the forefront of the Gothic Revival movement. He added medieval-style towers, battlements, pointed windows and moulded Tudor chimneys to his Georgian house at Strawberry Hill in Twickenham, thereby giving its name to a new style of architecture: Strawberry Hill Gothic.

The author, art critic and socialist John Ruskin was amongst those who promoted the architecture of the thirteenth century, in particular its stylized carvings. He believed this reflected the medieval mason's freedom of expression, as opposed to the Victorian factory worker, circumscribed by having to mass-produce goods. His opinions had a major impact on the later Arts and Crafts movement. By the 1850s steep-pitched roofs, pointed arches, forward-facing gables, carved foliage capitals and patterned brickwork were popular on a wide range of houses and other buildings.

Later architects looked to old manor and farmhouses for inspiration, using mock timber framing, hanging tiles, and terracotta for decoration. By the second half of the nineteenth century distinctive features were asymmetrical buildings, with steep pitched roofs, forward-facing gables, pointed arches and exposed brick with patterns of different colours.

With the repeal of the Brick Tax in 1850 and the increasing popularity of the Gothic style, brick began to be widely exposed on the outside of buildings and used as a decorative feature. One of the most popular styles from the 1860s onwards was the use of a dark red brick stone trimming and walls broken up by bands of different coloured bricks. This also reflected the growth of mass-produced bricks, as handmade bricks made out of different coloured clays and textures were being replaced. The expansion of the railways helped fuel the spread of these designs as it enabled cheaper mass-produced materials to be transported across the country.

This did not mean an end to the Classical or Italianate styles, as is shown by the distinctive flat roofs, bracketed eaves and semi-circular headed window sets still popular in the middle of the century. Fine-cut stone was fashionable but expensive, so brick exteriors were increasingly covered in stucco.

The growth of industrial towns influenced the growth of lower-status housing close to the emerging factories, especially in the Midlands and north of England. Building programmes would have been a combination of private enterprise with commercial support, characterized by rows of workers' cottages springing up on the outskirts of towns near to the factories to form industrial suburbs. In rural areas a number of villages were rebuilt on different sites as estates were redesigned to create large parks and enclosed fields. The new houses were often picturesque with rustic features. One such example of a workers' estate can be seen in Halton in Buckinghamshire, built by the Baron de Rothschild.

During the nineteenth century the general condition of houses improved, especially for the lower classes, with working families likely to be living in a small two-up two-down house by the time Victoria died in 1901. The rapidly growing middle classes emulated their social superiors. This was reflected in a desire by people to live in their own house. Speculative builders and landlords built on this desire and the Victorian era saw a rapid growth in semi-detached villas, large terraces and two-up two-down houses in urban areas. Most people were tenants with widespread property ownership only becoming the norm after the First World War. Working-class housing, however, continued to be regionally varied and often poor quality.

The Victorian period is often equated with the spread of terraced housing. Terraces tended to feature vertical sliding sash windows, with early Victorian sash windows often divided by a number of thin glazing bars with panes or lights. As large sheets of glass became more easily available, cheaper sash windows with just two panes became more popular. Roofs became a dominant feature rather than being hidden behind a parapet. One popular style was steep-pitched roofs with gables (the triangular-shaped top of a wall). Plain or decorative bargeboards often edged the gable and top of dormer windows, with some of these having elaborate carvings. From the 1860s patterns formed from different coloured tiles or slates were very popular, often finished off with ridge decorations made from terracotta or iron and an ornamental finial at the end.

Houses built for the upper and middle classes favoured Bath stone, with embellishments in marble and other materials, especially on columns, pilasters and friezes. Towards the end of the nineteenth century the fashion for Flemish, Dutch or Queen Anne styles, with delicate detailing in brick, terracotta and other materials, was becoming more apparent and generally used high-quality Welsh slates in roofing.

However, houses built for ordinary people were of brick, and of varying quality.

Ordinary cement, known as Portland cement, first came into use in 1824. However, it was not widely used in domestic building until after the Second World War. Brick or stone buildings used a lime mortar for pointing, with lime plaster on the interior, as Victorian houses relied upon the porous nature of their building materials to allow condensation to evaporate through the walls.

Houses in town centres were restricted for space and the general form of terraces changed little, other than perhaps becoming taller, with some including a half-basement, which raised the ground floor so it had to be accessed by steps. The gradual move to separate servants from the family, plus a general demand for additional rooms, resulted in the spread of rear extensions, or even mews buildings in the rear yard if there was space.

Terraces also tended to have their front doors set in pairs, rather than to the same side along a row as had been popular before. Plate glass came into production in 1832. This led to the small pane windows of the Georgian period being replaced by four- and six-pane vertical sliding sash windows.

Another distinctive feature was the growth of suburbs, with adjacent villages and hamlets losing their separate identities as they became subsumed into the city by the spread of building. For example, Norwich in 1801 had a population of 36,000, which had grown to over 100,000 by 1900. When comparing the tithe map of 1839 for what was the separate hamlet of Heigham and the first Ordnance Survey map of 1886, it is possible to see how the Victorian street plan follows the original field boundaries.

For the first time suburbs were deliberately built in distinct and planned styles. The first of these was Bedford Park, built on the west side of London in the 1870s, followed by Hampstead Garden Suburb and Portlight in Merseyside. Late Victorian England also saw blocks of flats specifically built for middle-class tenants, with the first being the Queen Anne's Mansions, built in 1873.

The later Victorian era still drew its inspiration from Britain's past, but began to be more influenced by the domestic than ecclesiastical. Many of the Revivalist features of this period can be seen in the spread of black and white timber-framed decoration and hung tiles above an exposed brick lower floor and the use of decorative panels and mouldings.

Building and health regulations also influenced the appearance of later Victorian buildings in response to epidemics such as cholera and typhoid (see the section on public health records). Ceiling heights were raised to improve the circulation of air, basements became less fashionable and rear extensions with more light became more popular as servants quarters. Houses were still raised slightly above ground level with vents in the

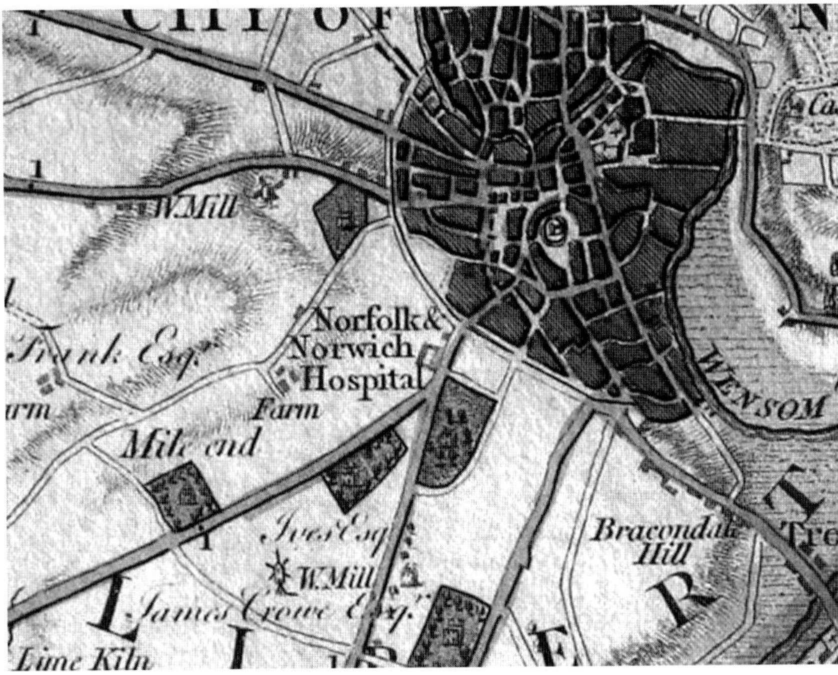

Faden's 1797 map showing the area near the old Norfolk and Norwich Hospital.

outer brickwork to allow air to move freely between floorboards, thereby reducing damp.

Bathrooms and kitchens tended to be strictly functional places. The centrepiece of kitchens was a large wooden table upon which food was prepared, with a scullery and walk-in larder. Chairs were also kept plain. The fashion in flooring was for rich, dark coloured carpets, heavily patterned with large three-dimensional designs celebrating elements of nature: birds, flowers or geometric patterns.

Victorian interiors were more cluttered, bold and colourful than before. Mass production and the growth of magazines and shops meant the middle classes could imitate the luxurious fittings of their social superiors and styles spread more rapidly across the country. The hall, drawing and dining rooms were kept for 'best', while upstairs out of sight the fittings tended to be plainer. Ceiling heights rose in most terraces and floors were raised up so that an air gap existed where there was no basement or cellar. Walls tended to be plain to begin with and had large skirting boards, although dado and picture rails later made a come-back.

Tiles were also highly patterned, with durable kiln-fired tiles made for use in corridors and entrances. Victorian fireplaces were ostentatious, elaborate pieces made of cast-iron, and frequently had material draped from the mantlepiece. Paintwork was limited to strong colours such as ruby reds and deep forest greens, with blue and purple coming in midway through the century. Artwork reflected notions of national identity and imperialism through regal portraits and romantic countryside scenes.

Furniture was overstuffed, ornate armchairs complemented by the odd chaise-longue. Wallpaper came into mass production in the 1840s and is perhaps the single most important feature in the interior of a Victorian property. Quality varied considerably, from mass-produced designs on wood-pulp paper to elaborate hand-printed motifs on rag paper. Elements of nature featured heavily, with birds and flowers in grand, elaborate designs.

Staircases at the beginning of the era tended to be elaborate, with twisting balustrades carved from a single piece of wood. These were later replaced by simpler designs. Front doors made of hardwood were left to a natural finish, while other woods considered inferior were painted. Four panels was the norm except where there were two panels of glass at the top. Later on these panels and internal doors were filled with stained or etched glass.

The introduction of steam-operated railways ushered in an impressive architectural heritage. Viaducts, tunnels, bridges and railway stations illustrate the marriage between buildings designed to serve a practical function that are architecturally important and influential in their own right.

Another significant architectural movement was what became known as 'Jacobethan'. This was a very popular style of house characterized by flattened arches, intricate brickwork, steep sloping gables and lighter patterned brickwork around windows. Victorian houses were further ornamented with pillars, balustrades and fortifications reminiscent of a castle dwelling. The style was later corrupted into 'Tudorbethan', which saw a softening, with the use of thatched roofs and half-timbering, reminiscent of a medieval cottage – commonly known as Tudor today.

The Arts and Crafts movement of the late nineteenth and early twentieth centuries occurred as a reaction against what was perceived as the soulless mechanization of the British workforce. Based on a vision of an idealized past, it encouraged quality over quantity, typified by the use of hand-painted ornamentation, personalized human touches, and the employment of craftspeople. The result was a style of architecture that made strong use of natural materials and harked back to the medieval house structures with sloping roofs, large gardens, timbering and small windows. Many buildings featured shallow-pitched hipped roofs, made possible by the availability of lightweight Welsh slate.

Buildings were often asymmetrical with low rooflines to give the impression of a rural cottage and had a front-facing gable (the upper triangular part of the wall that terminates a pitched roof) at the end of a building rather than in the centre. The craft of building was also celebrated, which resulted in the start of the style whereby construction methods such as exposed brick and stone work were left for all to see. Some architects and builders used roughcast render and pebbledash when finishing walls, whilst others employed lots of timber and created sloping roofs, small windows and expansive gardens.

The design of interiors was considered equally important in Arts and Crafts houses, even down to the wallpaper, furnishings and features such as fireplaces and door knockers. Space was planned in order to make the most aesthetic use of light and space and wallpapers such as those designed by William Morris drew strongly upon the natural world.

The Arts and Crafts movement benefitted from cheaper land costs, which allowed suburban detached (villa) and semi-detached properties to be built set back from the road and surrounded by gardens and walls. This was also, in part, a response to middle-class Victorians wanting more privacy and space within their homes as they adopted the lifestyle of the upper classes. The suburban villa took its name from an earlier eighteenth-century renaissance style of house, often built for country gentlemen and generally used to describe two-storey buildings with bedrooms over living rooms, with an extra wing for service rooms. By the nineteenth century 'villa' was used to describe compact new properties set in their own grounds, usually built in the suburbs. Villa styles did, however, vary enormously, with Regency, Gothic, Mock Tudor and other styles appearing widely.

This nostalgic harking back was not unique to Arts and Crafts, as the architecture evolved in the Victorian era had diverse influences, from religion to architectural philosophies. Mock Tudor, Gothic Revival, Queen Anne and Arts and Crafts are all products of this period.

Edwardian, 1901–1910

The Edwardian period was one of great social and political change, and saw the first serious attempts to solve the problem of working-class housing. By the time Queen Victoria died in January 1901 Britain had become the world's leading industrial and economic power. Living standards had generally improved for most people. The spread of a cheap suburban rail network meant middle-class families could live further out of town on cheaper land, which in turn meant they could afford a bigger house with a garden. Speculative builders built thousands of new houses, usually small semi-detached properties or better-quality terraces.

Architecturally, the Edwardian era was very eclectic. Most houses were inspired by architects from an earlier period, with replica Jacobean and Tudor buildings being immensely fashionable. Houses were taller and

Edwardian house built with strong Arts and Crafts influence on its design.

deeper than a hundred years before, with gardens being in great demand. Popular features include mock-timber gables; balconies with French windows; pebbledashed walls; leaded lights, stained-glass windows and skylights in doors; decorative tiles in porches; brass letterboxes and hanging terracotta tiles. New working-class houses often had small gardens and a separate privy. Electric heating and lighting became cheaper and easier to use. Cleanliness also meant lighter colours could be used in wallpaper and paint.

The Arts and Crafts movement, which had emerged in the late Victorian era, continued to have a huge impact, characterized by William Morris-designed textiles, wallpaper, decorative glass and murals. Art Nouveau, which lasted from around 1880 to 1914, had its main influence on furniture and interiors, characterized by the use of intertwined stems, leaves and flowers in an organic form and an emphasis on the sensuous female form. In architecture it took practical items such as iron gates and turned them into works of art. Other major developments included the growth of garden cities and planned communities (see separate section), whilst Modernist architecture made its first appearance.

Modern, Modernist and Post-Modernist

The interwar years saw a number of initiatives in towns and cities to tackle poor housing stock, and the related problem of poor public health. Schemes such as 'Homes Fit for Heroes' were the first attempts at a national programme of local authority housing. Large numbers of houses were built, mostly in the suburbs and areas in which new industries producing cars, electrical appliances and chemicals were based. Large-scale building companies emerged, aided by government subsidies and cheap land costs.

Modernism emerged in Paris in the 1920s. It emphasized everything modern, including construction materials. Modernism took off in Britain under the influence of Hungarian architect Ernö Goldfinger and the home he built for himself at 2 Willow Road in Hampstead. Ironically, despite the rejection of history that underpinned modernist philosophy, the Willow Road house was in fact a reworking of a Georgian house, with its emphasis on order and simplicity.

From the 1930s new architectural styles tried to highlight the formal qualities of a building by using contrasting colours and textures and artificial materials such as stainless steel, alongside natural resources such as wood, stone and brick. The 1930s semi-detached house is still one of the most popular British house styles of all time.

Art Deco lasted from 1925 to 1939 and is perceived to have developed as a response to the horrors and destruction of the First World War. It reflected the jazz and flapper era, with Hollywood films fuelling people's interest in the style. It was originally known as the Jazz or Moderne movement, with the term Art Deco only being used from 1966. Simplicity was the key. It was characterized by straight lines, right angles, geometric curves and highly stylized figures, often set against a distinctive sunray pattern motif or chevrons.

Architecturally, Art Deco styles were reflected in the greater use of render and the use of round-ended bays on the suburban semi. Roofs were usually flat or very shallow, or hidden behind parapets to give the impression of flatness. Windows were metal-framed and often curved in shape, standing out from the house, or in some cases sited on the corner of the house. Furniture and fittings used straight lines and sweeping curves in wood, stainless steel, aluminum, Bakelite and lacquer.

The Garden City movement continued to exert an influence, in particular after the Second World War, when the New Towns initiative began to replace homes destroyed by wartime bombing. The second half of the twentieth century is characterized by massive housing developments and urban renewal. Many people express surprise at the idea of investigating the history of modern buildings and the sites they were built on. Yet they are as much a part of our history as a medieval manor house or Tudor cottage.

Modern architecture comes in for much criticism, especially on the grounds of blandness and uniformity. Yet much modern housing in Britain was radical in concept and driven by innovation. There is also an argument that much of what we see as traditional housing may have been seen as radical, ugly or controversial at the time it was built.

Modern housing still has strong links with the past, as we can see the effects of nineteenth and early twentieth century social and political reforms on design, facilities and attitudes to housing provision. We have also seen a massive shift in the same period away from tenancies as the norm for the majority of people, to owner-occupancy and buy-to-let schemes.

Model Villages, Philanthropic Schemes, Garden Cities, New Towns and Council Housing

Planned housing developments built for workers, the poor, the sick and needy have been found in all eras, ranging from villages created on the country estates of the landed gentry to almshouses for the poor, elderly and sick and purpose-built communities for workers close to factories and mills. If you live in a house or flat that was part of one of these projects, or even just in the same area, they have a fascinating, even unique history of their own.

All were built to provide 'decent' affordable homes for those in 'need' in some way. Such schemes became much more commonplace from the nineteenth century as philanthropic housing developments by those such as Shaftesbury or Peabody, and slum clearance programmes, aimed to provide affordable, decent and integrated communities, usually for the 'labouring' or 'working' classes.

Generally described as 'social housing', the impact of such schemes on the communities in which we live cannot be underestimated. They had a long-term impact on town planning schemes up to the present day, through the influence of their architectural designs and the way in which people began to think about how communities could or should develop, as well as public and private housing development schemes. In the process they raised living standards and expectations and laid the groundwork for the council housing programmes of the twentieth century. Some commentators have gone so far as to argue that these were the first buildings specifically designed with the working classes in mind, as opposed to being something the working classes happened to find themselves living in.

One of the earliest projects was the Chartist Lands Purchase Scheme, which operated between 1845 and 1851. This was founded by the Chartist reformer Feargus O'Connor to enable workers to gain the right to vote by being able to buy their own land and homes. People were encouraged to buy small shares. The money from this was then used to buy land, which was in turn allocated to some of the shareholders by ballot. Land was bought in Hertfordshire, Gloucestershire, Oxfordshire and Worcestershire. The scheme folded due to mismanagement in 1851.

Housing specifically built for workers has existed from at least the eighteenth century, but became much more widespread in the nineteenth century. Famous examples include the homes built for workers near Richard Arkwright's mill at Cromford and those of Josiah Wedgwood's pottery workers at Etruria in Staffordshire. Building homes for workers guaranteed employers a supply of labour and helped instill loyalty amongst the workforce. Robert Owen is the person most often associated with model villages as he provided his New Lanark cotton mill workers with an infant school, free medical care, a crèche for working mothers and a pleasant working environment. A thriving social life was seen as an important part of building this community, with concerts, dances, a night school, library and reading room.

The idea of model villages was slow to spread. Most of the enthusiasm for it during the Victorian era was encouraged by concerns over public health rather than the idea of creating a community. Poverty, disease and squalor were rife in the overcrowded and rapidly expanding cities and towns. Another major influence was an anti-urbanism philosophy which manifested itself in a love of nature and rural values. This was in marked contrast with other European countries where the city was the desirable place to live. Writers and philosophers such as Robert Owen were convinced that the miseries of the industrial poor could only be relieved by a fresh start in an environment that broke away from the excessive size, density and centralization of the city.

Another aim behind model villages was to encourage property developers to improve what they offered, as they were deliberately designed to be attractive. However, whilst the homes were a vast improvement, most had restrictions such as no alcohol placed on the residents and some paternalistic owners, such as William Lever, attempted to control many aspects of the residents' personal lives. Nevertheless, many villagers accepted these conditions in return for the vastly improved quality of life.

Model villages led to the rise of the garden city movement, which aimed to create a healthy and wholesome city without slums and smoke. These were first proposed by Ebenezer Howard in 1900 as pre-planned towns with residential, commercial and industrial areas. Arranged

Plan of Letchworth Garden City, 1910 (Letchworth Museum).
Communal housing for business women in Letchworth, 1916–1925.

1905 Model Competition Cottages, characterized by white rough-cast walls, steeply pitched roofs and dormer windows.

around green public spaces and connected to public transport, these were intended to provide an affordable and beneficial working and living environment for the artisan working classes.

In 1903, work began on the first garden city at Letchworth in Hertfordshire, with Welwyn Garden City following later. Its founder, Ebenezer Howard, believed humans needed both the 'bosom of mother earth' and the civilising opportunities and sophisticated entertainment of the town. This could be provided through the creation of Garden Cities of limited size, surrounded by a permanent belt of agricultural land which would relocate people from slums and overcrowded centres to sparsely settled rural districts. Houses were spaciously laid out on tree-lined avenues to give light, air and a wholesome lifestyle away from the pollution of factories.

Howard's 'Three Magnets' ring and radial pattern illustrated how a model garden city of around 32,000 people should be laid out over 6,000 acres. The ground plan included six boulevards, each 120 feet wide, running from centre to circumference. There would be a beautiful and well-watered central garden circular space of around five and a half acres. Surrounding this and standing in their own ample grounds would be larger public buildings: town, concert and lecture halls, theatre, library, museum, picture gallery and hospital. The rest of the public space would be a large public park and recreation grounds within easy access of all the people, with a wide glass arcade, called the 'Crystal Palace', opening onto the park.

Houses were perceived as serving an almost biological function that facilitated reproduction, nutrition and recreation in order to serve primary physiological requirements of space for social companionship, play and study. Special attention was therefore paid to the width of streets, verges and general design. Houses were to be of good material, grouped harmoniously together with well-insulated walls. They were to include hot water and heating; cooking, laundry and drying facilities; as few stairs as possible and be within easy reach of schools, shops, social centres and work.

Letchworth became a place of pilgrimage for town planners from all over the world, whilst Port Sunlight and Bourneville attracted thousands of visitors. In 1905, a Cheap Cottages Exhibition, sponsored by the *Daily Mail,* was held in Letchworth, which attracted over 60,000 visitors. This proved so popular that the newspaper launched its first Ideal Home Exhibition, which aimed to improve 'the comfort, convenience, entertainment, health and well-being of home life'.

Various groups continued to try to address the problem of overcrowding and poor housing in cities and large towns, and the influence of Letchworth can be seen as early as 1921, when a government committee recommended garden cities be built under state assistance to relieve congestion in slum areas. Despite their egalitarian principles, most of these planned communities became middle-class centres and had little impact on city slums. Nevertheless, the idea grew and directly led to the later building of new towns, council housing initiatives and planning legislation which took physical environment into consideration.

After the First World War, the 'Homes fit for Heroes' schemes resulted in large working-class estates with rows of identical houses and little provision for community life. This, and fears over private developments eating into land around major towns, led the Garden City Association to change its name to the Town and Country Planning Association, and persuade London County Council to set up a commission on the location of industrial development. Their subsequent report recommended building 'satellite towns' and resulted in a plan that formed the basis of the New Towns initiative after the Second World War. Howard's

Postcard of Three Bridges village, 1908.
1947 Designation Plan for Crawley showing Ifield and industrial areas (Courtesy Crawley Museum Society).

emphasis on the importance of a permanent 'girdle' of open and agricultural land around the town thus became part of British planning doctrine, now known as the Green Belt.

Philosophically and politically this programme to build a better Britain linked in with the new Welfare State, which would provide health care and housing from 'cradle to grave', regardless of ability to pay. In the 1950s, 1960s and 1970s slum clearance began again as part of a programme of planned housing developments. Much of this was in the form of high-rise flats, which suffered from their own social problems. In the late twentieth century the emphasis shifted away from demolishing old housing and turned back towards renovating old buildings.

New Towns and modern developments have a special history of their own and are often described as the children of the earlier garden city movement, which produced Letchworth and Welwyn Garden City. Under the New Towns Act of 1946 the Government created eight self-supporting towns in a circle between twenty and thirty miles from the heart of London. At the time new towns represented the logical alternative to the massive congestion and outward sprawl of the capital. They promised employment, decent housing in a green environment, and an end to daily commuting.

Crawley in West Sussex, where I lived for seven years, was one of the original eight new towns built after the Second World War and was designated on 9 January 1947. It offers a slightly different perspective, and to me more interesting, as it was not purpose-built from scratch like most of the others, but around the three existing villages of Three Bridges, Ifield and Crawley.

The key social concepts for new towns were 'self-containment' and 'integration'. Divided by wide park areas, it was believed each neighbourhood would develop its own character, despite having the same basic structure of local shops, primary school, church, community centre, pub and homes for the elderly and disabled. Class segregation was avoided by providing homes for various income groups. Industry would be attracted by the reserves of labour and cost-effective purpose-built units. As such, Crawley promised financial security for Londoners in need of accommodation, the prospect of good jobs, training and pleasant homes in a clean and open setting.

Crawley planners originally envisaged nine residential neighbourhoods over nearly 6,000 acres, each based on a village concept and grouped around a town centre with an industrial estate to the north. The master plan for the Crawley New Town passed in 1950 proposed a total population of 60,000, a much larger figure than originally suggested.

Each area was given a name reflecting local history. The influence of the original garden city can be seen in the –use of wide park lands and public spaces within each industrial and residential area, with highways curving

Purpose-built corporation houses in Southgate.
Houses in Three Bridges converted from existing housing stock in the first phase of building.

around the town and arteries within the town following the parks. However, much of the original green space was gradually filled in. Today, with a population of around 100,000 and proposals for a fourteenth neighbourhood to the north-east of the town, Crawley is the largest inland town in West Sussex.

Architecturally, Crawley and other new towns embraced the new. This was reflected in a trend for local authorities to become the new patrons of architecture and one of the dominating forces in British architecture. Signature materials and designs included the use of prefabricated elements, metal frames, concrete cladding and absence of decoration. The experimental character of new towns encouraged architects who thrived on innovations to enhance their reputations, which in turn tended to be expensive, at least initially. As with Letchworth, new towns became places of pilgrimage for organizations across the world interested in town planning.

Letchworth has undoubtedly had a major impact on the design and ethos of modern town developments globally, but its success lies more in its influence than in its practical implementation. Although it seems obvious today to be aware of basic human needs, Letchworth was the first place this was put into practice on any large scale and thereby fundamentally changed the nature of town planning. One direct result was the new towns policy of the 1940s to provide for the growing demands of city populations. Some, such as Macfadyen in the 1930s, even went so far as to claim that decent well-planned housing played a crucial role in preventing the growth of communism.

Finding Resources for Model Villages and Philanthropic and Council Housing

Records of the Chartist Lands Purchase Scheme and those for workers' houses built by nationalized industries are held at The National Archives. Ministry of Housing files at The National Archives also contain much detail about local authority housing and tied housing built by other organizations which became government property.

The Letchworth Garden City website includes much information about its history, including photographs and Howard's original plans. **www.letchworthgardencity.net**

Port Sunlight Museum & Garden Village tells the story of life in the village. 23 King George's Drive, Port Sunlight, CH62 5DX. **www.portsunlightvillage.com** Visitors can also tour the village.

Villages of Vision by Gillian Darley (Five Leaves Publications, 2007) is a comprehensive account of model villages and utopian communities.

Details of the history of Robert Owen's New Lanark community can be found at: **www.newlanark.org**

Milton Keynes Living Archive has produced over twenty books, several major documentary plays, numerous songs and a large number of films about its history. Exhibitions of the city's heritage can be seen at Discover Milton Keynes, a retail unit in the City Centre Shopping Building. The archive is held at: The Living Archive, The Old Bath House, 205 Stratford Road, Wolverton, Milton Keynes MK12 5RL. **www.livingarchive.org.uk**

Crawley New Town Museum has produced a history of the town and the influence of Letchworth on it. Exhibition material includes background material on the development of new towns generally.

Local and national newspapers are immensely helpful for finding out more about big developments, government schemes and so on. The Times Digital Archive, for instance, has thousands of reports into Letchworth and other garden cities, the development of new towns, slum clearance programmes, and so on.

Public Health and Slum Clearance Resources

A related set of resources are the records relating to public health and schemes to improve living and housing conditions. These provide some fascinating insights into the social history of different communities as well as specific buildings. Historically, slum clearance and redevelopment needs to be seen in the context of philanthropic housing movements and other reforms aimed at improving the conditions of the working class. Nevertheless, in terms of researching individual properties, there are some specific records which relate to slum clearance and redevelopment of problem areas.

Poor housing conditions and epidemics are not new, but the widespread recording of them really dates from the nineteenth century. Obviously, houses were not built as slums, even if many were poorly constructed. Understanding how and why an area or individual property became a slum therefore forms part of understanding the history of the area in which it was built.

Public health became a huge political issue in the early Victorian period. By the 1840s social and religious campaigners were pushing for action against the high levels of infant mortality and poor housing. In towns and cities the prevalence of waterborne diseases such as typhus and cholera were endemic until the discovery of the link between sanitation and public health in the nineteenth century provided the impetus for developments in public hygiene and indoor plumbing, which helped eliminate them. In 1842, a Royal Commission was appointed to investigate 'the Health of Towns and Populous Places'. Two reports were published in 1844 and 1845 that led to the passing of the 1848 Public Health Act. This established the General Board of Health, which could in turn set up local boards of health in problem areas.

Before each board of health was created the General Board of Health would hold a public enquiry into sanitary conditions, overseen by an inspector. The published inspectors' findings provide a fascinating account of local housing conditions including statistics and quotations from witnesses. The witnesses included doctors, surgeons, clergymen, overseers of the poor, nuisance inspectors and other people aware of the unhealthiest areas where they lived.

More than 400 formal reports were published between 1848 and 1857. Around a hundred were follow-up studies from an earlier report. The metropolitan area of London was specifically excluded from the jurisdiction of the General Health Board, but some parishes on the edge of London, such as Southwark, were subject to enquiries. Statistics were gathered on death rates and disease, as well as levels of overcrowding and details of the squalor in which some people lived. Places surveyed ranged from small market towns to large industrial areas across the country. The published reports included tables and charts, plans and drawings to illustrate the worst areas.

Such reports can be cross-referenced with other sources, such as Ordnance Survey maps, census returns, newspaper reports, births, deaths and marriages and parish registers. Another useful set of records which link to these are the maps and records created for the supply of amenities such as water, gas, sewers and electricity, which can also provide some interesting social and local history context.

Following the 1848 Public Health Act every house had to have some kind of sanitary arrangement, whether a toilet, privy or ash pit, and five million pounds was invested into research and the building of a modern sewer system, although outside wells were still being used in rural areas well into the mid-twentieth century, and it is commonplace to see mention of them on house deeds; usually in clauses about maintenance and access.

Sewerage and drainage became the responsibility of new local boards of health, who created maps of the new systems. Gradually, records began to be kept of houses being connected to the new drainage pipes. These can list the applicant's name, whether they were the owner or occupier, the name of the builder and details of the pipes needed. Some are accompanied by architectural plans. Subsequent changes to the building are also noted. Even where there are no drainage records, the local authority minute books record many such applications.

The Poor Law Commission originally had responsibility for local housing issues, especially slum clearance. They were succeeded by the Local Government Board in 1871. Its Sanitary Board was responsible for housing until 1910, when it became the responsibility of the Board's Town Planning Department. Another change occurred after the First World War when housing was transferred to the Ministry of Health. Powers to compulsorily purchase slums were given to local authorities in 1875. The Town and Country Planning Act of 1947 was introduced to deal with the effects of bomb damage, slum housing and town planning and to regulate the building of new homes.

Finding Public Health, Redevelopment and Slum Clearance Records

The British Library, 96 Euston Road, London NW1 2DB **www.bl.uk** has the largest collection of General Health Reports, though it is not complete. Listings can be found on their online catalogue by putting in 'General Board of Health, and the location at **http://catalogue.bl.uk**. Many city reference and local history libraries hold copies of reports for their area.

Local and national newspapers contain many reports into slum clearance and redevelopment schemes and planning applications.

Planning applications and associated records can be found amongst town, borough and city council records held in county archives. A great example of what can be found in local record offices are the King's Lynn Slum Clearance records, including copies of newspaper reports, for the period 1934 to 1939, held at the King's Lynn branch of the Norfolk Record Office. These provide a fascinating account of the areas being cleared, including many individual houses. The documents include clearance papers; plans; photographs; and descriptions of individual unfit dwellings with lists of occupiers; objection letters and plans of the proposed replacement housing.

Local record offices have many records from the local Boards of Health and their successors, whilst some are still kept at local authority offices. Maps of local amenities and social surveys of poverty, disease and crime can be found at county record offices and in the British Library.

Records from the Royal Commission on the Health of Towns and Populous Places, established in 1848, can be found at The National Archives. The National Archives also has records, including plans of buildings, from the earliest schemes operated by local authorities amongst the Poor Law Commissioners' papers, to those granted under the Ministry of Health.

HOUSING ACT, 1936.

King's Lynn Borough Council.

Guanock Fields Clearance Order, 1936.

Situation and Description of Property - Nos. 4,5,6 & 7, Guanock Fields, King's Lynn.

Facts alleged to be the principal grounds on which the Council are satisfied that the buildings included in the Order under the reference mentioned above are unfit for human habitation.

No. 4, Guanock Fields.

DEFECTS:)

Ground floor. Living room.	Window area and opening space deficient; brick floor damp; walls damp.
First floor. Bedroom.	Window area and opening space deficient; top sash fixed; floor boards defective; ceiling plaster defective.
External.	External walls defective and perished.
Cement.	Roof fillet defective.
Sanitary Accommodation.	The sanitary accommodation is joint, two water closets in the yard are provided for the use of Nos. 4,5,6 and 7 (one cannot be used because of its dilapidated condition); the water closets' systons are defective; brick work defective; absence of eaves gutters and rain water pipes.
Yard paving.	Approach to washhouse unpaved.
Washhouse.	Door and door frame defective; brick floor defective absence of eaves gutters and rain water pipes; brick work defective.
Ventilation.	No through ventilation (no windows in rear walls).
Storage of food.	No proper ventilated cupboards are provided for the storage of foodstuffs.
Dampness.	Serious dampness is in evidence owing to the absence of a damp proof course.
Sink.	No sink is provided.
Water supply.	The water supply is joint, one tap in the Yard is for the use of 4 houses.

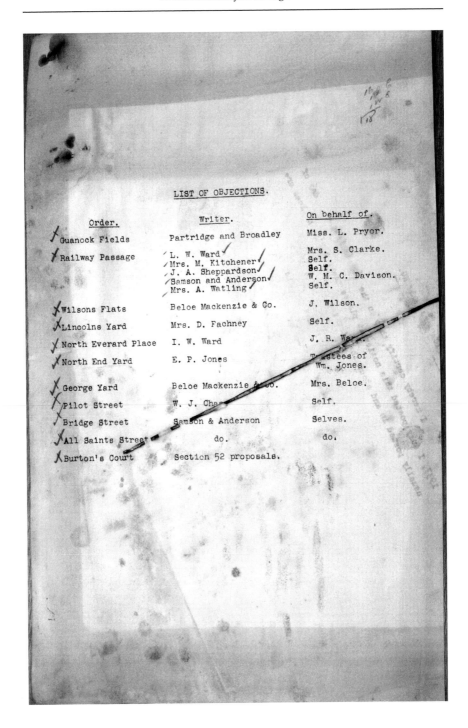

LIST OF OBJECTIONS.

Order.	Writer.	On behalf of.
Guanock Fields	Partridge and Broadley	Miss. L. Pryor.
Railway Passage	L. W. Ward	Mrs. S. Clarke.
	Mrs. M. Kitchener	Self.
	J. A. Sheppardson	Self.
	Samson and Anderson	W. M. C. Davison.
	Mrs. A. Watling	Self.
Wilsons Flats	Beloe Mackenzie & Co.	J. Wilson.
Lincolns Yard	Mrs. D. Fachney	Self.
North Everard Place	I. W. Ward	J. R. Wa[illegible]
North End Yard	E. P. Jones	Trustees of Wm. Jones.
George Yard	Beloe Mackenzie & Co.	Mrs. Beloe.
Pilot Street	W. J. Cha[illegible]	Self.
Bridge Street	Samson & Anderson	Selves.
All Saints Street	do.	do.
Burton's Court	Section 52 proposals.	

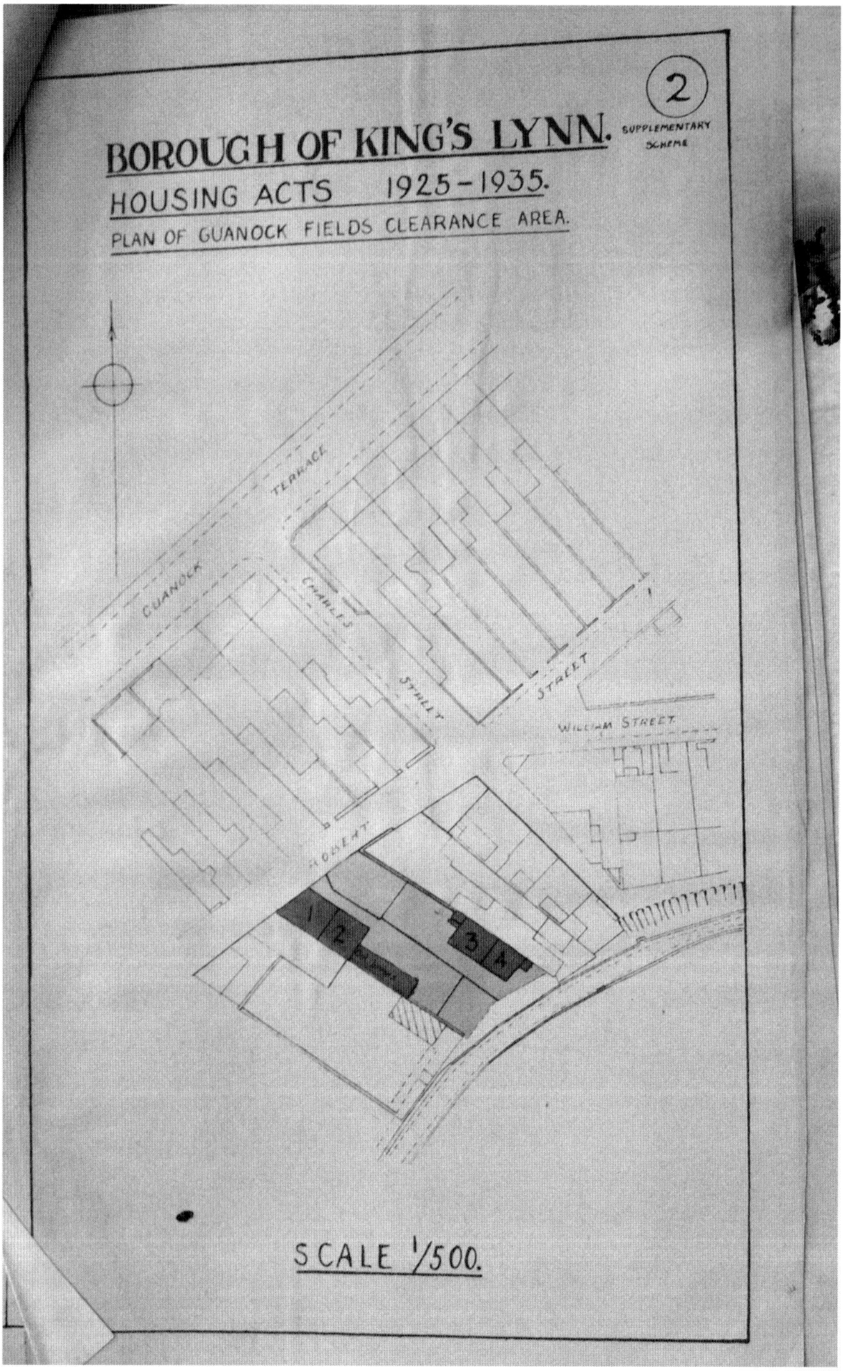
2
BOROUGH OF KING'S LYNN.
SUPPLEMENTARY SCHEME
HOUSING ACTS 1925-1935.
PLAN OF GUANOCK FIELDS CLEARANCE AREA.
GUANOCK TERRACE
CHARLES STREET
STREET
WILLIAM STREET
ROBERT
1
2
3
4
SCALE 1/500.

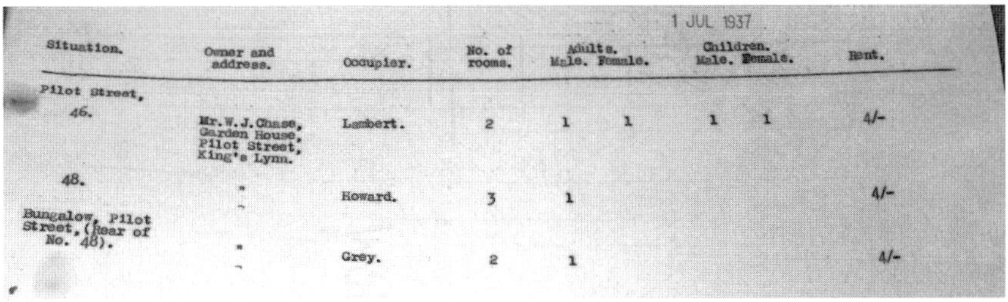

1 JUL 1937

Situation.	Owner and address.	Occupier.	No. of rooms.	Adults. Male.	Adults. Female.	Children. Male.	Children. Female.	Rent.
Pilot Street, 46.	Mr. W. J. Chase, Garden House, Pilot Street, King's Lynn.	Lambert.	2	1	1	1	1	4/-
48.	"	Howard.	3	1				4/-
Bungalow, Pilot Street, (Rear of No. 48).	"	Grey.	2	1				4/-

(Pages 52, 53, 54 and 55) Plan, descriptions of property and list of objections from the slum clearance records for the Guanock Fields area in King's Lynn, 1934–1938. (NRO King's Lynn Borough Archives: King's Lynn Slum Clearance Records, 1934–1938. Box 1)

Chapter 4

BUILDING LOCAL KNOWLEDGE

It is not possible to separate the history of a house from its geography, landscape and local history. Without that sense of place we are left with a shadow history. Oral histories, stories, legends and local gossip play a crucial part in building up a picture of your home within its community, as do old postcards and photographs, paintings, sketches and newspaper reports into local people and events. Literature, art and even poetry all add to our knowledge, as can be seen in this extract from a poem written by Richard Taylor in the eighteenth century about 'Old Edenbridge' in Kent:

> 'Tis a long street of hogpounds with old things behind 'em
> The people call houses, but trust me, you'll find 'em
> Such crazy old hutches, so cold and so damp,
> They'll give you the rheumatism, ague, and cramp . . .

Many houses have tales associated with them such as underground tunnels, ghosts, dastardly deeds or famous characters. Whilst you need to cast a critical eye over such tales and some local histories they can add 'colour' and may lead to historical sources which prove or disprove them. In the case of one house on the Norfolk coast, for instance, I found a book of smugglers' tales for the county taken from court records and newspaper reports. Whilst there was no specific reference to this house, it did mention events in the area and some people who were related to the occupants.

Histories, biographies, autobiographies and transcriptions of original records such as diaries and letters of people from the area you live will also add that all important context. For example, the fifteenth-century Norfolk Paston family letters refer to the financial side of a parson's life, whilst a document drawn up by Margaret Paston in 1478, when the Oxnede living was vacant, sets out at length details of the rectory grounds and their value:

There belongs to the said parsonage in free land, arable, pasture and meadow adjoining to the said parsonage, 22 acres or more, whereof every acre is worth 2s. to let £3. 0s. 4d (Paston Letters, p.219)

Some heritage organizations have used such records to help recreate the interiors of particular buildings, whilst many people research a

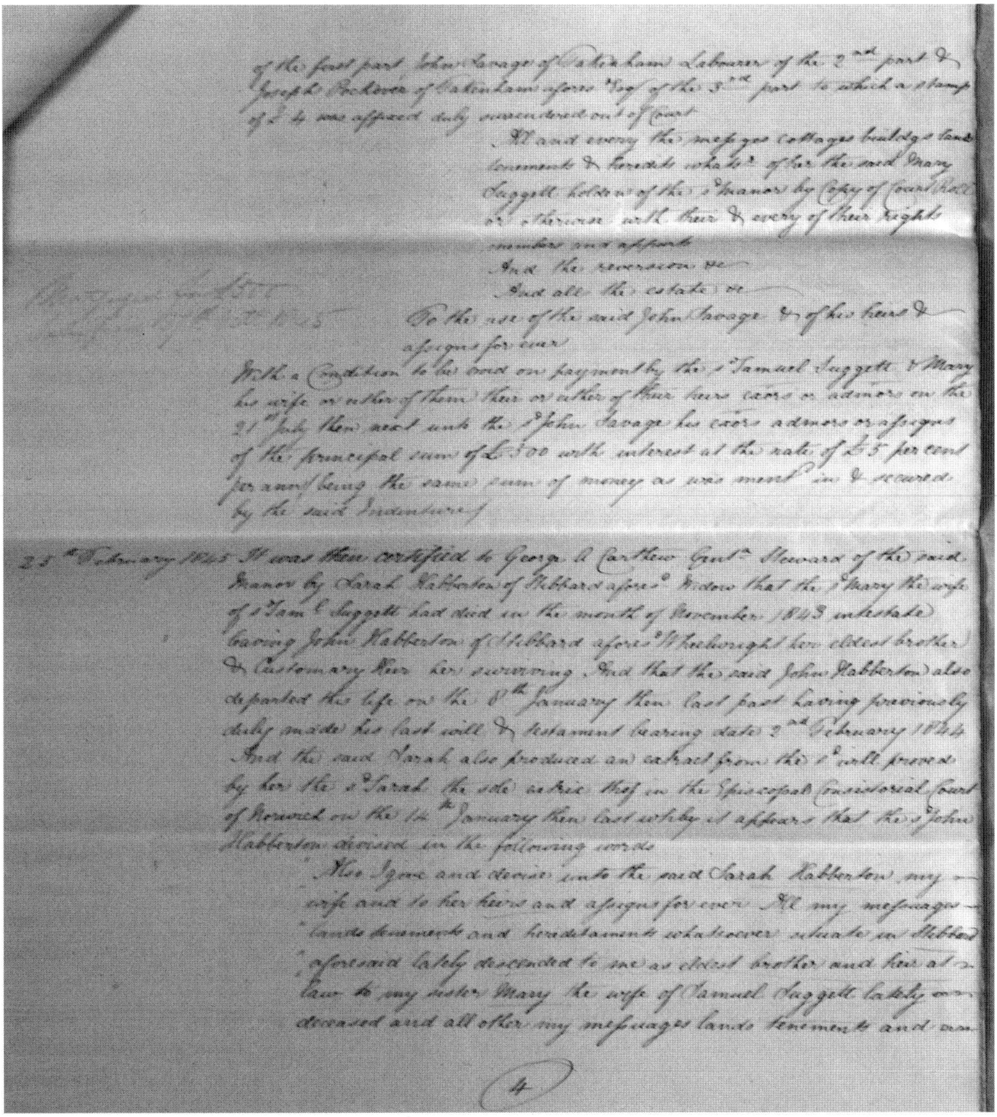

of the first part John Savage of Watenham Labourer of the 2nd part & Joseph Bolton of Watenham afores^d Esq of the 3rd part to which a stamp of £4 was affixed duly surrendered out of Court

All and every the messuages Cottages buildings lands tenements & hereditaments whatso^r of her the said Mary Suggett holden of the s^d Manor by Copy of Court Roll or otherwise with their & every of their rights members and appurts

And the reversion &c

And all the estate &c

To the use of the said John Savage & of his heirs & assigns for ever

With a Condition to be void on payment by the s^d Samuel Suggett & Mary his wife or either of them their or either of their heirs exors or admors on the 21st July then next unto the s^d John Savage his exors admors or assigns of the principal sum of £300 with interest at the rate of £5 per cent per ann being the same sum of money as was ment^d in & secured by the said Indenture

25th February 1845 It was then certified to George A Carthew Gent^n Steward of the said Manor by Sarah Habberton of Hebbard afores^d Widow that the s^d Mary the wife of s^d Saml Suggett had died in the month of November 1843 intestate leaving John Habberton of Hebbard afores^d Wheelwright her eldest brother & Customary heir her surviving. And that the said John Habberton also departed this life on the 8th January then last past having previously duly made his last will & testament bearing date 2nd February 1844 And the said Sarah also produced an extract from the s^d will proved by her the s^d Sarah the sole extrix thereof in the Episcopal Consistorial Court of Norwich on the 14th January then last whereby it appears that the s^d John Habberton devised in the following words

Also I give and devise unto the said Sarah Habberton my wife and to her heirs and assigns for ever All my messuages lands tenements and hereditaments whatsoever situate in Hebbard aforesaid lately descended to me as eldest brother and heir at law to my sister Mary the wife of Samuel Suggett lately deceased and all other my messuages lands tenements and

4

Abstract of Title from the Suggett Deeds. (Courtesy of John Bartle)

building's history in order to gain insights into the lives of their ancestors. This was the case with the Suggett family of Stibbard in Norfolk. A bundle of nineteenth-century title deeds relating to this family includes wills, extracts of manorial records and an abstract of title to properties. Such documents allow us to build up a mental picture of the interior of a home and workplace, thereby bringing the building to life. In this case we catch some glimpses of the day-to-day life of a wheelwright's home and business place as items of cherished furniture and important tools and equipment are mentioned in the wills. This illustrates how it is possible to find out more about a building by following the people associated with it.

The abstract of title in the same bundle of deeds also provides a summary of who owned this messuage and the land it stood on back to 1796, by recording the various sales, mortgages and inheritances between 1790 and 1845. Through these it is possible to trace ownership of this house from 1790. From Michael Habberton it passed to his daughter Mary, who married Samuel Suggett and, following her death in 1843, the house and part of the land passed to her brother's family and then on to the Bartles.

'Social survey maps' are mentioned in the separate maps and public health sections. Such maps also play a crucial part in researching the history of a community, as concerns with the health and social welfare of the poor in the Victorian era led to their creation from the 1830s onwards.

Local Histories

Local historians both amateur and academic have long been passionate about recording the history of local areas. Many such accounts have been produced from at least the seventeenth century onwards. They often record items of interest about buildings and archaeological remains, as well as pedigrees of notable people and landowners. These do need to be treated with caution, as the wealth of genealogical material now available was not easily accessible, so you may discover inaccuracies and contradictions. The opposite can also be true, as the writers may have had access to records long since damaged or destroyed. Blomefield's 'History of Norfolk', originally written in the early 1700s, and updated in the early 1800s, for example, provides details of manor houses being passed on through sale or inheritance.

Occasionally a building or piece of land may have already been researched by someone else. Old pubs, schools, vicarages, almshouses, manor houses and large farmhouses are often mentioned in local histories of a city, town or village. A local history of Sidbury in Devon, for instance, describes buildings and the people who lived in them accompanied by old photographs (*Within the Bounds: Sidbury Parish Past and Present* by Barbara Softly, West Country Books, 1998).

The *Victoria County History* (VCH) series is always worth checking for such details. *The Victoria County History* was founded in 1899 as an encyclopaedic record of England's places and people from the earliest times. It covers cities, towns and parishes across the country. More than 240 volumes have been published, providing an invaluable resource of local history. Many record offices and reference libraries have copies for their county. A full list can be found at their website as well as links to those available online as PDF copies **www.victoriacountyhistory.ac.uk**.

Literary references to buildings are another source that brings our homes to life. The words of Dickens, Austen, the Brontë sisters and other contemporary authors weave a mental picture of buildings, their furnishings, decoration, social status, physical position and so much more. Some may be directly relevant to where you live, whilst others will simply give a flavour of similar buildings at certain points in time. Charles Dickens, for example, featured Shoreditch in his works, with Mr Micawber living at Windsor Terrace, City Road (now demolished) and Oliver Twist living in south Shoreditch.

Oral Histories, Local Tales, Legends

Another important element of local history is the stories associated with a house. An amazing amount of detail regarding properties and the people who lived in them can be obtained from local histories. Some of these may prove inaccurate, but others will have at least a grain of truth in them. Talking to local people, especially those who have lived there a long time, and investigating the local history of the area can reveal details you won't find in official documents. Whilst some of these stories may never be substantiated, others may take you in directions you would not have otherwise thought to research. When researching a house in Swan Street in Boxford in Suffolk, I found local histories of the village invaluable when trying to discover what this house and its neighbours had been used for over time.

Finding out More about Local History

An immense amount of local history is available locally, nationally and online. Local studies libraries and heritage centres collect both published and unpublished material for each county. Photographs, postcards, newspapers, local history ephemera, oral histories, unpublished memoirs, biographies and autobiographies, posters, drawings, sales particulars and so on can all be found there.

There is often one (or more) person who is the 'village historian'. A variation on this is the Online Parish Clerk (OPC) project, which acts as a conduit for transcribing and indexing projects. This involves a worldwide group of volunteers gathering transcriptions and name indexes relating to individual parishes which are not already readily available elsewhere, such as land tax assessments and census information. Links to local OPCs can be found on GENUKI **www.genuki.org.uk/indexes/OPC.html**.

Vision of Britain is one of my favourite websites as it provides historical information on individual places over a two-hundred-year period. These include historic maps dating from the early 1800s, travel writings from people such as Daniel Defoe, statistics and other general data **www.visionofbritain.org.uk**.

Local history groups flourish across the country. *The Family and Local History Handbook* is a directory of a vast number of such organizations, whilst the Local History organization has a list of all groups affiliated with it.

There are now a huge number of parish and local history websites online which can be found simply by putting the name of a place and 'local history' into a search engine. Some exist only online, whilst others have been created by local groups. Whilst this book obviously cannot list them all, looking at some of those I have come across will give you an idea of what might be out there.

One fantastic example is the Foxearth District Local History Society, which publishes research materials relating to the area around the parishes of Borley, Foxearth, Liston and Pentlow in Essex and Suffolk. Their website includes a vast amount of local history material from directories, newspapers, contemporary accounts, photographs, drawings, parish records and so on. One fascinating example is their reproduction of the account of 'The Old Timbered Houses of Sudbury', complete with illustrations, which was originally published by William Hodson in 1887 in the Suffolk Institute of Archaeology and Natural History.

Other historical information on houses and streets in Sudbury can be found on this site in transcripts of a wide range records originally collected by David Lindley from parish registers and records; trade directories; the listed buildings register; nineteenth and early twentieth-century planning committee minutes; newspapers; census returns; manorial records; wills and photographs. Number 8 Hungate, for instance, is described as an eighteenth-century building, two storeys high, with painted bricks, a rather steep slated roof and a mid-nineteenth-century shop front designed by Arthur Pellis in 1891. Further information lists some of the occupiers from 1600, as well as who bought and sold or inherited it. **www.foxearth.org.uk/index.html**

Lincolnshire is one county that has catalogues and photographs online. Their local studies library catalogue can be searched at: **www.lincolnshire.gov.uk/index** There is also a joint illustrations database from the archives and library collections of over 50,000 photographs including buildings and topographical views. Contact Lincolnshire Archives or email **illustrations_index@lincolnshire.go.uk**.

A fantastic website to find links and information on places is the Modern History Sourcebook site. This has articles and documentary sources on the social and economic changes occurring throughout the nineteenth and twentieth centuries. **www.fordham.edu/halsall/mod/modsbook20.html**

The Dictionary of National Biography can be very useful for background information on prominent people associated with properties.

It was fashionable in the eighteenth and nineteenth centuries for gentlemen to travel round the British Isles, in a homegrown version of the grand tour, recording their observations in letters, diaries and publications, often accompanied by sketches. Some of the best known are Daniel Defoe, who described villages, buildings and people on his tour of Eastern England in 1722 and Richard Cobbold's *Rural Rides* across England in 1821–26. Some historical accounts such as Defoe's can be found online, often published by Gutenberg books or on the Vision of Britain website.

If you are interested in how people lived in the seventeenth century, for instance, a fascinating glimpse into day-to-day life in seventeenth-century London can be seen in Pepys' *Diary* **www.pepysdiary.com** Other accounts, such as a history of Little Walsingham in Norfolk in the Lee-Warner collection at Norfolk Record Office, can be found amongst private collections held in local archives.

Other groups and individuals have been involved with collecting, producing and preserving local histories, oral histories, memoirs, biographies and autobiographies. These range from the Women's Institute (WI) to vicars. Novelists of the past also drew on the stories and history of certain areas. Amongst these you may be fortunate enough to find specific mention of your property or others nearby. If not, you will at least gain a greater knowledge about some of the people and events which shaped the place in which your property is situated.

Finding Societies, Groups and Information

Local archives and local history libraries have huge amounts of local history material, much of it unpublished. A search for information on Ebbw Vale by local researcher Greg Howes produced copies of local histories, magazines from the steelworks, photographs of houses and newspaper articles. Amongst these were magazines produced by the Ebbw Vale Steelworks from 1923 and 1927 and the Ebbw Vale Official Guide of 1936 extolling the quality of houses for workers.

Family history societies often collect local histories, as knowledge of family and local history go hand in hand. This means there may already

(This page and opposite) Official Guide to Ebbw Vale, 1936. (Ebbw Vale Pictorial Collection, Gwent Archives)

EBBW VALE

(MONMOUTHSHIRE)

An Industrial Town of present importance, and with great possibilities of future development

Official Handbook

(Second Edition)

Produced for the
Town Development Committee of
The Ebbw Vale Urban District Council

Copyright

Ed. J. Burrow & Co. Ltd., Imperial House, Cheltenham
and 125 Strand, London, W C.2

E.B. *Printed in Great Britain*

be a huge amount of information on people and places from across your region readily available. Many of these would be hard, if not impossible, to find elsewhere.

A huge number of village, town and city history websites can be found online, as well as some associated with particular buildings, such as stately homes, pubs and hotels. People in Boltby in Yorkshire, for example, produced a history of the village a few years ago full of photographs, copies of maps, details of buildings and people. Local Histories acts as an umbrella for details of local groups **www.localhistories.org.**

Burke's Peerage and *Burke's Landed Gentry* are helpful if a building was connected with prominent people. **www.burkes-peerage.net**.

Whitmore and Marshall detail bibliographical references to the sixteenth and seventeenth-century heraldic pedigrees.

A very useful journal is 'The Family and Local History Handbook' published by Robert Blatchford annually. This lists local history societies, archives, local studies libraries, museums and other organizations as well as interesting articles on a range of subjects. **www.genealogical.co.uk /index.html**

Three major publishers of books on local history are Phillimore **www.phillimore.co.uk**, Sutton publishing **www.suttonpublishing.co.uk** and Pen & Sword Books **www.pen-and-sword.co.uk**.

The British Association for Local History is based at PO Box 6549, Somersal Herbert, Ashbourne, Derbyshire, DE6 5WH **www.balh.co.uk**.

If your home was built in the Victorian period, then the Family and Community Historical Research Society (FACHRS) publish research into all aspects of Victorian social, family and local history. **www.fachrs.com**.

The British History Online website has much useful general historical information and can be searched by place. **www.british-history.ac.uk**

Another interesting local history project is **www.ideal-homes.org.uk** which has galleries of maps and images from south-east London arranged by borough.

The History Pin website allows people to add their own photographs of houses and streets **www.historypin.com**

The BBC History website has a gateway page to social, political history and local history links. **www.bbc.co.uk/history/trail**

Great Britain Historical Geographical Information System (GIS) – details of Britain's localities from census reports, historical gazetteers and maps at: **www.port.ac.uk/research/gbhgis**

The *Victoria County History* series (VCH) includes descriptions of parishes. Most large reference libraries and local history libraries have copies for their area. A full collection can be seen at the Society of Genealogists and several counties are available online at **www.victoria-countyhistory.ac.uk**

There are also many local initiatives, some of which are published privately. Some family history societies collect such histories. To find your nearest family history society, check the Federation of Family History Societies. **www.ffhs.org.uk**

Record Societies were founded for the purpose of publishing editions of original documents and unavailable printed works and historical maps for each county in order to make them more accessible (see Resource Directory for contact details). For example, the charter series published by Suffolk Record Society includes those for the village of Stanton near Bury St Edmunds from around 1215 to 1678 (The Boydell Press, 2009). Most of the documents were written for or involved local peasants and farmers. Grants, sales of leases of land and property feature prominently and also illustrate the social and economic history of this village, and Suffolk generally. Archaeological societies can also be very useful when it comes to researching buildings, although they often feature just one particular building or site.

Photographs, Postcards, Paintings and Drawings

Finding visual images or descriptions of your home in the past is one of the most exciting discoveries. These could be paintings, old photographs or drawings. If you are very fortunate these will feature the building you are researching. Even if they don't show your home, other buildings nearby and features of interest can be located. Descriptions, drawings and paintings of buildings can turn up in some unexpected places. For example, the editor of the *Children's Encyclopedia*, Arthur Mee, wrote an interesting account of how his own house was built, with accompanying drawings, in the encyclopedia of 1925.

The first photographs were taken in 1839 and the first British studio opened in London in 1841. Picture postcards began in the 1870s or 1880s. How wonderful to find one such as the one from Bacton-on-Sea sent by 'May C' on 4 July 1910, featuring Holme Cottage and entitled 'postcard of "our house"'.

An example of some of the hundreds of thousands of sketches to be found in collections in county archives is the eighteenth-century *Features of Wortham* in Suffolk. Drawings and descriptions of every type of house in the village were produced by the local rector, Richard Cobbold, over the fifty years he was incumbent and can be seen at the Suffolk Record Office in Suffolk. Some of these can be seen in his 1860 *Biography of A Victorian Village,* which has been published. Although this is just one small place, the detail helps us envisage what similar homes elsewhere looked like at the same time, and gives us insights into the living conditions at that time. Another example from Suffolk Record Office is the plans and elevations of buildings in the Tollemach collection, which include many pubs.

Taking photographs of the area around your home is also essential as it highlights the changes that have occurred and captures remnants of the past. In the case of a house on New Inn Yard in Shoreditch traced for its owner's descendants, the house itself no longer survives, although New Inn Yard does. Much of the Shoreditch area has been redeveloped

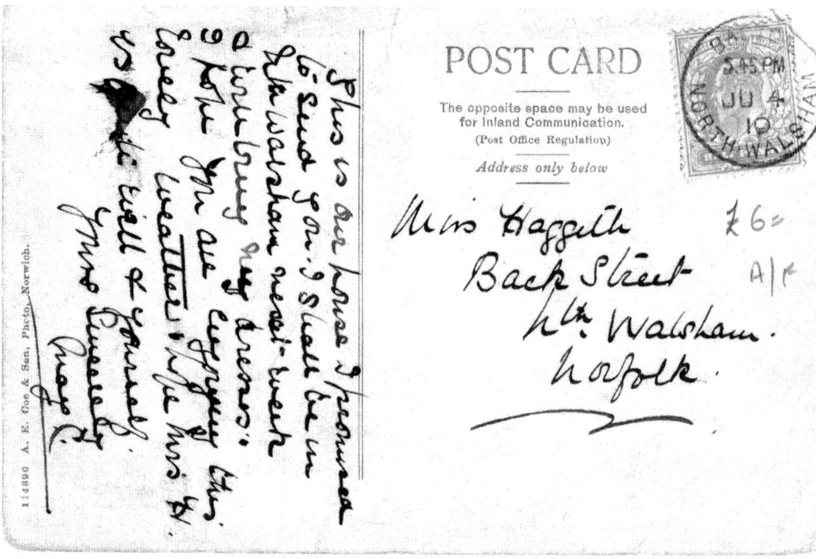

Postcard of Bacton-on-Sea.

in the last fifty years and a recent visit revealed that all except one of the houses had been demolished prior to a new redevelopment. Photographs of the remaining house in this yard and the new development thereby provided a postscript to the history of the house being investigated.

Finding Images

Local history libraries, record offices, The National Archives and the National Library of Wales all have large collections of old photographs and other material which might show how your house or neighbourhood looked in the past. Paintings and drawings of buildings from the great to small can be found in archives, galleries and private collections.

Original works by famous artists are most often found in museums and galleries, but reproductions can be bought, or even found free online. Artwork can also be found in books, magazines and private collections. Painting and drawing have been popular hobbies for many generations, so it is always worth checking local museums, heritage centres and local history libraries for information on local artists and whether there are any known works relating to where you live.

Check the collections of the landowners and prominent people at record offices. When searching for information on property in Brent Eleigh in Suffolk, for example, a bundle of family papers included some notes about the history of the house which formed the basis of an article that appeared in *Country Life* magazine. An illustrated book created by a member of the same family in the same collection also included photographs and drawings of the house.

The Hulton Getty picture collection at Unique House, 21–31 Woodfield Road, London W9 2BA, is considered one of the world's greatest libraries of photographs and other images dating from the 1800s. **www.gettyimages.co.uk/creative/frontdoor/hultonarchive**

The National Monuments Centre (NMR), Great Western Village, Kemble Drive, Swindon, SN2 2GZ, has a huge collection of material of use when researching the history of a building. This includes a photographic collection of buildings taken by the National Buildings Record (NBR), which began in 1941 and was the forerunner to the NMR. Its original aim was to record the architecture of buildings that were likely to be targeted during the Blitz and has resulted in a photographic record of many buildings that were subsequently destroyed. **www.english-heritage.org.uk/professional/archives-and-collections/nmr**

There are a number of online collections, some free and others commercial. One of the best known is the Francis Frith archive, founded in 1860, which has over 365,000 photographs of around 7,000 British towns and villages. **www.francisfrith.co.uk** There is also the Dixon-Scott

Photograph of a house in Brent Eleigh in Suffolk. (SRO: Bury St. Edmunds HD 27/13409)

Photographic Collection, 1915–1948, held at The National Archives and available online: **www.nationalarchives.gov.uk**

Many local history libraries and record offices are placing images online. A very good example is the excellent collection of old postcards and photographs from the Centre for Buckinghamshire Studies. **www.buckscc.gov.uk/bcc/museum/ea_buckinghamshire_photos.page**

Postcard dealers advertise locally and nationally and there are several with online galleries such as Footsteps in Time. Many dealers also attend family and local history or antique fairs.

English Heritage maintains the database of English buildings listed as of historic or architectural importance. Each one has a description. A nine-year project coordinated between the Royal Photographic Society and local camera clubs resulted in a photograph of each one up to the year 2008. **www.english-heritage.org.uk/professional/protection/process/national-heritage-list-for-england** They also have a huge collection of general photographs dating from the earliest days of photography. Their online database lists some of these at: **www.english-heritage.org.uk/viewfinder**

Survey of London is part of the English Heritage Archive. As mentioned in the section on maps it carries out detailed architectural studies of London, which are published. These include many descriptions of buildings, accompanied by contemporary and historical drawings and photographs. The survey can be consulted at the English Heritage archive in Swindon. **www.english-heritage.org.uk**. The Survey of London is also available online via the Institute of Historical Research's British History Online website, which hosts a wide range of digitized primary and secondary printed sources for medieval and modern history. **www.british-history.ac.uk**

When looking for information on a house called Crewes Hurst in the village of Warlingham in Surrey the British History website provided an interesting description of the village. This was taken from a history of Surrey written in 1912 and specifically mentions Crewes farm house as being the old manor house 'which, though modernized, contains ancient portions'. Further details on Warlingham and many of its buildings, including photographs, were found on a website called 'Exploring Surrey's Past', which reproduces details from parish histories written by a local churchwarden between 1898 and 1925. **www.exploringsurreyspast.org.uk**

Aerial Surveys

Aerial surveys are very helpful in identifying changes in the structure of buildings as well as putting buildings into their physical context very clearly. In addition, boundary markings, the remains of older buildings and changes in the shape of rooflines or shape of exterior walls all show up from the air in a way that can be hard to see clearly from the ground. Archaeological mapping from the air began in the early 1900s, and O.G.S. Crawford's 1928 book *Wessex from the Air* demonstrated its true potential from flights he had taken across Dorset, Hampshire and Wiltshire in 1924.

RCHME and English Heritage launched a programme of archaeological mapping from aerial photographs in 1988 – the National Mapping Programme. The aim was to map, interpret and record all archaeological features on aerial photographs to a consistent standard and produce a map of England's prehistoric and historic landscape.

Finding Aerial Surveys

The Royal Commission on the Historic Monuments of England (RCHME) established an Air Photographs Unit as part of its National Monuments Records. The unit has carried out its own flights throughout England since 1967. The archive was taken over by English Heritage in 1999 and is home to around three million aerial photographs. Some photographs can be found on their website **www.english-heritage.org.uk/professional/research/landscapes-and-areas/national-mapping-programme**

Many local archives hold copies of the Aerial Survey conducted by the Royal Air Force in 1945–46 to help with the revision of maps as well as highways and planning work. Copies of many historical aerial photographs can be found online at Multimap **www.multimap.com**. Many are included on village and town websites and local museum and archaeological websites.

Listed Buildings, Environmental and Heritage Surveys

The first legal attempt to preserve old and interesting buildings was the Ancient Monuments Protection Act of 1882. A number of other Acts followed and the 1944 Town and Country Planning Act empowered the Ministry of Town and Country Planning to draw up lists of historic buildings and other constructions for local authorities classified in grades of importance. The listings often include relevant social and local history details.

The Royal Commission on Historical Monuments of England (RCHME) was set up in 1908 to compile and publish an inventory of all ancient and historical monuments by county and parish. The Historic Building and Monuments Commission for England was set up in 1963 and later renamed English Heritage. It merged with RCHME in 1999 and their joint archives are held at the National Monuments Centre. These include over 70,000 building files for individual buildings with photographs, drawings, notes and reports and inventories created by inspectors visiting parishes making a note of buildings that might be of merit and published between 1910 and 1993. These were not all listed buildings. **www.englishheritagearchives.org.uk**

Many local record offices and reference libraries have lists of listed buildings and other historically important buildings for their area. The county of Kent, for example, has a Historic Buildings Committee which has produced a series of indexes covering a wide number of districts across the county. These include notes on listed buildings, ancient monuments and other buildings of interest.

A great resource for finding out about an area and individual properties are the numerous environmental and heritage surveys that have been carried out across the UK. These can include the results of archaeological digs, items relating to the local history of an area and any sites of special architectural interest past and present. Information on listed buildings is often recorded in some detail. Some surveys are conducted for a particular purpose, such as levels and risk of subsidence or industrial contamination, which means they may only record details relevant to their purpose.

Nevertheless, such surveys are always worth looking at as they will help you build up knowledge of an area and may contain details relevant to your property or others nearby. For example, a search for information on the Upper King Street area of Norwich at the Norfolk Heritage Centre came up with information on the history and ownership of neighbouring buildings, including some no longer there or significantly altered over time. The environment record included archaeological surveys; copies of maps from the sixteenth to twentieth centuries; information from Taylor's *Index Monasticus* published in 1821; notes from the 1568–1570 Norwich landgable (a survey of ground rents payable to the king) and the 1570–72 census of the poor.

A fantastic online example is the Norfolk Heritage Explorer website, which includes the *Norfolk Historic Environment Record* database, which describes the archaeology of Norfolk from the Palaeolithic period to the modern day.

Finding Listed Buildings and Environmental and Heritage Surveys

All listed buildings up to the year 2000 are included on the 'Images of England' website **www.imagesofengland.org.uk** This includes photographs, the century of construction and important technical details. Past owners are sometimes recorded.

British Listed Buildings is an online database of buildings and structures that are listed as being of special architectural and historic interest. As well as reading the official listing data for each building, you can also view the location on a map, and, where possible, browse for listed buildings by country, county and parish/locality. **www.britishlistedbuildings.co.uk**

The National Monuments Record Centre in Swindon provides details on old buildings. **www.swindon.gov.uk.nmro**

English Heritage is responsible for administering the list of 'Buildings of Special Architectural or Historical Interest'. A nine-year project to add photographs in collaboration with the Royal Photographic Society and local camera clubs was completed in 2008 and can be seen on Images of England **www.english-heritage.org.uk/professional/protection/process/national-heritage-list-for-england**

Some local record offices have lists of listed buildings in their area. Local environmental surveys can also be found in reference and local studies libraries, museums and record offices. Many are published online.

The English Heritage 'Red Box' Collection has over 500,000 miscellaneous architectural items, mainly photographs of buildings, from the 1870s to the 1980s. These are particularly good for church buildings and country houses, but do include other homes, shops, schools and other buildings.

PastScape describes around 400,000 archaeological and architectural records with information about their sites. **www.pastscape.org.uk**

Chapter 5

RESOURCES

Whatever the age of your home there are certain records and steps everyone can and should take. Most of all, understanding the documents used for tracing the history of a house is absolutely essential. Whilst some refer to particular time periods, others may cover several hundred years, or be something you revisit over and over again in order to find out more about your property and the people who lived in it.

The resources section of this guide will take you alphabetically through the main types of documents you need to research the history of your home. However, when starting out you need to access the deeds to your home, obtain details from the land registry and to look at modern electoral registers and local histories. Going back from the twenty-first century to the beginning of the twentieth the main resources will be modern Ordnance Survey maps; electoral registers; trade and street directories which list many people living in particular places; the National Farm Survey of 1944; local histories describing places and people; sales particulars advertising properties for sale; the Inland Revenue Survey of 1910–15 which recorded every property and who owned and lived in it and the 1911 and 1901 census returns showing who was in every household in Britain on the night it was taken. If you wish to find out more about the people living in your home in this period then you will also need birth, marriage and death certificates, parish registers and wills.

Stepping back from the twentieth century into the nineteenth, all the resources mentioned above will still prove relevant. In this period you can add further census returns back to 1841 (and sometimes back to 1801); poll books showing who people voted for up to 1872 and electoral registers listing everyone who could vote from 1832 to the present day. The national survey of owners of land over an acre in size taken between 1873 and 1876 may also prove helpful. Local parish registers of baptisms, marriages and burials become especially important in this period as there was no national registration of births, deaths and marriages until 1837 and many omissions until the 1870s. Parish registers can also save you money as buying certificates can prove very expensive.

It is virtually impossible to research a building of any kind thoroughly without using maps. The nineteenth century saw an explosion of maps being produced. Those of most use to the family historian are those created by the Ordnance Survey and the tithe maps and their accompanying apportionments listing everyone who paid tithes to the church, which began in 1836. Although enclosure maps can be found as early as the 1500s, the main series began in 1801 and shows owners and sometimes occupiers of large areas of former common land and fields which had been divided into individual strips.

You will find that as you go further back in time to the seventeen and sixteen hundreds and before that you revisit many of these resources. Some which either only exist or are most useful in this period are the hearth tax records of 1662–69, the land tax records which began in 1692 and window tax records of 1697–1851.

Resources relevant to particular types of properties such as mills or pubs and the occupations of those who lived in them are not necessarily tied to a specific time period. These include business, occupational records and court records. If you live in a house built on land once owned by the church then their glebe records may reveal more. A major resource is the wills and administrations of people owning or renting property. These can be found from the thirteen hundreds up to the present day.

Manorial and estate records are a resource that can cover several hundred years. Manorial records can provide information on ownership of copyhold land (around one third of all land in England and Wales) from the thirteen hundreds up to 1922. Fire Insurance records, taxes and the records held in the parish chest all feature. These generally tell you about the owners and occupiers who took care to protect their buildings and had to pay rates and taxes. Once you have exhausted these records, the earliest record you are likely to use is the Domesday Book of 1086.

Below is a timeline which includes a summary list of the different documentary resources which can be used in house history. It also makes reference to key events or pieces of legislation that impacted on how buildings developed.

Dates	**Time Periods, Key Events and Types of Records**
From *c.*1200s	Wills, administrations and inventories
1235–1649	Inquisitions post mortem
*c.*1300–1920s	Manorial records
1361–1971	Quarter Sessions records
*c.*1400–1750	Older borough records
1479	First map of Bristol
1485–1558	Tudor Period
1500s–1980s	Rate records
1538–present	Parish registers

1534–mid-1500s	Records of Dissolution of Monasteries
*c.*1500s–1960	Enclosures of common land
1560	Cunningham's map of Norwich published
1560	The Agas map of London published
1574–1579	Saxton's county maps
1660–1850s	Glebe terriers recording church lands and properties
*c.*1660s present	Newspapers and Broadsheets widely published
1663–1920	Bedford Level Corporation records survive
1662–1688	Hearth Tax
1677	First London directory
1680–1968	Fire insurance records
1683	Ogilby and Morgans maps of London published
1693–1963	Land Tax
1696–1851	Window Tax
1696–1872	Poll Books – list voters in county elections
1700–1799	Many town, county, estate and country maps
1701	First English local newspaper published in Norwich
1702	Publication of the first national newspaper – *The Daily Courier*
1704	Queen Anne Bounty introduced to provide loans for the purchase of parsonage houses
1708	Land registries begin in the East Riding of Yorkshire and Ireland
1709	Opening of Middlesex deeds registry
1716	Sun Fire Insurance Office established
1732	General adoption of English instead of Latin in legal records
1736	Opening of North Riding of Yorkshire deeds registry
1747	Window Tax reinforced
1780–1832	Main period that land tax records survive for 1785
1785–1985	The Times Newspaper is first published
1798	Land Tax Perpetuation Act – everyone liable to pay land tax is listed
1800–1910	Records of planning, street names, sewers etc.
*c.*1800–1930s	Most county and city trade and street directories are published
1801	First Ordnance Survey 1 inch = 1 mile
1801	First Parliamentary Enclosure Act
1801–1831	Some census returns available – mostly local records
1830	William IV lifted tax on beer. Many pubs named after him
1832	Reform Act
1832–present	Annual electoral registers compiled
1836–1856	Tithe Maps and Apportionments compiled

July 1837–present	National registration of births, deaths and marriages in England and Wales
1839	First daguerreotype
1841–1911	Annual Census Returns – show who was living in a household decade by decade
1843	First Ordnance Survey 5 inch = 1 mile
1850	First Ordnance Survey 10 inch = 1 mile
	Repeal of Brick Tax
1854–1967	Rent charge apportionments
1854	First Ordnance Survey 25 inch = 1 mile
From 1858	National civil system for proving wills and administrations
1862	National Land Registry begins
1872	Introduction of secret ballot ends compilation of voters lists
1873–1876	Land Valuation Survey
1880s–present	Telephone directories
1882	The first Ancient Monuments Protection Act passed
1899	Land registry compulsory in London
1901–1911	Annual Census Returns – show who was living in a household in the first two decades of the twentieth century
1903	Booth's Survey of London Poverty
1910–1920	Inland Revenue Valuation Office Survey (aka Lloyd George Domesday)
1918	Extension of right to vote means all men over 18 and women included in electoral registers
1922	Law of Property Act ends the copyhold system of land tenure
1924–1969	Houses and Inhabited House Tax
1925	Law of Property Act – the seller of a house only has to provide title for the previous 30 years
1928	Street numbers begin to be included in electoral registers
1941–1943	National Farm Survey
1944	Town and Country Planning Act enabled the Ministry of Town and Country Planning to draw up lists of historic buildings
1971	Electoral Registers include everyone over 17 years old
2003	Compulsory to register all properties with the Land Registry

Births, Marriages and Deaths

You cannot research the history of a house without finding out about the people connected to it. Once a building is created and used it becomes unique, even if a thousand others look the same on the outside. This is because people are the heart of every building, whether it is domestic or commercial. It is their lives, feelings, beliefs, attitudes, actions and experiences as well as what led them there that creates a home's personality.

One of the key sources for tracing people from July 1837 onwards is births, marriages and deaths. A national system known as civil registration was introduced at that date to record births, marriages and deaths. Indexes to these can be searched free, but individual certificates have to be purchased.

You will find that certificates start to include more detail as time goes on. Many of the early ones, particularly in rural areas, do not include addresses. They can, however, be used in conjunction with other records such as electoral registers; parish registers; census returns and trade directories in order to narrow down when people moved in and out of a property. For example, when researching a house which had stood empty for some years I knew that two different families lived there when the 1861 and 1871 census returns were taken, but not when the later occupants moved in. This couple's marriage certificate in the mid–1860s gave a different address, but by the time their first child was born two years later they were shown as living at the house.

Finding Birth, Marriage and Death Certificates

Indexes can be found locally, nationally and online and copies of certificates can be bought online for £9.25 each or from local registrars for £10.

FreeBMD is a free index to the original indexes of English and Welsh births, marriages and deaths from 1837 up to the early part of the twentieth century. **www.freebmd.org.uk**

There are a number of commercial websites that host their own versions of the indexes from 1837 to within the last few years. Some have copies of the original indexes which can be checked and searched independently. Access costs vary and the main companies are Find my Past at **www.findmypast.com.uk** and Ancestry at **www.ancestry.co.uk**. Ancestry is available free at most libraries in the UK.

The cheapest and quickest way to buy a certificate is to use the online ordering service at: **www.gro.gov.uk/gro/content/certificates** Certificates can be ordered by post from: General Register Office, Postal Application Section, PO Box 2, Southport, Merseyside, PR8 2JD.

Contact details for local registry offices can be found via telephone directories and **www.192.com** and registry offices in your area. The GENUKI site also lists local offices at: **www.genuki.org.uk/big/eng/RegOffice**

Business and Occupational Records

Work and home were much more intertwined in the past, with large numbers of people working from home or close by. Hundreds of thousands of homes before the early to mid–1800s housed the cottage industries of weavers, lace-makers, carpenters, cobblers and so on. Other business premises such as factories, mills or public houses have since been converted. This means that searching for business and work records can form an integral part of research into a property's history. Many businesses have their roots in a local community so their history also reflects the history of that place. An example is Tombland Bookshop in Norwich, which has been a doctor's home and butcher's shop, amongst other things, in the past. Your home too may have had more than one type of use.

Every collection of business records is unique and can include anything relating to a company's history, some of which are listed separately in this guide in their own right. These include mortgages; sales particulars; marriage contracts; employee records; accounts; newspaper cuttings; promotional material and photographs.

Brewery records are a great example of how business records can be used. Virtually every city, town, village and parish has had at least one public house, inn, tavern or beer house during its existence. Brewery records tend to be administrative, financial or legal and can include minute books; accounts ledgers; wages books; pension, letter and estate books giving details of sites, tenure, rentals and so on. Records for pubs owned by Watney Mann in Norwich are a good example as they include estate books from 1837 of city and county public houses listing their sign and situation, tenure, rentals and annual deliveries. A survey of all the brewery premises provides an overall estimated value, with a summary of each property. There are also some records of property sales detailing the reason for disposal, name of buyer and prices. This collection also has some photographs of brewery workers and public houses used in a souvenir booklet

Many breweries merged, so the big companies still in existence often have records from smaller breweries that no longer exist. This can mean there is more than one series of records to look in. For instance, whilst searching for details on a pub once owned by Steward and Patteson in Norfolk I found some were listed under Steward and Patteson, whilst others formed part of the Pockthorpe Brewery collection, which was at the Steward and Patteson headquarters.

It is very common for pubs to change names or even reuse a name once

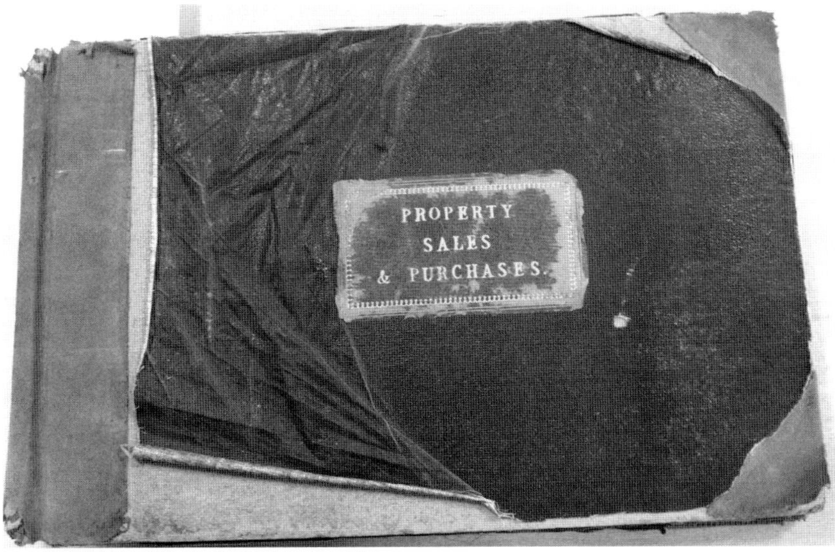

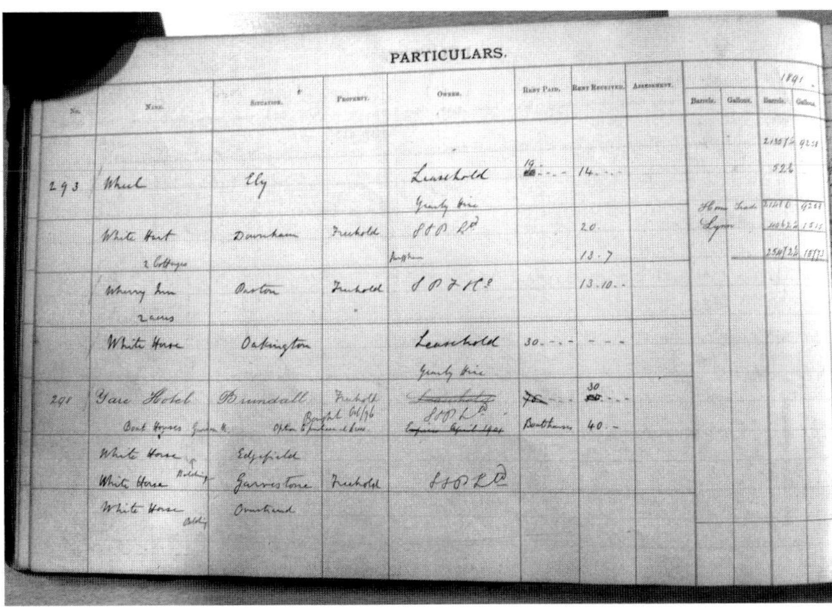

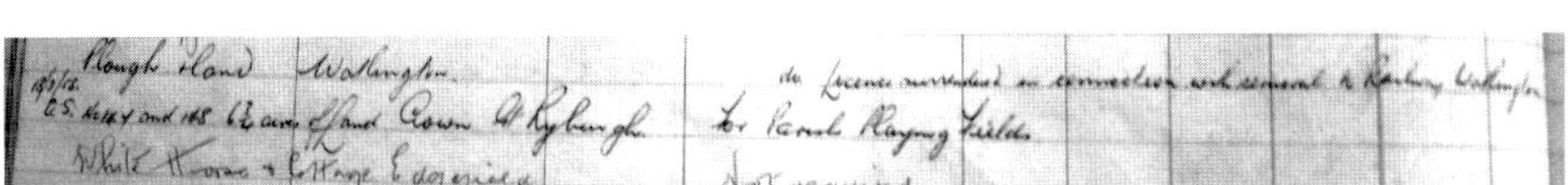

Watney Mann records giving details of a pub in Edgefield in Norfolk. (NRO: BR 259/26/1)

used by another pub in the same area. Brewery records, the tithe map of 1845, Ordnance Survey maps, the electoral register, trade directories and other sources show how a Robert Broughton went from leasing a cottage, blacksmith's shop and foundry at Cross Green in Edgefield to buying it in 1861. He then built a pub on the side of the blacksmith's workshop. This became the White Horse, after another pub of the same name on The Street in a completely different part of the village.

The brewery records contain deeds for the White Horse that describe how in 1812 Thomas Barber and wife Rebecca sold one rod of land to William Bacon of Edgefield. They go on to detail how, sometime between 1812 and 1827, William Bacon sold the land to John Pegg of Edgefield for £20 and John Pegg subsequently built 'a substantial house and blacksmith's shop' there. In 1827 John Pegg mortgaged the land with house for £100. In 1830, John Pegg defaulted on paying the principal on the mortgage, but had paid the interest. He then sold the property to John Richardson of Heydon. After the death of John Richardson in 1849 the property was put in trust for his son John Soame Richardson until aged twenty-one. It was sold to Robert Broughton in 1861.

The brewery records (NRO: BR 1/148 and BR 259/26) also provide much information on what subsequently happened to the White Horse pub in Edgefield. A undated note on the wrapper of the deeds states it was sold to 'Steward and Pattason Limited'[sic]. An entry found in an index of public houses they owned lists the amount of land on the site and shows that the pub and cottages nearby were sold to the Swaffham Brewery in 1895. Delivery particulars for the period 1890 to 1902 show the number of barrels and gallons delivered from 1892 onwards, along with the notation 'Home Trade Swaffham Lynn'. A separate property sales and purchases register lists 'White Horse and cottage' at Edgefield as being sold to the tenant, A. Ellis, for £1100 in 1957.

Occupational records for the people who lived and worked in your home can also add to its history. Apprenticeship indentures, for example, can survive from 1563 onwards and will give the names of both master and apprentice being bound. Although these are most helpful for following up on people you know lived in a property, such records can also add to your knowledge of what occupations were carried on there and people's living conditions.

Every town and village has had at least one vicarage or rectory. These were rarely purpose-built before Queen Anne's Bounty of 1704 provided loans for clergy to buy parsonage houses. This scheme was extended under the Gilbert Act of 1776, which allowed incumbents to mortgage glebe land to build new parsonages or outbuildings or to improve existing ones. The money raised was entrusted to a third party, or nominee, who supervised the work. Incumbents were responsible for the maintenance and repair of the parsonage, and under the Dilapidations

Act of 1871, surveyors were appointed to inspect glebe buildings. Parish records show how Reverend Hayter of Burnham Sutton made good use of these arrangements when, with the assistance of the Church Commissioners, he took out a mortgage to buy a house and various pieces of land at Burnham Sutton for £1035.

Finding Business and Occupational Records

The National Register of Archives (NRA) includes the results of several individual and industry-based surveys conducted by the Business Archives Council and Historical Manuscripts Commission **www .nationalarchives.gov.uk/nra** The NRA also provides useful links to other online resources which may have additional information, such as Access to Archives (A2A), the Archives Hub and electronic catalogues from individual record offices and archives.

The majority of business records are still local records. This means they are held close to where the business originated, with around seventy per cent held in city or county record offices. Contact details for each repository can be found on ARCHON, the online directory of archive repositories **www.nationalarchives.gov.uk/archon** (also linked to the NRA).

Most local record offices have indexes to individual businesses. However, some business records are mixed in with other personal or family papers and some business names have changed over the years. This means you may need to do a certain amount of cross-referencing to find the full scope of records, but many record offices have a designated business archivist who can advise you.

A large number of big companies have their own archives. Where these businesses have become part of bigger parent organizations, as Colman's Mustard did when bought by the Reckitt Company, their records may end up held in the parent companies' archives. In the case of Colman's there are some records held locally, and a catalogue of others held by their head office in Yorkshire.

The National Archives, ARCHON and Access to Archives (A2A) all have lists and catalogues of business records. The commercial website Find my Past also includes a list of business records **www .findmypast.co.uk**

Many businesses still hold their own records. They may charge for access, but I have found several very accommodating, especially if you provide information in return. Some include historical information on their websites or have produced a company history.

Companies House holds details of live and recently dissolved companies. Basic information about listed companies is free. This includes the company's registered office.

Some companies which no longer trade still exist as legal entities for practical reasons, especially where there are property and assets still needing management, or to prevent a company name being reused by someone else. Where companies have been dissolved there should be some basic information in the files of dissolved companies at The National Archives. Other records which can be found at The National Archives include rail and canal companies nationalized in 1948.

Trade and street directories provide invaluable lists of businesses across the UK from the eighteenth to the late twentieth century. Not only do they list many small tradespeople, but their potted histories of each parish also often refer to businesses, the buildings they were housed in and the people who formed them. Other buildings which have since been converted to domestic use, such as schools and chapels, will also be listed. The Society of Genealogists has an extensive collection **www.sog.org.uk**. Many directories can be found online at **www.historicaldirectories.org**

Specialist archives which collect records from particular businesses include the Guildhall Library, Aldermanbury, London EC2P 2EJ, which holds those from City of London companies. The Museum of English Rural Life, University of Reading, PO Box 229, Whiteknights, Reading, RG6 6AG, has records of farms, agricultural engineers and related businesses **www.merl.org.uk**.

The Museum of Science and Industry in Manchester, Collections and Information Department, Liverpool Road, Manchester, M3 4JP, has records of many businesses in the North West, especially those from the engineering trades.

If you live on or near a former dock, wharf or quay or your house was connected to shipbuilding, then many records relating to shipping and shipbuilding companies can be found at the National Maritime Museum, Manuscripts Section, London, SE10 9NF **www.nmm.ac.uk** and the Tyne and Wear Archives, Blandford House, Blandford Square, Newcastle upon Tyne, NE1 4JA **www.tyneandweararchives.org.uk**.

The Victoria and Albert Museum, Archive of Art and Design, 23 Blythe Road, London, W14 0QX, looks after the archives of many firms connected to the manufacture and sale of furniture, textiles, precious metalwares and other areas **www.vam.ac.uk/resources/archives/aad**.

The Modern Records Centre, Warwick University, Coventry, CV4 7AL, holds material about the motor manufacture industry as well as records of trade unions and business organizations.

Local record offices have many brewery records, whilst some of the larger companies have their own archives. There are also a large number of websites dedicated to pub histories; many of these have indexes and transcripts to licence agreements, trade directories, newspaper reports, photographs, postcards and other sources, whilst details of licences can be found in quarter sessions records.

Museums of trade and business and living history sites can give you a real insight into what the interior of your home was like when it was a business or trade. The Bridewell Museum in Norwich, for example, specifically features artefacts and information from local businesses.

Local school records before the 1870s are very scarce and where they do survive they vary enormously in detail. It is, however, possible to find references in lists to parish records. These lists also include references to more recent records where the parish still had (or has) some kind of involvement. Some local authority records of schools which were taken over when a national system was introduced do include earlier records from before their amalgamation. As a result it is important to check both parish records and local education records held at record offices.

Apprenticeship records can be found locally, nationally and online. Parishes were responsible for arranging apprenticeships for local paupers until 1834 and on behalf of charities they managed. These are generally held in county record offices in parish records collections. Workhouses also arranged many apprenticeships and these too are held locally. Cities and boroughs tend to have very good collections of apprenticeship records and indexes as one of the means by which someone gained the freedom to trade was by serving an apprenticeship to a freeman. Many of these can be found in county record offices and/or amongst the records of the guilds for particular trades. Some of these guilds still hold their own records, but many have been deposited at the Guildhall Library in London and The National Archives.

The Society of Genealogists (SoG) has a collection of around 18,000 apprenticeship indentures dating from 1641 to 1888. The SoG also has copies of published indexes and extracts from apprenticeship indentures from a wide range of sources, including some guild records, in their library.

An Act of 1710 made stamp duty payable on apprenticeship indentures except for pauper and charity ones. Registers of the money received were kept up to 1811. The original registers can be seen at The National Archives. Indexes can be found at the SoG and digitized copies of various dates can be viewed online at Ancestry and Find my Past.

Local parish records and glebe records held at record offices can provide useful information on loans granted to clergymen to buy or maintain parsonages.

Census Returns

Census records can provide a snapshot of who lived in a house from the early 1800s to the early 1900s. They are also one of the most accessible resources, as all those between 1841 and 1911 can be found online, whilst local archives have copies on microfilm or microfiche for most years. Whilst the online versions are hosted by commercial companies, those on Ancestry can be accessed free at the majority of libraries in England and Wales and others such as Find my Past and The Genealogist offer free trial periods.

From 1801 onwards a national census has been taken every ten years in England and Wales, except for 1941 when the UK was at war. Currently available up to 1911 due to a 100-year closure rule, those from 1841 list who was in every property in a parish on the night the census was taken, including lodgers, live-in servants and visitors. Some specifically mention empty properties, whilst others simply omit them. The first page of each return describes the area covered in each district, with some describing the direction or route the enumerators took. Some city census returns have accompanying enumerators' maps. These can be found at The National Archives, whilst some local archives have copies.

Each time the census was taken more and more detail was required. In 1891 people had to list the number of rooms they occupied if it was less than five, and whether people were employers, employed or neither, thereby giving some idea of whether their home was also their workplace. From 1911, the number of rooms in all households was noted and separate household schedules listing owners and heads of household are available.

Nevertheless, it can be surprisingly tricky to identify particular properties, especially on the earlier returns. You must avoid the trap of assuming the schedule number recording each household corresponds with locations, especially as there were no street numbers given on the early census returns. Many small rural areas still had no street numbering in the late 1900s. You may therefore find just the name of a street, or worse, just the parish name, with no street names at all. There was also no set pattern in which the enumerators collected the forms from each household and then copied them into books.

Even where street numbers are included these need to be treated with caution, as many houses were renumbered for a variety of reasons over time, whilst many streets have had gaps filled in with additional buildings, which may change or affect the numbering system. It can therefore appear that someone has moved house, flat or street, and maybe even moved back again, when it is simply the number or name that has changed. This was the case with a house in New Inn Yard in Shoreditch, London, where the Knightly family who owned it are shown on various census returns as living at numbers 7, 8 and 9.

Such problems in identifying properties can often be overcome by looking at the neighbours, identifying and double-checking against known inhabitants over several years and in relation to fixed points such

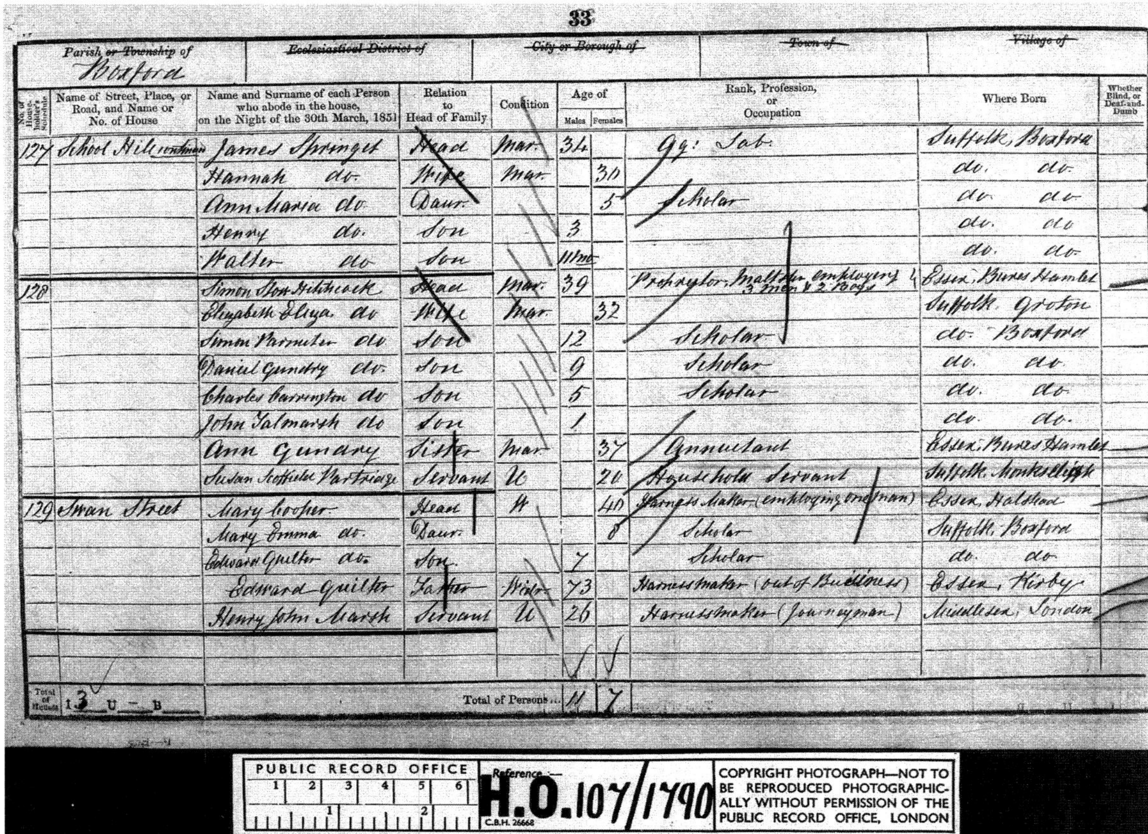

33

Parish ~~or Township~~ of Boxford	~~Ecclesiastical District of~~	~~City or Borough of~~	~~Town of~~	~~Village of~~

No. of Householder's Schedule	Name of Street, Place, or Road, and Name or No. of House	Name and Surname of each Person who abode in the house, on the Night of the 30th March, 1851	Relation to Head of Family	Condition	Age of Males	Age of Females	Rank, Profession, or Occupation	Where Born	Whether Blind, or Deaf-and-Dumb
127	School Hill continued	James Springet	Head	Mar.	34		Ag: Lab	Suffolk, Boxford	
		Hannah do	Wife	Mar.		30		do. do	
		Ann Maria do	Daur.			5	Scholar	do do	
		Henry do	Son		3			do. do	
		Walter do	Son		11 mo			do. do	
128		Simon Stow Hitchcock	Head	Mar.	39		Proprietor, Maltster employing 3 men & 2 boys	Essex, Bures Hamlet	
		Elizabeth Eliza do	Wife	Mar.		32		Suffolk, Groton	
		Simon Parmiter do	Son		12		Scholar	do. Boxford	
		Daniel Gundry do	Son		9		Scholar	do. do	
		Charles Carrington do	Son		5		Scholar	do. do	
		John Talmarsh do	Son		1			do. do.	
		Ann Gundry	Sister	Mar.		37	Annuitant	Essex, Bures Hamlet	
		Susan Scofield Partridge	Servant	U		20	Household Servant	Suffolk, Monks Eleigh	
129	Swan Street	Mary Cooper	Head	W		40	Stays Maker (employing one man)	Essex, Halstead	
		Mary Emma do	Daur.			8	Scholar	Suffolk, Boxford	
		Edward Quilter do	Son		7		Scholar	do. do	
		Edward Quilter	Father	Widr	73		Harnessmaker (out of Business)	Essex, Kirby	
		Henry John Marsh	Servant	U	26		Harnessmaker (Journeyman)	Middlesex, London	
Total of Houses	3 U – B			Total of Persons...	11	7			

PUBLIC RECORD OFFICE 1 2 3 4 5 6

Reference — H.O. 107/1790

C.B.H. 26668

1851 Census Return for Boxford in Suffolk showing the end of School Hill and the beginning of Swan Street.

as a pub. This can be enhanced by comparing census returns with other sources such as trade directories, maps, rate books and electoral registers.

The census returns for Swan Street in Boxford in Suffolk are a good example of how it is sometimes possible to identify which house is which when street numbers and house names are lacking. In this case it was possible to work out the route taken by the enumerators by using the Swan Inn as an anchor point and identifying features on census returns which could be compared with the 1840 tithe map and apportionment, trade directories and parish rate books. The 1851 census return makes it clear that the enumerators followed a route from the bottom of the road as it lists people on School Hill, then houses opposite the church on Swan Street. In 1851 the Swan Inn was occupied by Robert Stevens (schedule number 136). His immediate neighbours were John Watson, a shoemaker, (schedule number 135) and John Herbert (schedule number 137).

The Tithe Map of 1840 has an enhanced section which specifically shows the side of Swan Street on which the Swan Inn stood. The inn stood on plot 175 and the accompanying tithe apportionment lists this as a house and garden owned by John Herbert and occupied by 'Herbert and Prentice'. The 1841 census lists Samuel Prentice as an innkeeper (although the inn is not named), thereby confirming this plot as part of the Swan Inn complex. Samuel Prentice and John Herbert are listed in other later trade directories as at Swan Inn.

It is important to remember that census returns will not tell you who owned a property, only who was living in it or visiting on one night in the year. The 1841 census will give you even less information, as it only lists who was in a household, but not their relationship to each other. Nevertheless, such problems should not deter you from using these records as you will find out invaluable information about the place they lived, who their neighbours were, occupations, the names of other locals, who the schoolteachers were and so on. All of this helps build a picture of a home within a living community.

Pre–1841 Census Returns

The returns collected between 1801 and 1831 only included statistical information, such as how many males or females in a parish. However, some enumerators did compile unofficial listings of people, whilst some parish officials were inspired to compile their own versions. These are generally kept with other parish records and they can vary enormously in what details are recorded. Some only include the name of the head of the household and the numbers of children, whilst others will include details of each parishioner's religion and where they lived. Occasionally, they include personal comments on the character and behaviour of local people, so you may find out more about the people who lived in your home.

One of these was very helpful when researching a house in Sedgeford in Norfolk. A census was compiled in September 1829 and originally kept with the parish records. This is now deposited at the Norfolk Record Office (reference NRO: MC 741) and has been transcribed by the Norfolk GENUKI page host. Not every household is listed, but it does describe a large number of properties in the village, their location, whether they were owned by the occupier, and if not, who they rented from and what they paid.

It also includes lots of personal comments, such as who people worked for, their relationships to each other and their health and personality traits. For example, the last two cottages on the right hand side of Sedgeford Lane were occupied by a Samuel and Susan Jennings, aged thirty-two and thirty-four respectively, and their two children. Samuel was a blacksmith and paying rent to 'Beckerton' of seven pounds and fifteen shillings. A John Beckerton is listed on the right hand side of Sedgeford Street as living in his own house and owning several cottages **www.origins.org.uk/genuki/NFK/places/s/sedgeford/census1829.shtml**.

Finding Census Returns

The National Archives (TNA) holds all census returns for England, Wales, the Isle of Man and Channel Islands. Copies for the whole of the UK can be used at the Hyde Park Family History Centre run by the LDS church **www.hydeparkfhc.org**. Microfilm copies for individual counties are widely available locally in record offices, libraries and LDS family history centres and some family history societies.

A number of commercial websites offer access to the census, with the most well known of these being Ancestry, Find my Past, the Origins Network and The Genealogist. A useful free-to-use website with transcripts from various census returns is FreeCen **www.freecen.org.uk**.

The pre–1841 census returns are usually found in local archives. A full listing can be found in Colin Chapman's *PRE–1841 Censuses and Population Listings* (Dursley, 1990). Another useful way of tracking down such local returns is to use the Access to Archives (A2A) website: **www.nationalarchives.gov.uk/a2a**. Some lists and transcripts to pre–1841 census returns can be found online on the county pages of GENUKI at **www.genuki.org.uk**.

There is lots of fascinating and relevant material on the 'Vision of Britain Through Time' website, including maps and historical descriptions, some of which is taken from census returns and enumerators reports **www.visionofbritain.org.uk/census/census**.

Deeds

House deeds are one of the most important places to start your research as they record how ownership of a particular property or piece of land was transferred over time. They can also give an idea of its changing value and the names of the other people who occupied it. Some, especially those which have been used for commercial reasons, such as pubs and shops, may include plans showing the layout.

A set of house deeds is literally a bundle of legal documents compiled to show who owned what and when. You may also see them referred to as title deeds or 'muniments of title'. Older deeds, especially those from before the early nineteenth century, were usually written on parchment. They may include copies or extracts from other documents relevant to the property transfer such as wills, manorial records, marriage contracts, maps and plans. Such extracts sometimes survive when the deeds don't. Property deeds vary enormously in their detail. Some may only go back a short period of time, even when a property is much older, whilst others give enormous amounts of information over many centuries. They may

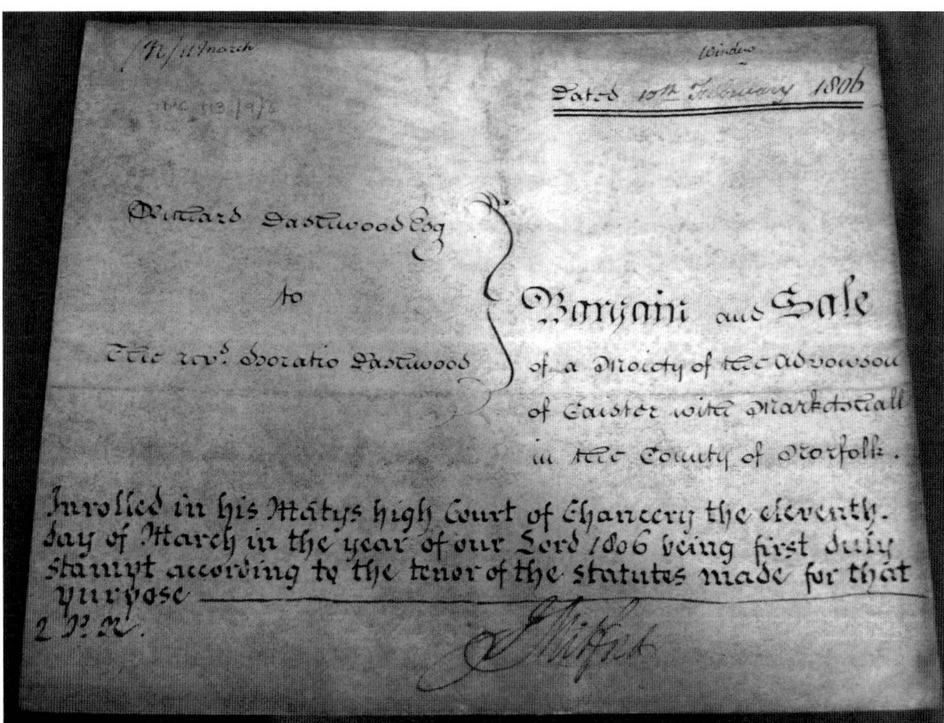
Dated 10th February 1806
Richard Eastwood Esq
to
The Revd. Horatio Eastwood
Bargain and Sale
of a Moiety of the Advowson
of Caistor with Markshall
in the County of Norfolk.
Inrolled in his Matys high Court of Chancery the eleventh day of March in the year of our Lord 1806 being first duly stampt according to the tenor of the statutes made for that purpose

(Pages 88, 89 and 90) Deeds for Caistor Hall. (NRO: MC 113/9/4, 576X7)

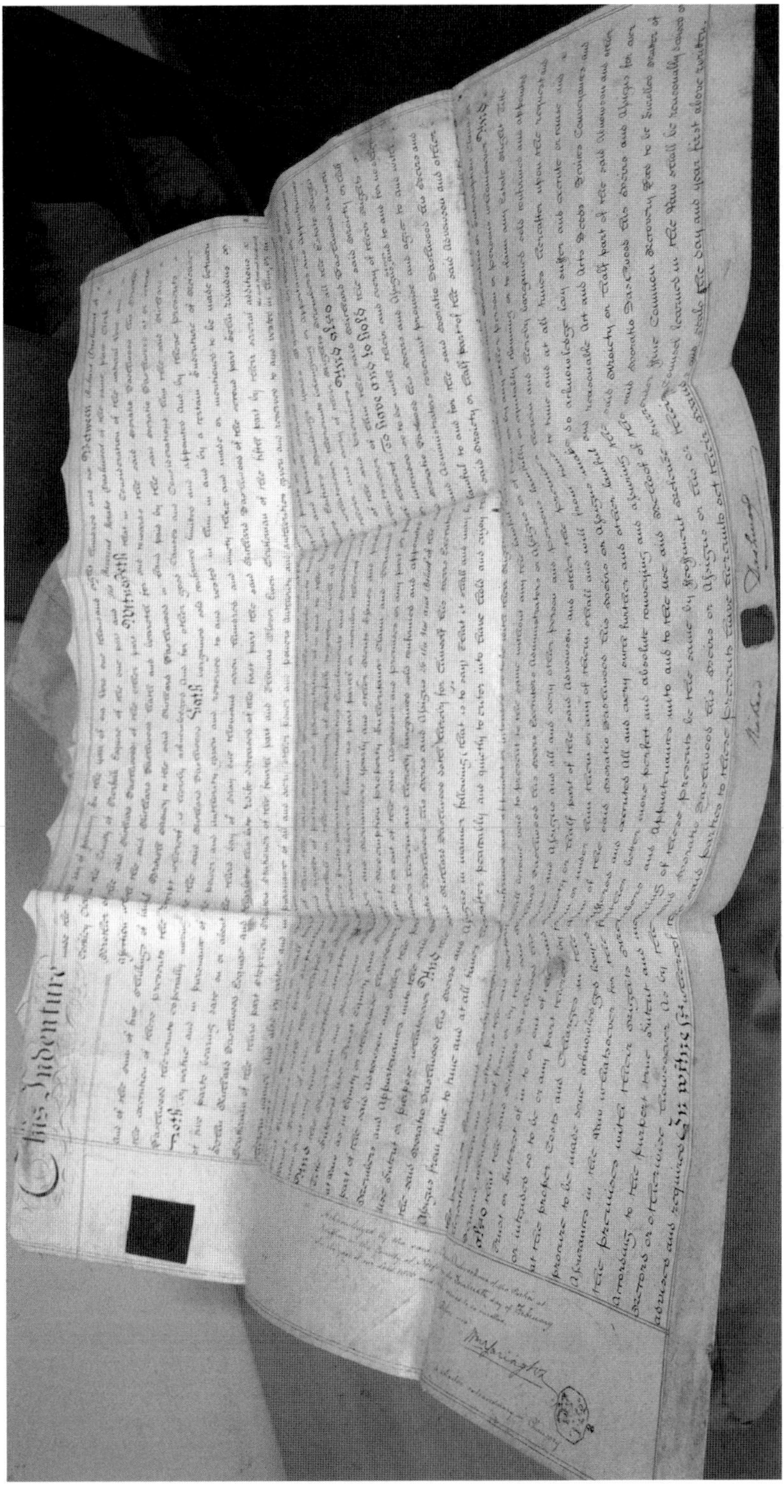
This Indenture

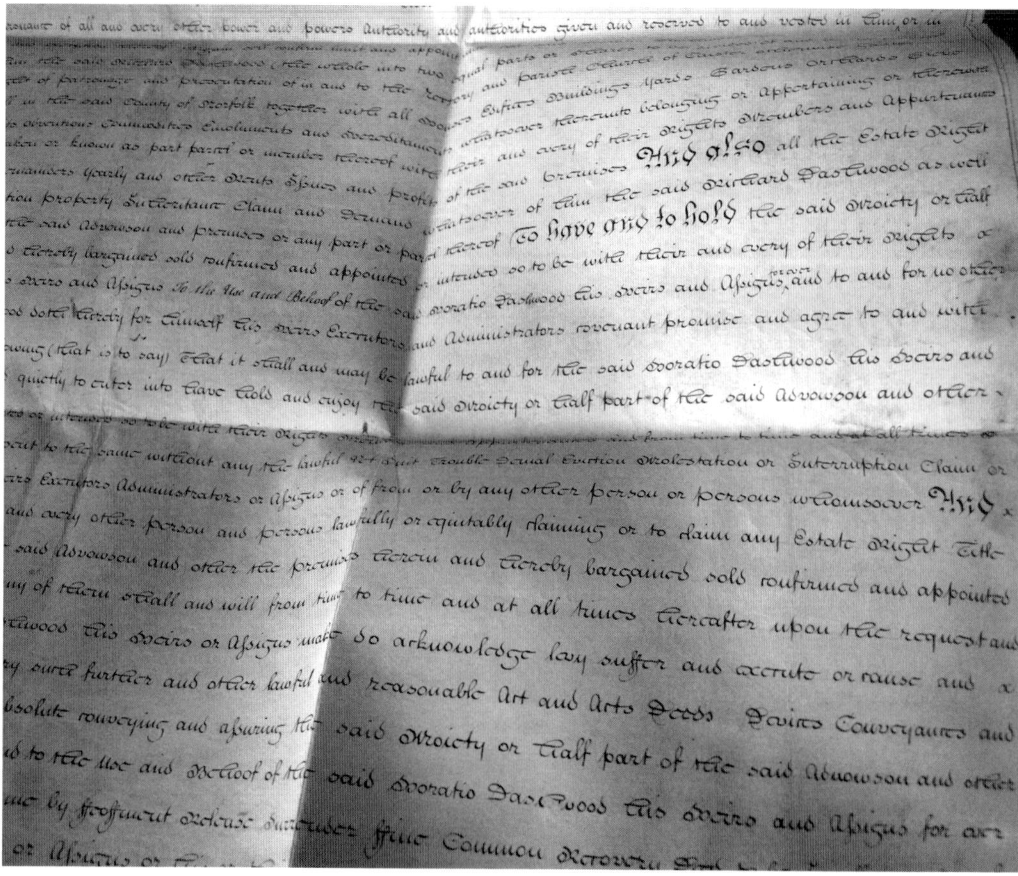
…venant of all and every other power and powers authority and authorities given and reserved to and vested in him or in
…and every of their rights … And also all the Estate Right
…ion property Such claim and Demand whatsoever of him the said Richard Eastwood as well
…the said Advowson and premises or any part or parcel thereof To have and to hold the said Moiety or half
…thereby bargained sold confirmed and appointed or intended so to be with their and every of their rights or
…Heirs and Assigns To the Use and Behoof of the said Horatio Eastwood his Heirs and Assigns forever and to and for no other
…does hereby for himself his heirs Executors and Administrators covenant promise and agree to and with
…(that is to say) That it shall and may be lawful to and for the said Horatio Eastwood his Heirs and
…quietly to enter into have hold and enjoy the said Moiety or half part of the said Advowson and other
…or intended so to be with their rights … and from time to time and at all times
…to the same without any the lawful let suit trouble denial eviction molestation or interruption claim or
…his Executors Administrators or Assigns or of from or by any other person or persons whomsoever And
…and every other person and persons lawfully or equitably claiming or to claim any Estate Right Title
…said Advowson and other the premises thereon and thereby bargained sold confirmed and appointed
…any of them shall and will from time to time and at all times hereafter upon the request and
…Eastwood his Heirs or Assigns make do acknowledge levy suffer and execute or cause and
…such further and other lawful and reasonable Act and Acts Deeds Devices Conveyances and
…absolute conveying and assuring the said Moiety or half part of the said Advowson and other
…to the Use and Behoof of the said Horatio Eastwood his Heirs and Assigns for ever
…by Feoffment Release Surrender Fine Common Recovery …

even include details about other properties which once belonged to previous owners. Interpreting deeds can be complex due to the legal terms involved and those before the 1730s may be in Latin. There are a number of good books and online guides that explain the terminology.

Unfortunately, many older deeds have been destroyed as the 1925 Law of Property Act stated that deeds were only needed to prove ownership for the previous thirty years. In 1970, this was reduced to fifteen years. Despite this, hundreds of thousands of deeds do survive in private hands and local and national archives. Even if the deeds you hold for your home do not go back very far you may still find others elsewhere or details of your property amongst those of other local properties.

Deeds do not usually state when a property was built, although they may assist in narrowing it down to within a very short period of time. When researching a house near Wendover in Buckinghamshire the title deeds referred to the sale of the land by the War Department in March

1923. The accompanying map shows the plots bought and the conveyance describes this as arable land in the parish of Wendover. Just over a year later, in July 1924, the owner resold part of these plots. Construction of the house can be dated to a seven-year period between the sale of the land in 1924 and 1931, when the first record of people living in it occurs in an electoral register.

Deeds usually start with an introduction giving the date and a list of parties to the deed, including their occupations and residence. Women are described as either a spinster, married woman (with her husband's name and occupation) or as a widow (often with her deceased husband's name and occupation). What follows are the details of the purchase monies, any mortgages and whether or not it is a lease, bargain and sale or release. To find details of the property you need to look for the words 'All that' which will be followed by a description of the property. This will include buildings, field names, acreages, cultivations and the names of adjacent property owners.

When researching the history of a house on Whitwell Street in Reepham in Norfolk, the deeds had no information before the late 1960s. A sales particular at the local record office stated it had previously been owned by the Burcham family. By following up on this I was able to locate documents relating to the property going back 150 years, and other information about the land pre-dating that. Another house researched in Reepham was an old pub owned by the Reepham Brewery (also owned by the Burcham family). Deeds held at the record office provided details of when it was first built and when it stopped being a pub, including a covenant that it could not be used as licensed premises ever again.

Many title deeds include an 'abstract of title', which summarises all the documents relating to its ownership without much of the legal wordiness of the original records. Such abstracts usually describe whether a property was bought or inherited, who from and under what terms. This was the case with a house in north Norfolk. An abstract of title drawn up in 1891, when William Wallace England inherited the house from his sister's estate, refers to an 1871 marriage contract between William's sister, Mary Ann England of Aylsham, spinster and William Mitchell of Burnham Westgate. A later reference in the house deeds refers to a coverture between Mary Ann and W.W. England (her father) in 1867. Under coverture wives could not control their own property unless specific provisions were made before marriage, as a wife was considered under the cover, influence, power and protection of her husband. These references indicate that the Mitchells bought the property in or before 1867.

Another example relating to a cottage in Barton Turf in Norfolk demonstrates how a collection of deeds may include other records. In this case the bundle of deeds included a pedigree from the early 1800s of family relationships, with dates of births, marriages and deaths as supporting evidence when the house passed on after the death of the owner. Many of these events took place outside the county and were too early to be recorded on the national indexes.

Much of the terminology in deeds also occurs in manorial records (see also the section on manorial documents). However, it is worth mentioning the main ones here. A 'Bargain and Sale' originated in the sixteenth century as a means of conveying property. It was a private agreement drawn up by a lawyer which had to be enrolled in a court within six months. It was gradually replaced by the 'Lease and Release', which was used up to 1845. In the first part of a lease and release, the purchaser leased the property for one year, thereby avoiding having to enroll the deed as they already occupied the property. The following day the seller released the reversion of the lease to the buyer and the transfer was complete.

You may also find a 'Bond', which is a two-part agreement to perform certain duties with a penalty for non-performance. The first part is the 'obligation', giving the penalty (in Latin until 1733). The second part is the 'condition' which states the commitment to be performed. In one case the earliest deed from 1688 specifically refers to the conditions put upon the bequest of her house by owner Joane Thurlow to her kinsman Henry Thurlow. If he did not carry out her wishes then the house was to go to his sister.

A 'Common Recovery' (these date from the fifteenth century to 1833) was a fictitious legal action in which the buyer (known as a 'recoverer') sued the seller (known as the 'tenant'), alleging the seller had no legal title and possessed the property only after a fictitious third party forced the recoverer out. These were used to get round property having to pass down a direct line of heirs. Such actions were held at the court of Common Pleas and often preceded by a deed to 'Lead the Uses of a Recovery'

Another record associated with these fictitious actions was a 'Final Concord' (known as a 'fine'). This was the final agreement to settle the fictitious cases used to transfer property. The case was brought by the purchaser (plaintiff) against the vendor (deforciant), claiming the purchaser had been deprived of the property. Before a judgement was made the two parties reached a compromise in which the purchaser received the property and the vendor received a sum of money which was the purchase price. The deed was an 'indenture tripartite' and consisted of three copies of the fine (final concord) on a single sheet. The copies were separated by wavy (indented) cuts and given to each party, with the third kept by the court. These copies are known as 'Foot of Fine' and these actions were often preceded by a deed to 'Levy a Fine'.

A 'Feoffment' is the oldest form of conveyance by a symbolic handover before witnesses, known as 'livery of seisin'. It was commonly used in the transfer of copyhold land, which is why it so commonly appears in manorial records as well as in bundles of title deeds. The document confirming this had to be endorsed to record the entry into the property otherwise it was invalid. Feoffments were later replaced by 'Bargain and Sales'.

House deeds can often include information about other properties once owned by the same owners that have nothing to do with the house being investigated. The deeds of one house investigated combined with an architectural assessment and manorial records in revealing that a Georgian house was literally built on the footprint of a much older property. The deeds date from 1674, which is at least 150 years before the present house was built, when they note that a tenement with garden measuring 70 feet by 16 feet was sold. What the architectural assessment showed was that the measurements of the plot mentioned in the deeds are an exact match to the present house. Later references in the deeds and manorial records confirm that the present house was built on the same plot and each time the house was sold, leased or inherited its measurements were included. Eventually, one manorial record from the early 1800s refers to the house as standing on the site of a former messuage on the same plot. Again, the measurements are included and match those of the earlier property.

Bedford Level Corporation

The Bedford Level Corporation records include a huge number of deeds and other records for land and property in the Isle of Ely area of Cambridgeshire and neighbouring counties. The north of Cambridgeshire, including the Isle of Ely and part of the Great Bedford Level, was once submerged in marsh. This was turned into farmland when the Fens were drained via a network of canals. The corporation and its predecessors administered the Great Level of the Fens from 1362 to 1920 and almost all the Bedford Level Corporation records from 1663 to 1920 have survived. These include a huge collection of maps, a registry of deeds and petitions from the mid-seventeenth century onwards regarding improvements to drains and access across land.

Chancery Deeds

Private individuals could enroll deeds in the Court of Chancery for a fee. 'Memorials' of property sales and transfers were copied onto the back of close rolls, but this method became less popular after a central Land Registry started to take off in the nineteenth century. The Close Rolls are particularly useful if the land was formerly owned under the terms of a charitable trust, something that occurred frequently with chapels and schools. Grants of land by the Crown in the medieval period were usually recorded in Charter Rolls, whilst later grants were entered in the Patent Rolls.

Finding Deeds

For general information on finding and interpreting deeds see Nat Alcock's book *Old Title Deeds* (Phillimore, 2001).

Until the land registry was formed there was no national list of property ownership. Whilst the land registry does record many deeds there are still huge numbers not listed with them. Title deeds may be kept by the solicitor who handled the sale of the house or a building society. If the house is still mortgaged it is unlikely the original deeds will be released, but the mortgagee should be able to provide photocopies, although they will probably charge. If you don't own your own home then ask the person that does for access. This won't be possible if it belongs to a council or housing association, but their development is well documented in other sources.

Once you have exhausted mortgage providers you need to check local record offices, as they have hundreds of thousands of title deeds deposited with them. Large numbers of these have been catalogued, with some of them appearing on record offices' own online catalogues or via the Access to Archives (A2A) website. When researching property owned by the Slade family of Hilmarton and Warminster in Wiltshire I found several references via A2A to deeds and other records held at Wiltshire and Swindon Archives. These contain a summary of details, as in this one:

> Deeds, etc. relating to property of the Slade family of Warminster in North Bradley and Warminster; including a mess. Near the Pound, Southwick, North Bradley 1722 and 1796. Property and land in Warminster including house at West end, newly built in 1722, house near the former George Inn and three houses, formerly the Dolphin Inn. Marriage settlements of John Slade of Warminster and Anne Davis of Studley, Trowbridge; Rev. Wm. Slade of Warminster and Ann Wyche of Salisbury; probate of the will of Rev. Wm. Slade 1845.

Court of Chancery records are held at The National Archives in Kew. Many of the deeds held by local record offices have come in from local solicitors, where they may have been stored for decades or even hundreds of years. Some collections may be still uncatalogued even though they were deposited many years ago. If no reference exists for your property or people you know were associated with it then look for collections relating to solicitors who practiced in that area. You may be able to narrow down who these were by looking in trade directories and at newspaper advertisements. Their name may also appear on more recent title deeds that you can access. From there you can check if there are any relevant uncatalogued collections in a record office.

As many lists of deeds do not include specific details you will need to look through the bundles of deeds for each place to see if your property is included. Whilst it may seem daunting to search through hundreds (or even thousands) of bundles, they are often organized into groups of years. Most title deeds also name the main parties and sometimes a property's name or address is on the reverse of each document, so the search time is lessened.

Old deeds sometimes turn up at auction houses, antique shops, antiquarian bookshops and family history fairs. There are also a number of private companies who buy and sell old deeds. The investigation of a house near Wendover in Buckinghamshire began with a collection of family documents bought at an auctioneer's, which the purchaser contacted the owners about. As well family memorabilia it contained photographs of the house and gardens in the 1920s and 1930s.

Whilst there is no overarching register of deeds, there are two counties in England that do have their own registers. Yorkshire and Middlesex are the only counties in England and Wales to have a register of deeds. These were established by Act of Parliament in what was planned to be the first stage of an experimental local system. The Yorkshire registry opened on 29 September 1704 in Wakefield in the West Riding. Registries for the North and East Ridings followed later and Middlesex opened in 1709.

Although most of the documents registered were deeds, any document related to a legal estate such as a will could be entered. Registration was not compulsory to begin with. The deeds registers compiled for Middlesex and Yorkshire do contain some deeds, but are mostly 'memorials'; in effect abstracts of the original documents. Separate indexes were created for each register. The originals for Yorkshire are held by the West Yorkshire Archive Service and the Middlesex registry is at the London Metropolitan Archives. Film copies of the indexes can be accessed via LDS family history centres.

Whilst searching for information on the farms where some of my own ancestors lived and worked in the Boltby and Thirsk area of Yorkshire I found a number of references in the register of deeds held at the North Yorkshire Record Office in North Allerton. Those for a Richard Knaggs of Skelton include an 1887 indenture and mortgage issued by the National Provincial Bank. The details of this mortgage refer to other documents dating from 1847 including a conveyance in that year and a fire insurance policy issued by Alliance Assurance Company in 1886. There is also a reference to his will, which was proved in 1893, which names the beneficiary, executors and witnesses. Another Knaggs who appears in this register of deeds was Robert Knaggs of Thirsk. For him there are details of indentures from 1905 to 1919 and a private mortgage taken out in

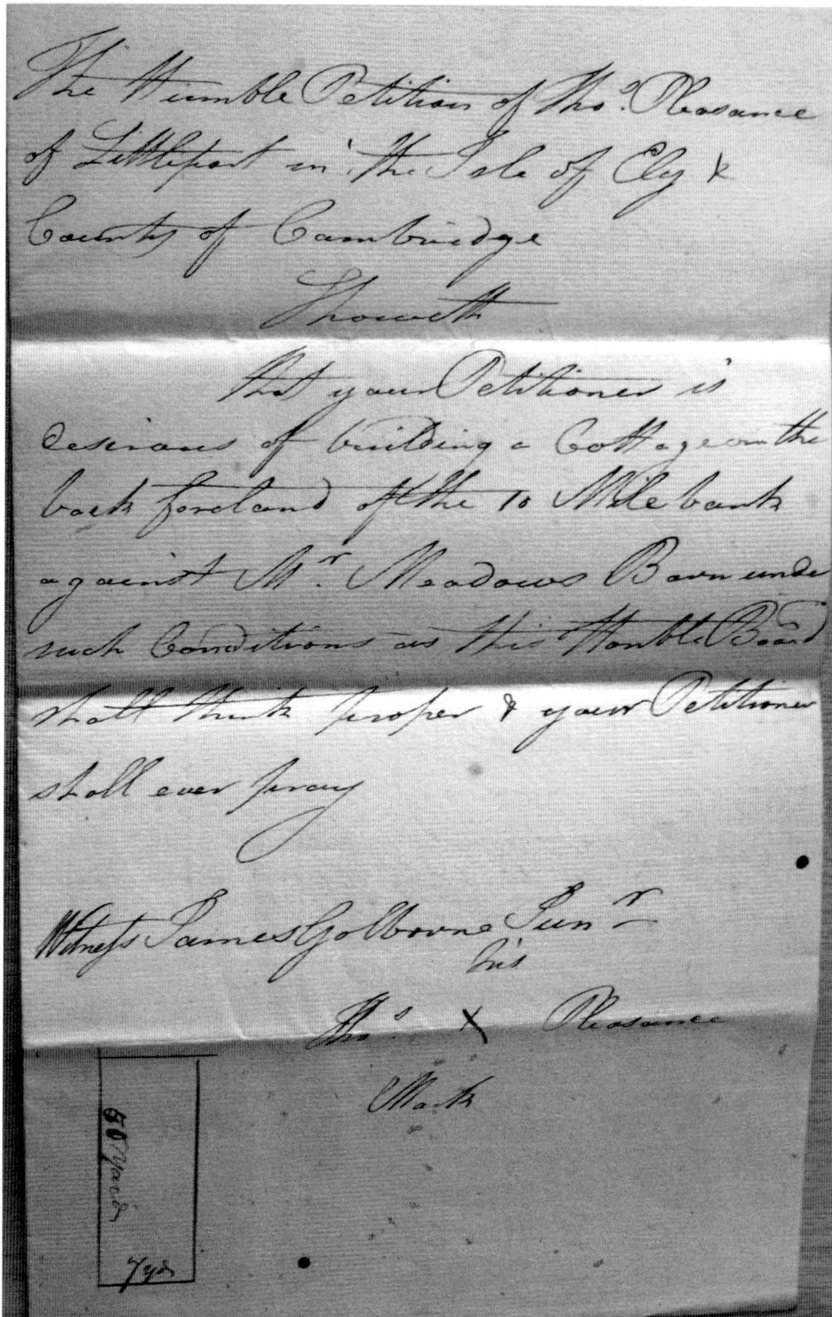

The Humble Petition of Thos. Pleasance
of Littleport in the Isle of Ely &
County of Cambridge
Showeth
That your Petitioner is
desirous of building a Cottage on the
back foreland of the 10 Mile bank
against Mr. Meadows Barn under
such Conditions as this Honble Board
shall think proper & your Petitioner
shall ever pray

Witness James Golborne Junr.
his
Thos. X Pleasance
Mark

Petition to the Bedford Level by Thomas Pleasance. (Cambridgeshire Archives Service: S/B/SP 952)

January 1905 relating to 'messuages, cottages and closes at Forby St Thirsk in the sum of £800 and interest'.

The deeds and petitions, plus many other records relating to the ownership and tenancies of property from the Bedford Level Corporation and other smaller drainage authorities, are held at Cambridge Record Office. An example of what can be found can be seen in this petition by Thomas Pleasance in 1812 to build a cottage on the Ten Mile Bank, which comes with a small sketch showing its proposed measurements as fifty yards by seven yards:

> The Humble Petition of Thos Pleasance of Littleport in the Isle of Ely County of Cambridge Showeth that your Petitioner is desireous of building a Cottage on the back foreland of the 10 Mile bank against Mr Meadow Barn under such Conditions as this Honble Board shall think proper & your Petitioner shall ever pray

Directories and Gazetteers

You will find trade directories and gazetteers mentioned in several different sections of this book. This is because directories are another source that provides a snapshot of local communities throughout time and can be used with a range of other resources to find out more about people and places. They are often referred to as 'trade directories' because they list people in trade – butchers, plumbers, innkeepers, dressmakers and so on.

Directories were originally produced to provide commercial travellers with a source of information as they made their rounds. As a result they include a short history and description of all cities, towns and villages, as well as listing major householders, professionals and prominent buildings. Although directories do not necessarily represent everyone with a business or trade, especially if they were employed by someone else, they do give a picture of changes within local communities throughout time.

Directories are particularly relevant if your home was originally used as commercial premises. They are also very helpful in tracing the more recent period, especially for the years where census returns are not available. However, it is important to remember that a directory may have been compiled anything up to a year before its publication, so the information included is always slightly out of date, whilst some information may have simply been copied from one publication to another.

Most directories date from the early nineteenth century and continued into the early part of the twentieth century. Cities and large towns continued to have street listings until well into the second half of the twentieth century. A number of companies produced directories, with some focusing on counties, whilst others only produced listings for certain cities and towns. The Post Office directories, for instance, often combined entries from neighbouring counties so you can find Essex, Suffolk and Cambridgeshire all together.

Although it varies from area to area, by about 1850 directories were frequently divided into one or more sections. These were a commercial section, which includes a general alphabetical listing of all traders; separate parish listings with topographical and historical descriptions plus lists of local traders; streets lists of tradespeople and residents, arranged by street, and the court section, which lists wealthier residents, local government and court officials or dignitaries, and, in London, central government officials.

Directories for cities such as London are slightly more complicated as many are split into two sections – trade and commercial. In these the trade section lists people in alphabetical order under their job or profession, whilst the commercial section lists the same information in alphabetical order by surname. These also include a street-by-street listing of residents. Many other cities and large towns adopted a similar format over time. Whilst these are a more comprehensive list of residences, they often only include the head of a household or main residents living there, so buildings in multiple occupancy will not list everyone. When searching for details of the farm my Knaggs ancestors lived on in Boltby in Yorkshire I found Bateson Knaggs described as: 'farmer, High Paradise'. The 1885 directory describes how Boltby was a township and village in Feliskirk parish and that the chief crops were oats, barley and wheat.

Gazetteers or Topographical Directories

A gazetteer is a bit like an expanded atlas listing all places, however small, in a specific geographical area. Depending on the gazetteer this could be a specific county, a country or the whole of the British Isles. They usually include useful information such as which parish and local government area a place is situated in. The most well known was produced by Samuel Lewis in 1833. It is particularly useful as you get a description of every parish before the boundary changes of the nineteenth century. One of the most comprehensive series is the Bartholomew's *Gazetteers*. Those published before the boundary changes of 1974 use the historic counties when listing places. This is very helpful when looking for place names in historic records in areas where boundaries have changed.

Telephone Directories

Although telephone directories are not as informative as trade directories, they are still helpful for locating names and addresses. The fact that someone had a telephone provides some indication of social status up until the mid-twentieth century when they started to become much more commonplace.

Finding Directories, Gazetteers and Telephone Directories

Most, if not all, record offices and local studies libraries have a collection of trade directories for their area, and often for neighbouring counties. The collection on the shelves at Cambridge Record Office, for instance, was very useful for narrowing down when one house was built, as it only appears after a certain year. The historical section also provided interesting historical information on the area and how it developed. In another case Cambridgeshire directories showed the same family running a pub in the city over several years and provided supporting evidence that the lane on which it was located had been named after them, rather than just being a coincidence of names.

Kelly's directories are the best known series of local directories. A full collection of these is housed at the London Metropolitan Archives (LMA): **www.cityoflondon.gov.uk/Corporation/LGNL_Services/Leisure_and_culture/Records_and_archives**

The Society of Genealogists (SoG) in London has a large collection of different directories from all over the country in their library. For further details check their catalogue at: **www.sog.org.uk/sogcat/access**

Many directories have been published in printed format or on microfiche and are increasingly being digitized and published on CD ROM/DVD or the internet. There are several commercial companies who sell these, whilst many family history societies have also published copies for their own areas. See for example, **www.ukgenealogyarchives.com/products/kelly.html** and **www.genealogysupplies.com**

A free digital library of local and trade directories for England and Wales from 1750 to 1918 can be found on Historical Directories. **www.historicaldirectories.org/hd**

The GENUKI website includes some transcripts of trade directories from various areas as well as some images. **www.genuki/org/big/eng** GENUKI also has a useful online Gazetteer. **www.genuki.org.uk/big/Gazetteer**

The National Gazetteer of Wales can be found at **http://homepage.ntlworld.com/geogdata/ngw/places.htm** Two nineteenth-century gazetteers covering Wales can be seen at Vision of Britain **www.visionofbritain.org.uk/descriptions/index.jsp**

The British Telecom Archives have an extensive collection of telephone directories, dating from 1880 to the present day, available on microfilm in their public searchroom. Contact BT Archives, Third Floor, Holborn Telephone Exchange, 268–270 High Holborn, London, WC1V 7EE. **www.bt.com/archivesonline**

The Ancestry website has a pay-to-view search facility for all British Phone Books from 1880 to 1984. See their link to 'Directories and Other Member Lists'. **www.ancestry.co.uk**

Domesday Book, 1086

The Domesday Book is probably the earliest record you will look at during your research. The Domesday Book was completed in 1086 after William the Conqueror ordered a survey of all landholdings and livestock in England so he could impose a tax. Most of the country except a few northern areas was covered, although the records for London and Winchester have not survived. Although very few buildings are specifically named, it includes such exciting details as how many mills and fisheries; wood, meadow and pasture; slaves, serfs and cattle there were and how much the whole area was worth in 1066 and 1086. For Naseby in Northamptonshire, for example, it reveals that Naseby Manor had been held by Gytha, the wife of Ralph, the Earl of Hereford (Edward the Confessor's nephew) before the Conquest. The manor then passed to William Peverel, the sheriff of Nottinghamshire and Derbyshire:

> William [Peverel] also holds 7 hides in Naseby Navesberie. Land for 14 ploughs. In Lordship 2.8 villagers with priest, 2 Freemen and 11 smallholders have 3 ploughs. Meadow, 8 acres. The value was 20s; now 60s.

Finding the Domesday Book

The Domesday Book is held at The National Archives. There have been a number of published versions, such as *The Domesday Book: England's Heritage, Then and Now* published by Bramley Books in 1997. Searchable digitized copies of the whole survey can be found on The National Archives website **www.nationalarchives.gov.uk/domesday**. Copies with accompanying transcriptions cost £3.50. There is an accompanying searchable map on The National Archives Labs site. **http://labs.nationalarchives.gov.uk/wordpress**

The PASE (Prosopography of Anglo-Saxon England database) Domesday project links the 1086 survey to free online mapping resources to document all recorded inhabitants of England from the late sixth to the end of the eleventh century **http://domesday.pase.ac.uk**.

Electoral Registers and Poll Books

Electoral registers and poll books allow you to find out who lived at a particular address over a couple of hundred years. They also give you

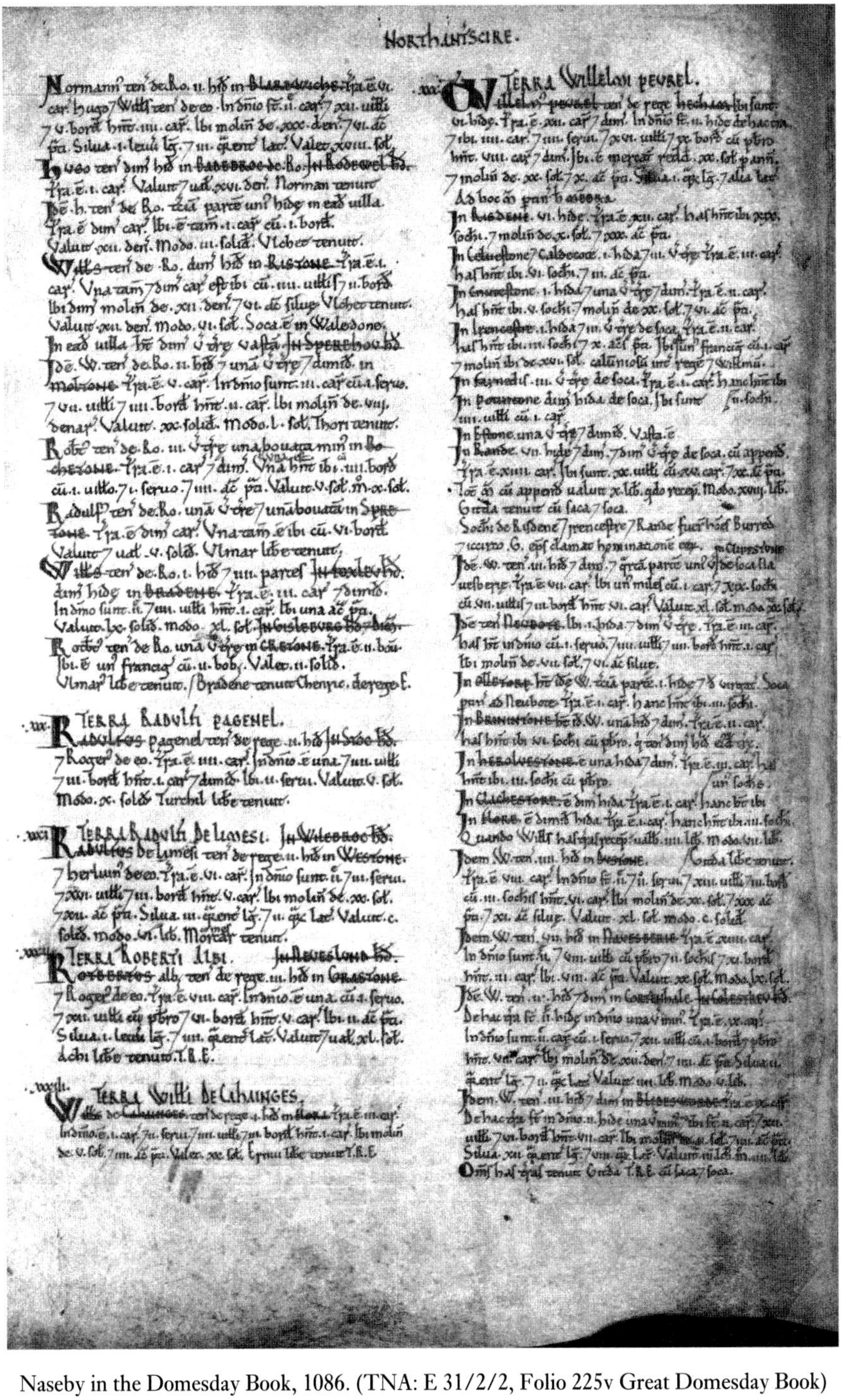
NORTHANTSCIRE.
TERRA WILLELMI PEVREL.
TERRA RADULFI PAGENEL.
TERRA RADULFI DE LIMESI.
TERRA ROBERTI ALBI.
TERRA WILLI DE CAHAINGES.

Naseby in the Domesday Book, 1086. (TNA: E 31/2/2, Folio 225v Great Domesday Book)

some idea of the social status of the people who occupied it and help you discover more about the type of property it was. It was only in the early part of the twentieth century that every adult was entitled to vote in parliamentary elections. As a result, electoral registers are by no means a complete record. Even if the people who lived in a property were not entitled to vote, their absence still tells you something about their social status.

The registers will show changes in occupancy from 1832 (but not ownership), when children became old enough to vote, changes in the franchise entitling different groups of people to vote and whether someone was serving in the armed forces. Registers for local authority elections are more revealing as women ratepayers are included even in the years before they could vote for a Member of Parliament (MP). They also list people living elsewhere who had an entitlement to vote due to owning property in a place. Whilst poll books merely list who people voted for up to 1872 they do pre-date electoral registers so may enable you to go further back in time. They also play a crucial role in building up knowledge about local communities.

Electoral Registers

The right to vote has always been linked to where people live. Electoral registers are therefore arranged by county, parish and polling districts. The records can be divided into two distinct phases: before and after 1832. There have been lists compiled of people entitled to vote since the seventeenth century. Before 1832, land tax assessments were kept as evidence of voting qualification and published poll books listed voters, their occupations, their voting qualification and who they voted for until the secret ballot was introduced in 1872.

Electoral registers date from 1832, when the Reform Act came into force, and list all those who were entitled to vote in parliamentary elections. This means that you can potentially track many of the people who lived in your house back to this date. The laws governing who could vote have changed many times, so that more and more people have been entitled to vote. When the Reform Act was introduced in 1832, only the male owners and tenants of larger properties could vote. A change in law in 1867 widened this to the male owners of property worth £5 per year and any tenants paying £12 per year. Further changes entitled an increasing number of men to vote for a Member of Parliament, but this right was still tied to owning or renting property worth over certain amounts.

Until 1918 women who paid rates could vote for local councillors, but not for Members of Parliament. It was only in 1918 that the property qualification was ended, and all men over twenty-one and women over thirty years old could vote. Finally, from 1928 all men and women over twenty-one years of age could vote on equal terms. The age was reduced to eighteen in 1969.

The electoral registers were (and still are) compiled by local authorities and are produced for 'Polling Districts', which correspond with parliamentary constituencies. Separate registers are produced for each constituency. Until 1918 electoral registers were compiled by parish overseers, and they were arranged in alphabetical order by parish. This started to change in 1978, when the parliamentary registers began to be merged with the registers for municipal (local) elections. The latter were effectively a list of ratepayers, and as rates were collected door-to-door, their arrangement was in street order, so gradually parliamentary registers followed this pattern. From 1928 they always include street names and numbers. Until the Juries Act of 1974, you can also find out if a property had a yearly rateable value of £30 or more, as this was the level at which the head of a household qualified for jury service.

When looking for details on a property in the village of Wood Dalling in Norfolk, the electoral registers for 1902 revealed some fascinating details about the whole community and clues as to where to go for more information. The freehold and copyhold houses and lands on Norton Corner indicated a certain status and that the manorial records would be worth pursuing for the latter. Some people were described as living 'near Red Pits' or 'near Plough'. One voter had a home address in Berkshire, but could vote because he owned a freehold house and land in the village. Other properties were described as 'tenements', 'dwelling houses' or just 'house'. Only a couple were specifically named or identified in some other

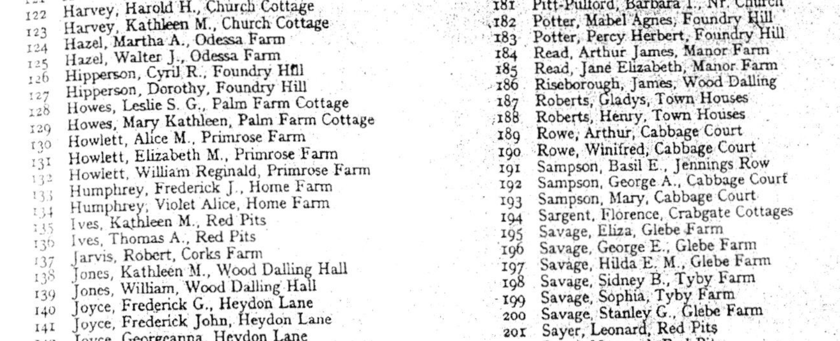
COUNTY OF NORFOLK—NORTHERN DIVISION—WOOD DALLING (BX) POLLING DISTRICT—REEPHAM

120 Harrison, Isabella, Red Pits
121 Harrison, William, Red Pits
122 Harvey, Harold H., Church Cottage
123 Harvey, Kathleen M., Church Cottage
124 Hazel, Martha A., Odessa Farm
125 Hazel, Walter J., Odessa Farm
126 Hipperson, Cyril R., Foundry Hill
127 Hipperson, Dorothy, Foundry Hill
128 Howes, Leslie S. G., Palm Farm Cottage
129 Howes, Mary Kathleen, Palm Farm Cottage
130 Howlett, Alice M., Primrose Farm
131 Howlett, Elizabeth M., Primrose Farm
132 Howlett, William Reginald, Primrose Farm
133 Humphrey, Frederick J., Home Farm
134 Humphrey, Violet Alice, Home Farm
135 Ives, Kathleen M., Red Pits
136 Ives, Thomas A., Red Pits
137 Jarvis, Robert, Corks Farm
138 Jones, Kathleen M., Wood Dalling Hall
139 Jones, William, Wood Dalling Hall
140 Joyce, Frederick G., Heydon Lane
141 Joyce, Frederick John, Heydon Lane
142 Joyce, Georgeanna, Heydon Lane
143 Kiddell, George R., Heydon Road

179 Pease, Ivy, Hall Cottage
180 Pestle, Harry W., Holly Grove Cottage
181 Pitt-Pulford, Barbara I., Nr. Church
182 Potter, Mabel Agnes, Foundry Hill
183 Potter, Percy Herbert, Foundry Hill
184 Read, Arthur James, Manor Farm
185 Read, Jane Elizabeth, Manor Farm
186 Riseborough, James, Wood Dalling
187 Roberts, Gladys, Town Houses
188 Roberts, Henry, Town Houses
189 Rowe, Arthur, Cabbage Court
190 Rowe, Winifred, Cabbage Court
191 Sampson, Basil E., Jennings Row
192 Sampson, George A., Cabbage Court
193 Sampson, Mary, Cabbage Court
194 Sargent, Florence, Crabgate Cottages
195 Savage, Eliza, Glebe Farm
196 Savage, George E., Glebe Farm
197 Savage, Hilda E. M., Glebe Farm
198 Savage, Sidney B., Tyby Farm
199 Savage, Sophia, Tyby Farm
200 Savage, Stanley G., Glebe Farm
201 Sayer, Leonard, Red Pits
202 Sayer, Maynard, Red Pits
[illegible], Wood Dalling Hall

Wood Dalling Electoral Register, 1945. (NRO: C/ERO 1/428)

way. By 1959 most of the properties in the same village had names or descriptions such as 'Crossway Cottage', 'Town Houses', 'Church Gate Farm' and 'Council Houses'. The inclusion of the council houses in itself marks an interesting period in the history of housing.

Poll Books

Poll books were first published in 1696 when sheriffs were required to compile lists of voters in county elections. These were usually divided by parish and list the names of each voter and the candidate they voted for before the introduction of the secret ballot in 1872. Their survival before 1711, when they had to be enrolled in the Quarter Sessions, is generally poor. But each county varies and you may be fortunate to find records from the 1600s. Once the secret ballot was introduced the poll books became redundant.

Poll books are also extremely useful when used in conjunction with land tax records (see also the section on land tax records). This is because one of the requirements to be able to vote was renting or owning freehold land or land above a certain value. They also give insights into the social status of the people listed and local political allegiances, which in themselves form part of the wider history of the area your home stands in.

Finding Electoral Registers and Poll Books

By law, your local authority has to make the electoral register available for anyone to look at in their council offices. However, under recent changes there are two versions of the register – full and edited, as people can choose whether or not to have their details included.

Electoral registers for the current year for the whole country are held at the Office for National Statistics, Segesworth Road, Titchfield, Fareham, Hampshire, PO15 5RR. **www.statistics.gov.uk** Earlier records are held at the British Library, 96 Euston Road, London, NW1 2DB **www.bl.uk** These will soon be available on the Find my Past website. **www.findmypast.co.uk**

Many local record offices and libraries have copies relating to their area. For further information on the whereabouts of surviving registers for particular areas see J. Gibson and C. Rogers *Electoral Registers since 1832* (FFHS, 1989). You can also use the listings on ARCHON and Access to Archives (A2A) for more information. The London Metropolitan Archive (LMA) holds a good selection of electoral registers and a large collection of poll books for the whole country. The British Library, record offices and libraries that hold copies will also have lists that show which parliamentary constituency a particular place came under over time.

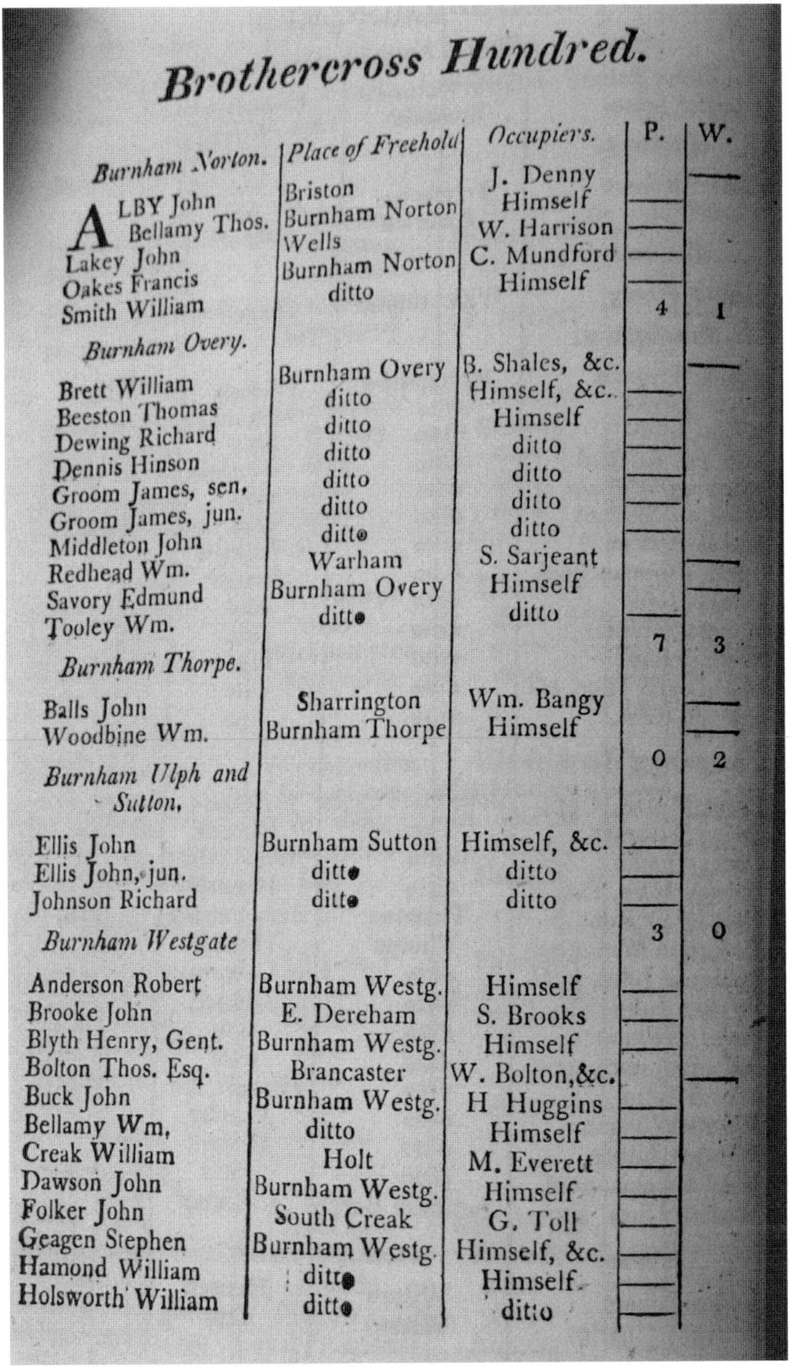

Brothercross Hundred.

Burnham Norton.	*Place of Freehold*	*Occupiers.*	P.	W.
ALBY John	Briston	J. Denny		—
Bellamy Thos.	Burnham Norton	Himself	—	
Lakey John	Wells	W. Harrison	—	
Oakes Francis	Burnham Norton	C. Mundford	—	
Smith William	ditto	Himself	—	
			4	1
Burnham Overy.				
Brett William	Burnham Overy	B. Shales, &c.		—
Beeston Thomas	ditto	Himself, &c.	—	
Dewing Richard	ditto	Himself	—	
Dennis Hinson	ditto	ditto	—	
Groom James, sen.	ditto	ditto	—	
Groom James, jun.	ditto	ditto	—	
Middleton John	ditto	ditto	—	
Redhead Wm.	Warham	S. Sarjeant		—
Savory Edmund	Burnham Overy	Himself		—
Tooley Wm.	ditto	ditto	—	
			7	3
Burnham Thorpe.				
Balls John	Sharrington	Wm. Bangy		—
Woodbine Wm.	Burnham Thorpe	Himself		—
			0	2
Burnham Ulph and Sutton.				
Ellis John	Burnham Sutton	Himself, &c.	—	
Ellis John, jun.	ditto	ditto	—	
Johnson Richard	ditto	ditto	—	
			3	0
Burnham Westgate				
Anderson Robert	Burnham Westg.	Himself	—	
Brooke John	E. Dereham	S. Brooks	—	
Blyth Henry, Gent.	Burnham Westg.	Himself	—	
Bolton Thos. Esq.	Brancaster	W. Bolton,&c.		—
Buck John	Burnham Westg.	H Huggins	—	
Bellamy Wm,	ditto	Himself	—	
Creak William	Holt	M. Everett	—	
Dawson John	Burnham Westg.	Himself	—	
Folker John	South Creak	G. Toll	—	
Geagen Stephen	Burnham Westg.	Himself, &c.	—	
Hamond William	ditto	Himself	—	
Holsworth William	ditto	ditto	—	

Poll Book, 1845. (Norfolk Heritage Centre)

Electoral registers can be searched online at **www.192.com**, whilst Ancestry has many for London at **www.ancestry.co.uk**.

Eroll is just one commercial company offering access to last year's electoral registers, searchable by surname and first name. **www.eroll.co.uk/?engine=adwords!7308&keyword=Electoral+Roll&match_type**

Copies of many poll books and modern transcripts can be found at the British Library, the Guildhall Library in London, at the Society of Genealogists and many local family history societies and local studies libraries and record offices. The Institute of Historical Research, University of London, Senate House, Malet Street, London, WC1 7HU, also has a substantial collection. **www.ihrinfo.co.uk**

Many poll books have been transcribed and published and are available on CD or online via commercial companies such as The Parish Chest. One online example is the transcripts for Norfolk on the GENUKI Norfolk page. The transcript of the 1835 poll book for Dunston, for instance, lists three men entitled to vote – Last Dring Carpenter, John Fish and Robert Churchman Long, parish clerk. All three held freehold land in the parish. Out of the four candidates, all three voted for both Walpole and Wodehouse. Additional information taken from census returns and trade directories has been added and tells us that Carpenter was a farmer and Long lived at the hall.

Estate Records

Estate records are a very important resource, particularly before the 1800s. They can incorporate a huge variety of different types of documents such as manorial records; maps; title deeds; accounts; surveys and tenancy agreements. As a result many of the records found amongst estate records also exist in their own right in other collections. Separate subject indexes to these at record offices can sometimes obscure the fact that they belonged to one person, family or large house. Examples of this are maps, title deeds, leases, manorial records and sales particulars.

The Walpole estate papers in Norfolk illustrate this overlap as the Walpole family owned several manors and large houses. They also leased out farms and other properties and land that does not appear in manorial records, as well as employing large numbers of people to work for them. One example is a rent book which includes details of all the payments made by a Jacob and Isaac Emerson for the 'Lands and Mannor house of Burnham Thorpe' from 1712 to 1725. The annual rent was £200 per year due each Michaelmas, with 'taxes and repairs all allowed to that time'. There is no record of a tenancy agreement for this property, and as the Manor House was a freehold property such agreements do not appear in the manorial records.

Another set of estate records in the neighbouring parish of Burnham

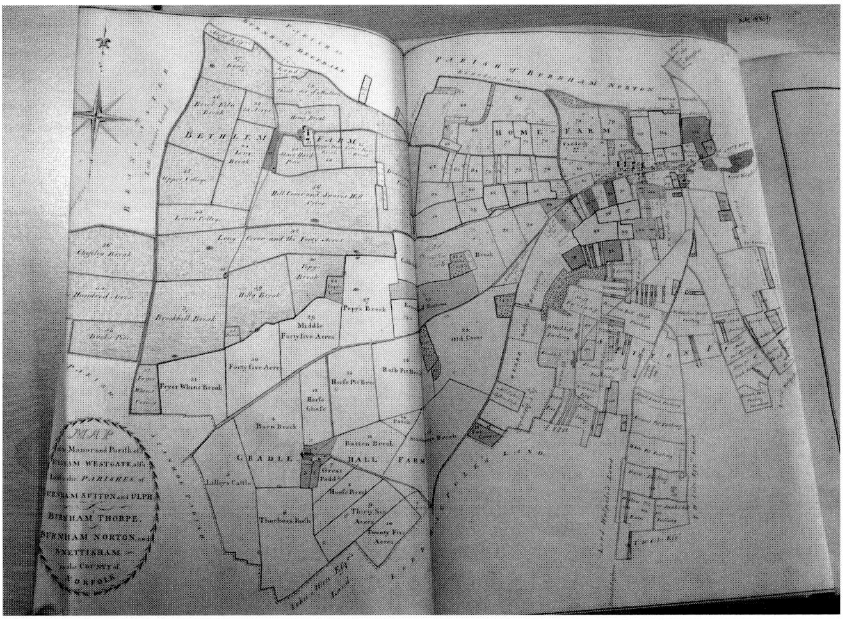

(Page 107 and 108) Cradle Hall Estate Survey, 1803. (NRO: MC 1830/1, 852X7)

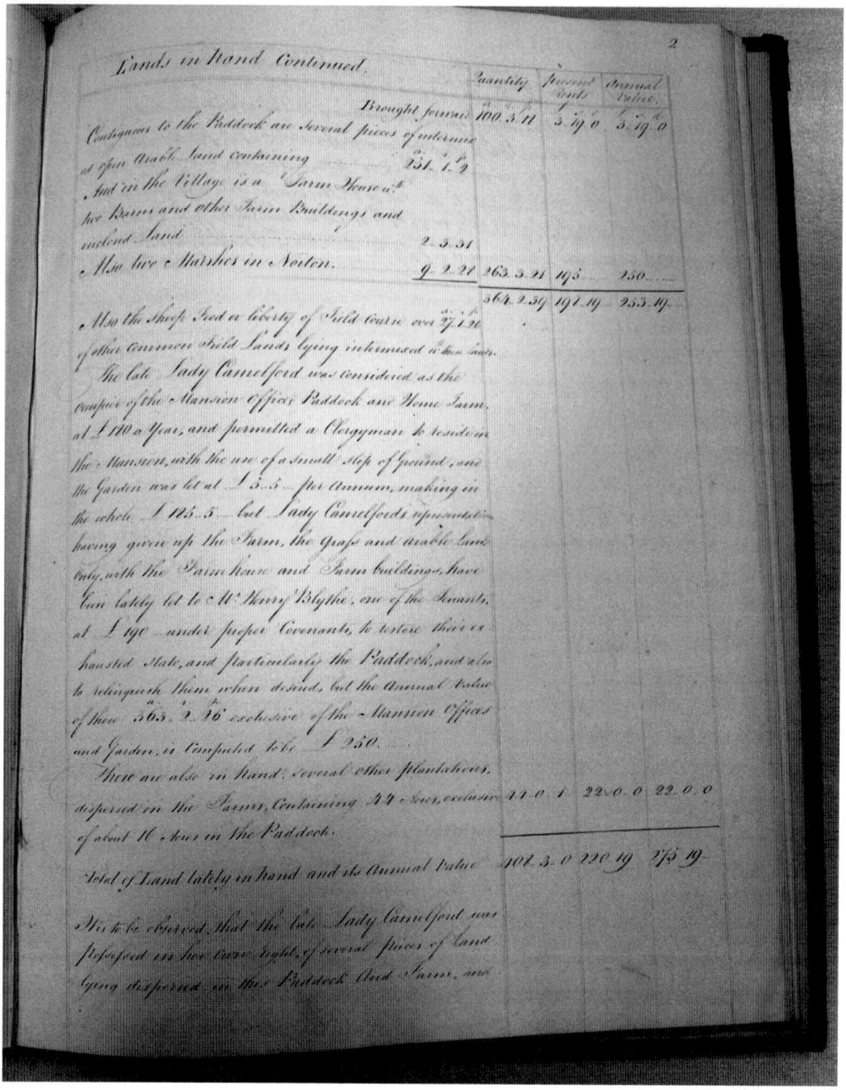

2

Lands in Hand Continued.

	Quantity	Present Rents	Annual Value
Brought forward	100. 3. 11	5. 19. 0	5. 19. 0
Contiguous to the Paddock are several pieces of intermixt open Arable land containing 251. 1. 9 And in the Village is a Farm House with two Barns and other Farm Buildings and inclosed Land 2. 3. 31 Also two Marshes in Norton. 9. 2. 21	263. 3. 21	195	250
	364. 2. 39	197. 19	255. 19

Also the Sheep Feed or liberty of Field Course over 27. 1. 26 of other Common Field Lands lying intermixed with their lands.

The late Lady Camelford was considered as the occupier of the Mansion Offices Paddock and Home Farm at £140 a Year, and permitted a Clergyman to reside in the Mansion, with the use of a small slip of ground, and the Garden was let at £5. 5 per Annum, making in the whole £125. 5 but Lady Camelfords representatives having given up the Farm, the Grass and arable land only, with the Farm house and Farm buildings, have been lately let to Mr Henry Blythe, one of the Tenants, at £190 under proper Covenants, to restore their exhausted State, and particularly the Paddock, and also to relinquish them when desired, but the Annual Value of them 363. 2. 26 exclusive of the Mansion Offices and Garden, is Computed to be £250.

	Quantity	Present Rents	Annual Value
There are also in Hand several other plantations, dispersed in the Farms, Containing 44 Acres, exclusive of about 16 Acres in the Paddock.	44. 0. 1	22. 0. 0	22. 0. 0
Total of Land lately in hand and its Annual Value	401. 3. 0	220. 19	275. 19

It is to be observed, that the late Lady Camelford was possessed in her own right, of several pieces of Land lying dispersed in this Paddock and Farm, and

Westgate includes an account of how the estate passed from one owner to another over a two hundred-year period. When this estate was sold in 1803 a survey of lands was taken which includes maps and the names of large numbers of other owners and tenants in the area.

Some records may have been created for or in relation to an estate by and for other people. Copies of sales particulars created by auctioneers, for instance, can often be found with title deeds and other legal papers. Enclosure maps and awards from before 1801 are another instance, as

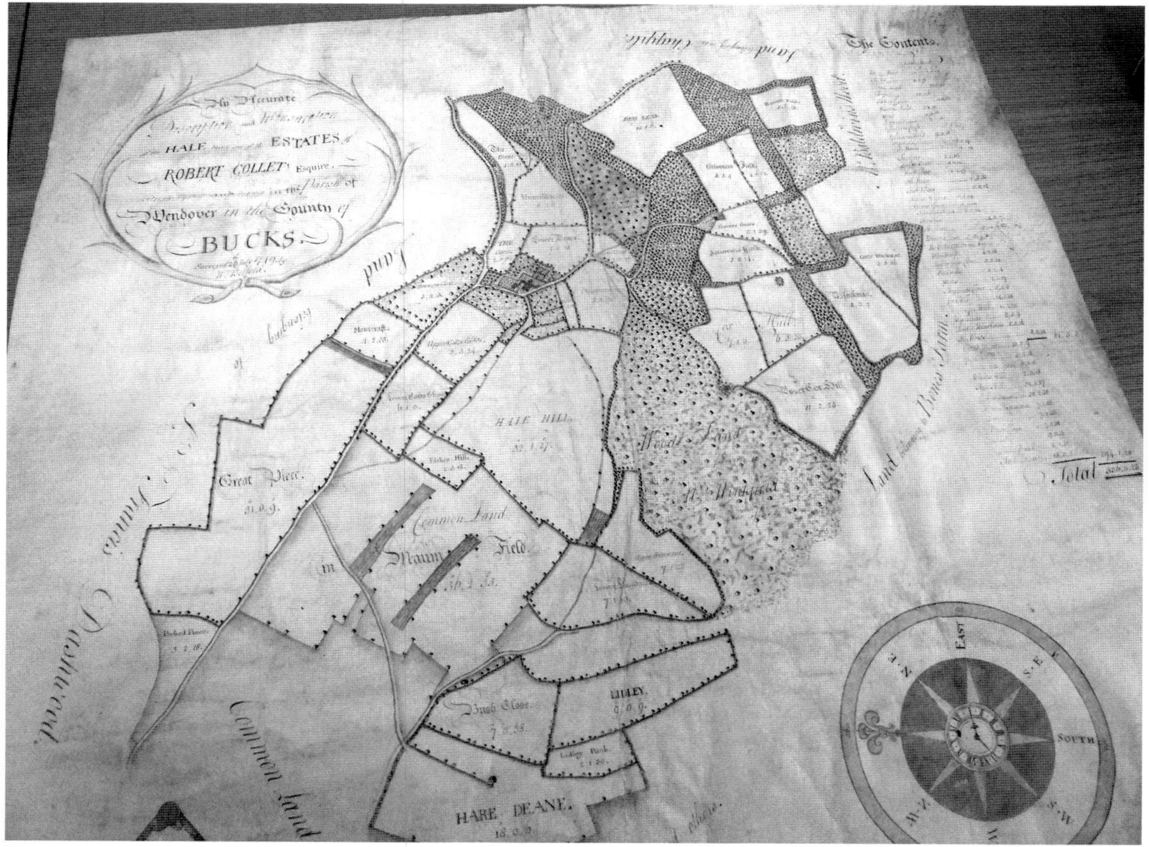

Map of the Hale, Buckinghamshire, Estate of Robert Collet, 1749. (BRO: MA 262/T)

these were often produced for more than one landowner in collaboration with each other. A map of the Hale in Buckinghamshire produced in 1749 showing the estate of Robert Collet is a great example of how landowners included the details of adjoining lands and their owners in order to define their own boundaries. The use of different colours on maps usually denotes different ownerships or uses, with the cartographer and person who commissioned it knowing what it meant. Although some of the colour on the map has faded over time, close inspection shows that the lands on Collet's estate are marked in a different colour to his neighbours whilst woods are coloured dark green. Some land is marked a light green and comparing this to the later enclosure map shows that all the light green plots were common land.

Finding Estate Records

Record offices across the country and The National Archives have large collections of estate records. Many large country houses have their own archives. Generally, the county record office for that area will have a list of private archive collections such as this. Some may even have copies of their catalogues.

Fire Insurance Records

Fire was a serious risk for many people until well into the seventeenth century as most buildings were built of timber and roofed with thatch. The Great Fire of London in 1666 and other major fires in other cities and towns led to the introduction of some building regulations, whilst the use of brick and tiles became more common. Several fire insurance companies were formed from the seventeenth century onwards. Fire brigades were linked to insurance companies, who issued metal plaques to be fixed to buildings to identify who had paid for insurance so that firefighters would know who had paid for their services when they arrived at a fire (see also the section on dating buildings).

Various insurance company records survive detailing people who had fire insurance from 1680 to 1968. One of best known was the Sun Fire Office, which began in 1710. Their registers generally provide the address of the insured property, the owner's name and occupation, any transfer of ownership and a brief description of the structure, including the materials it was made of. When Peter Conway, the tenant of a house in Essex, took out insurance in 1803, the household goods and wearing apparel in his brick and tiled house and adjoining offices was valued at up to £100. His stock, utensils, implements of husbandry and farm machinery were valued separately at up to £40 with 'the usual Average Charge NB Free from loss on such Hay or Corn as shall be destroyed or damaged by

Sun Fire Insurance plaque on a house in Essex.

normal heating'. The fire plaque issued by the company – numbered 737813 – is still placed next to the front door.

In many cases there are accompanying fire insurance plans, which provide a fascinating insight into how large towns and cities in Britain have developed between the 1880s and 1970s. From 1885 to 1968 a company called Chas E. Goad Ltd was employed to make insurance plans for the whole country on a scale of forty feet to the inch, which were updated roughly every five years.

Finding Fire Insurance Records

The Guildhall Library, Aldermanbury, London, EC2V 7HH, has a collection of fire insurance records including those of the Sun Fire Office and the Hand in Hand, which both began in 1710, the London Assurance from 1720 and the Royal Exchange Insurance, which survive from 1773. **www.cityoflondon.gov.uk/guildhalllibrary**

There is an ongoing project to place the Sun Fire Insurance policies online for the period 1787 to 1838. Although this database is not yet complete, it does provide hundreds of thousands of names, addresses and occupations of owners, and sometimes occupiers of insured properties. Some registers are online and can be searched by name, place or occupation. For example, the Sun policy register Ms 11936/419-560 for the period 1800 to 1838 can be searched at The National Archives website. See **www.history.ac.uk/gh/sun.htm** or **www.nationalarchives.gov.uk/a2a**

The Goad insurance maps dating from 1885 to 1968 can be found at the British Library. **www.bl.uk/collections/map_fire_insurance.html**

References to fire insurance records can also be found with title deeds and other property records. The register of deeds for Yorkshire already mentioned includes many such records. Another example is a set of deeds held at Norfolk Record Office for the former White Horse pub in Edgefield in Norfolk, which contains details of a 'policy of Insurance for £100 in the Norwich Equitable Fire Insurance Company' in 1866.

Glebe Records

Glebe was land used to financially support the incumbent (vicar or rector) of each parish. It could be cultivated by the incumbent or leased to tenants. Glebe terriers are detailed inventories of the land or property belonging to the Church of England and take their name from the Latin for land or earth. They began in 1571 when each bishop was directed to make sure that terriers of glebe land for each church were compiled and deposited in their archives. From then on terriers were compiled every few years by the incumbent, churchwardens and older parishioners and were presented at the Bishop's visitation when he reviewed the business of each parish, although they rarely exist before 1604. As a result, terriers also give us insights into how people lived and the wide role the church played in everyday life.

Terriers usually list everything within the church, such as furniture, plate bells and books; those responsible for repairing churchyard walls and fences; any rights, profits, customary fees and income from other sources; the parsonage; cottages; farms and parcels of land. This can be a very long list where land was divided into strips, or parishes owned extensive property. Other buildings such as barns and the names of tenants may also be mentioned. As it was crucial to note the extent and boundaries of all land the owners and occupiers of adjoining lands are often included, which can be helpful if you live near a piece of glebe land. Some parishes relied more on the income from tithes (see the section on tithe records). Even where this was the case some terriers describe how the income from tithes and fees was calculated and collected.

The format and detail of glebe terriers was largely left to each incumbent, so it can vary enormously. Some are very detailed, even going so far as to state whether the parsonage house was made of brick, tile, wattle and daub, plaster and so on. More rarely, they describe the rooms inside,

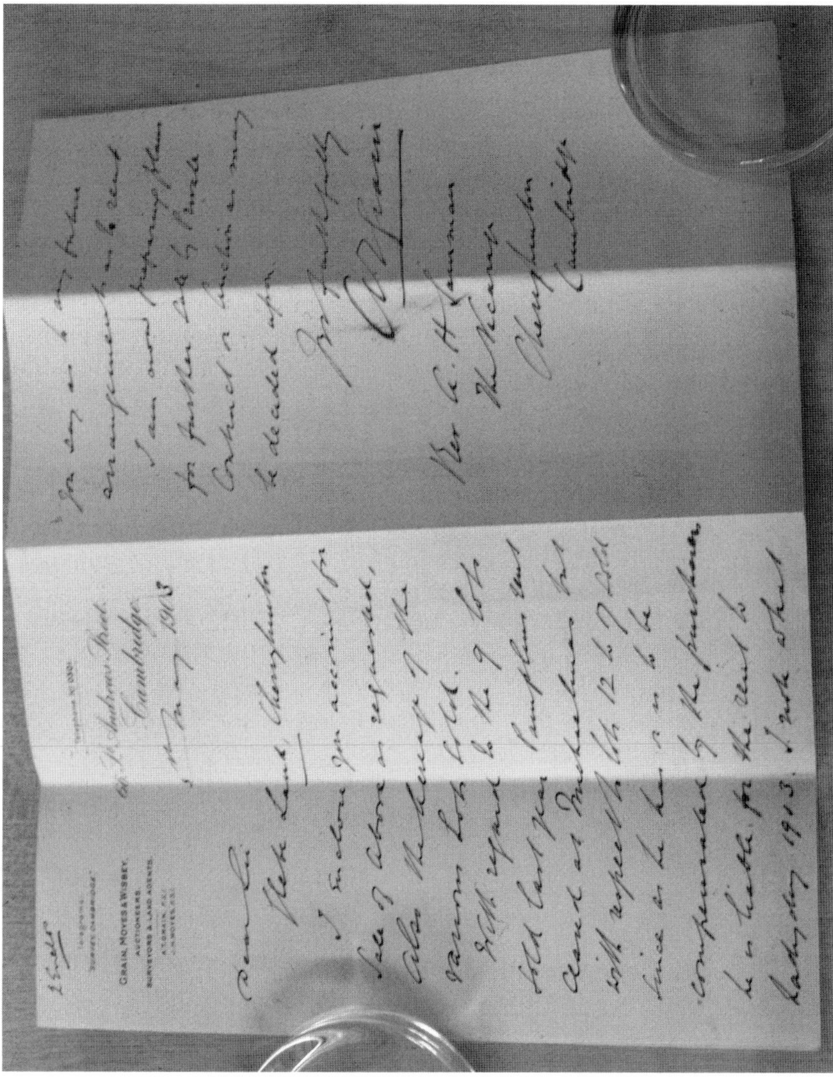
GRAIN, MOYES & WISBEY,
AUCTIONEERS,
SURVEYORS & LAND AGENTS.

(Pages 113 and 114)
Correspondence with Board of Agriculture about sale of glebe land in Cherry Hinton, Cambridgeshire, and an account of the sales of seventeen lots, 1901–1903. (Cambridgeshire Archives Service: P39/3/12)

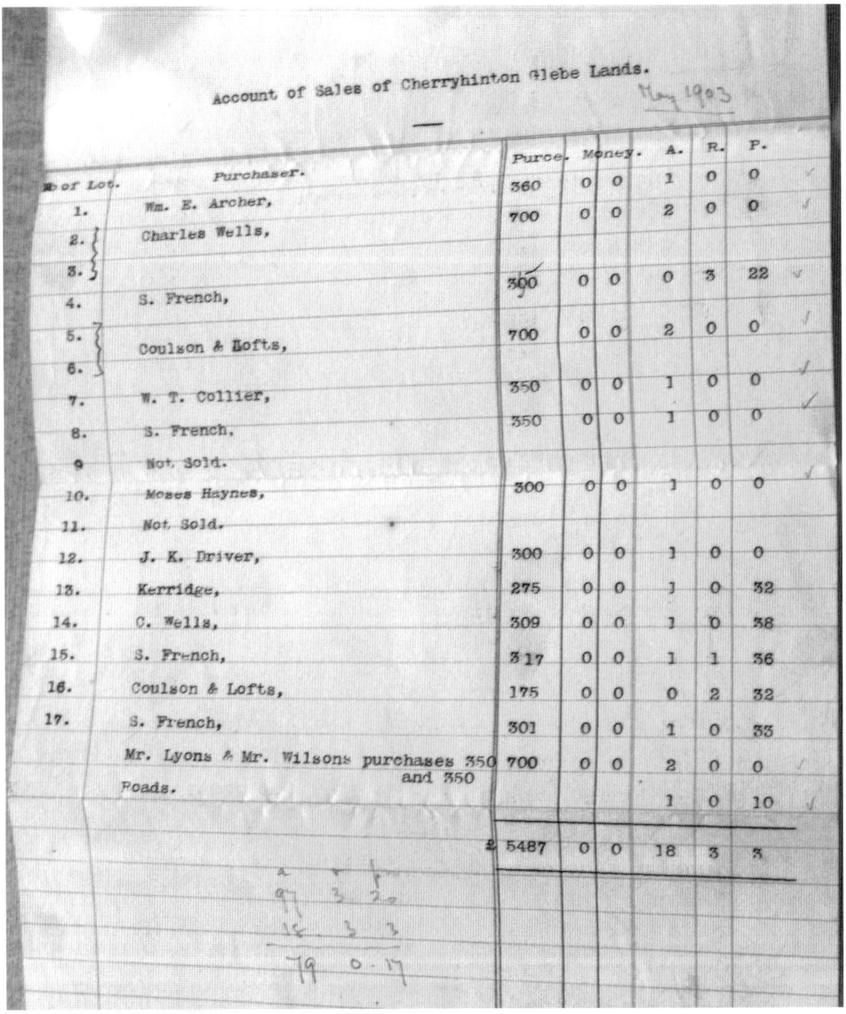

Account of Sales of Cherryhinton Glebe Lands. May 1903

No. of Lot.	Purchaser.	Purce. Money.			A.	R.	P.
1.	Wm. E. Archer,	360	0	0	1	0	0
2. } 3. }	Charles Wells,	700	0	0	2	0	0
4.	S. French,	300	0	0	0	3	22
5. } 6. }	Coulson & Lofts,	700	0	0	2	0	0
7.	W. T. Collier,	350	0	0	1	0	0
8.	S. French,	350	0	0	1	0	0
9	Not Sold.						
10.	Moses Haynes,	300	0	0	1	0	0
11.	Not Sold.						
12.	J. K. Driver,	300	0	0	1	0	0
13.	Kerridge,	275	0	0	1	0	32
14.	C. Wells,	309	0	0	1	0	38
15.	S. French,	317	0	0	1	1	36
16.	Coulson & Lofts,	175	0	0	0	2	32
17.	S. French,	301	0	0	1	0	33
	Mr. Lyons & Mr. Wilsons purchases 350 and 350	700	0	0	2	0	0
	Roads.				1	0	10
		£ 5487	0	0	18	3	3

a r p
97 3 22
18 3 3
79 0 19

such as the 1812 terrier for Cranworth with Letton in Norfolk copied into the baptismal and burial register. This has drawings of the old parsonage house as it was in 1802 with 'walls of clay'. Additions made in 1812 show the kitchen, dairy and other rooms and plans of new drains. A note dated 1813 states: 'the Lean to Part was new roofed when the wall was raised 4 feet & a small Chamber obtained'.

Glebe terriers were produced until well into the twentieth century. In the case of Cherry Hinton in Cambridgeshire a terrier was drawn up in 1902 in preparation for the sale of glebe lands. This is filed with a series of correspondence detailing the sale of this land in 1903, and how the proceeds were to be invested by the Reverend Samman in Government stocks in order to provide him with an income.

Where to find Glebe Terriers and Related Records

Bundles or registers of terriers are usually deposited in local record offices with other diocesan (bishop's) records. Some record offices have separate lists of diocesan terriers, whilst others list them under each parish. Copies of each terrier were often kept in the parish, either as loose sheets or copied onto spare pages in the parish registers.

Glebe properties are often described in early electoral registers, although the detail given does vary.

Some copies of glebe terriers, such as those hosted on the Leicester University website, can be found online. Others, such as those for Staffordshire from 1585 to 1885, have been published by local record societies. See *Staffordshire Glebe Terriers 1585–1885* edited by Sylvia Watts (Staffordshire Record Society, Volumes 22 and 23).

Hearth and Window Taxes

Hearth Tax, 1662–1689

The Hearth Tax was introduced in 1662 during a financial crisis. Every householder whose house worth more than 20 shillings a year at local rates had to pay one shilling for each hearth (fireplace) in their property twice a year, starting at Michaelmas 1662. Payments were collected each Michaelmas (29 September) and Lady Day (25 March). The original Act of Parliament was revised in 1663 and 1664, and collection continued until it was repealed in 1689.

Hearth tax records do not identify individual properties, so are of most help if you have an idea who lived there at the time. They do, however, give an idea of the relative status of different properties in that time period by providing the names of those paying and the number of hearths. However, this does not necessarily correspond to the number of rooms, as many rooms in old houses were unheated, whilst inns had larger numbers of hearths than the average house.

Administration of the tax was extremely complex, and assessment and collection methods changed radically over time. The tax was collected using the administrative divisions of the time – counties, hundreds, boroughs and parishes. The majority of surviving documents relate to the periods 1662–1666 and 1669–1674, when the tax was administered directly by royal officials, who returned their records to the Exchequer. The rest of the time it was collected by private tax collectors, who paid a fixed sum to the government in return for the privilege of doing so. They were not required to send their assessments into the Exchequer, although a few returns from these periods do survive.

Large numbers of people were exempt from payment. These included paupers and people inhabiting houses worth less than 20 shillings a year who did not have any other property over that value, or an income of over £100 a year. Charitable institutions with an annual income of less than £100, and industrial hearths such as kilns and furnaces (but not smithies and bakeries) were also exempt. People not liable to pay the hearth tax were required to obtain a certificate of exemption from the parish officials, countersigned by two Justices of the Peace.

After the revising Act of 1663, hearth tax officials had to list those chargeable and not chargeable (exempt). Some assessments contain the names of exempt individuals, whilst others simply record the total number. From 1670, printed exemption forms were introduced, but the rules for exemption seem to have been applied differently according to the local officials concerned. Due to the varying assessment methods employed, some documents contain information for an entire county, while others cover only one town or village.

Window Tax, 1697–1851

The Window Tax was introduced in 1697, eight years after the Hearth Tax was abolished, in order to cover the cost of re-minting the coinage. This tax was applied to every inhabited dwelling house. The usual levy was two shillings for up to ten windows, eight shillings for ten to twenty windows and ten shillings for twenty or more windows. In 1709, the rates were increased for larger houses, but exempted those too poor to pay church or poor rates. From the mid-eighteenth century, the rates were often increased for houses with more than ten windows. From 1825, occupiers of houses with less than eight windows were exempt and the tax was abolished altogether in 1851.

As with hearth tax, the surviving records are of most use when you know the names of people living in your home. This tax had a major impact on the architecture of buildings as windows were blocked up to cut costs. The 'blind' (fake) window, which balanced the look of buildings, became a popular feature.

Finding Hearth and Window Tax Records

Hearth Tax records for the period 1662 to 1689 have the best survival rate. The surviving records, including exemption certificates, are deposited in The National Archives in the E 179 series. Roehampton University's Centre for Hearth Tax Research provides free access to records of the Hearth Tax for England and Wales. This includes invaluable analyses which will help you to understand a household's status. The index can be searched by place, date and document type and will eventually host indexes and transcriptions to all the records with contextual maps and statistics. **www.hearthtax.org.uk**

Some paperwork relating to the administration involved in compiling such lists also turns up amongst parish records. Many held nationally have been published by the British Record Society, which exists to publish and make available transcripts of archive material.

Some local collections have also been published, often by family history societies or local historians, as is the case with the 1664 and 1674 returns for Cambridgeshire transcribed by Susan Rose and Nesta Evans respectively, which can be found at the record office. The Society of Genealogists in London also has a large collection of published indexes.

Further information can also be found in J. Gibson, *The Hearth Tax and other later Stuart Tax Lists* (FFHS, 1996), which gives county-by-county lists of document references held at TNA and elsewhere.

Window taxes were collected by the land tax commissioners. From 1767–1832 window taxes, along with land tax, were stored in annual bundles by hundreds with quarter sessions court records. Survival tends to be very poor, but what there is can be found in local record offices. Some collections have been indexed and transcribed by local family or local history societies.

Land Registry

The Land Registry was established in 1862 so that property transactions could be recorded in one central place. It was a voluntary scheme to begin with. As a result only a small percentage of property transactions are included before it became compulsory. The first compulsory scheme began in London in 1899, gradually spreading to other towns and cities, but it only became compulsory everywhere in England and Wales in 1990 (1979 for Scotland and 2003 for Northern Ireland). Even where it was compulsory it will only include properties that have changed hands after compulsory registration began. This means that there is still a significant percentage of houses and other buildings which are not registered, although that is gradually diminishing.

The Land Registry records the present owners of all properties and to some extent the past owners. Their records are easy to access and should be one of the first places to start your research.

The Land Registry records for a cottage in Reepham in Norfolk only listed owners from 1991, the first date it was sold after compulsory registration. However, access rights to the other cottages meant other historical details were recorded with the plan showing the access route that gave information about the ownership of all four cottages going back several decades.

Finding Land Registry Records

Check what is included with your house deeds. You can apply for a copy of the registration documents for your home for a small fee from Kingston-Upon-Hull Land Registry, Earle House, Portland Street, Hull, HU2 8JN. These list any sales since the house was registered, the current owner, any current mortgages and plans showing boundaries. They can also include older information that has been computerized such as older deeds containing clauses that still affect the property. **www.landreg.gov.uk**

Land Tax

Land tax was introduced in 1692 and remained in force until 1963. The assessments can be used to locate owners and occupiers of property throughout this period. At their most complete from 1780 to 1832, they are helpful for filling the gap in between enclosure records and the tithe survey beginning in 1836, or where no tithe or enclosure records exist.

Land tax was payable on any property worth more than 20 shillings rent a year. From 1698 the government decided on the amount of funding it required from the country as a whole. This total was then broken down into individual amounts for each county, then for each hundred within that county, before being broken down again for each parish. Local officials would assess the land holders in each parish to determine how much they should pay, with Roman Catholics charged double the normal rate up to 1832. However, rates do not appear to have been applied consistently across the country.

Assessments were produced either annually or quarterly. Most include the annual rateable value and amount of tax due, the names of owners from 1692 and owners and occupiers from 1772, although multiple occupancies in the same property may not all be mentioned. The rental value was originally assessed in 1698. In most areas there were no more taken, which means that the later assessments do not necessarily reflect their real value. Nevertheless, comparing the different values gives an indication of people's social status within a parish. This in turn can help with identifying your property.

The amount of land tax payable was imposed annually by vote of Parliament until 1798. From 1798, the rate was fixed at a level of four shillings in the pound. Significantly, this Act allowed land holders to commute future tax requirements by making a one-off payment equivalent to fifteen years' worth of tax. As land tax records were used to assess a person's right to vote, entries for people who commuted payment were still recorded up until 1832. Post–1798 land tax records do not usually provide detailed addresses, but do list landlords and tenants and the value of the assessment. This Act also introduced printed forms standardizing the type of information included.

Survival of land tax records is quite patchy, except for the period 1780 to 1832 when copies were made and lodged with the Clerk of the Peace for each county. These were used to verify voting rights, which were based on owning freehold property worth a rental of at least £2 a year. You may still find odd years missing from this period, but it is a more continuous run of years. Their use for this purpose became increasingly redundant after the Reform Act of 1832, so survival is once more very variable. In Suffolk, for example, some parishes have land tax records up until the 1940s or later, whilst neighbouring Norfolk has very little after 1832. The exception is borough records, as the right to vote in a borough was not dependent on payment of land tax.

Land tax records do not always provide a clear picture. Ownership may have changed within a short period of time and many records don't identify properties, or only one or two. Owners may be recorded as occupying more than one property at the same time, presumably because the assessors did not bother to record each one separately. The term 'owner' can also be a quite fluid description, and may refer to a leaseholder or occupier of copyhold lands.

Recording information over a span of years will make it easier to identify a property. By noting other properties and taking copies to see whether there is a pattern in how properties are recorded you may be able to identify it through its rateable value, unchanging position on the page or other details, and/or comparing this information to the tithe survey, census returns or house deeds. In particular, many of the owners and occupiers listed on the tithe apportionments beginning in 1836 will be found in land tax assessments.

In the case of a house in Heigham, the tithe map of 1842 and apportionment of 1843 describe the size of plot and name the owner and occupier. The land tax records do not specifically identify the same plot, but a plot of the same size and value is noted in a number of years and provided details of its value and additional information on other occupiers. Between 1807 and 1811, for instance, the owner was a Reverend John Humphrey and the occupier a 'Golding'. The rent was £98 and the 'Sums Assessed and Not Exonerated: £19. S.12. D.0'. Humphrey continues to be listed as the owner from 1812 up to 1828, with a tenant called Neale, although there are some years in between where no tenant's names are given at all. Confirmation that this was the same plot came when matching details of this plot size and these earlier owners' and occupiers' names were found in manorial records.

Finding Land Tax Assessments

The *Gibson Guide to Land and Window Tax Assessments* (FFHS, 1998) provides a comprehensive overview of these records, where they are held across the country and how they can be used.

The majority of land tax records are held locally. Surviving records from 1780 to 1832 are filed with the quarter sessions records at county record offices. These are usually stored and listed separately under 'land tax', or the name of individual parishes. Others may be found with parish records or in estate or family collections.

A number of London parishes have early records which can be found at the Guildhall Library.

The Essex Family History Society is one local group that has published indexes to land tax records, which can be accessed through them or at the record office. Many of these local publications can be found on the parish chest website **www.parishchest.com**.

The returns of 1798 are particularly comprehensive, as the tax commissioners created a list of everyone liable to pay tax in that year, whether owners or occupiers. These records cover all of England and Wales apart from Flintshire, and can be seen at The National Archives, with digitized copies available on the Ancestry website (see Land Tax Redemption records). These redemption records record the amount assessed and sometimes a redemption date **www.ancestry.co.uk**.

Manorial Records

What is most exciting about manorial court records is that every time copyhold land was sold, rented out or inherited, the details of how it was passed on from one person to another are recorded. They can therefore provide a wonderful resource for tracing property and land over several hundred years up to 1922, when the copyhold system of land tenure was abolished. However, the very word 'manor' seems to deter many people from going any further as the records are perceived as difficult to use. Whilst this can be true, manorial records are well worth the effort. In the case of land in Rickinghall in Suffolk, for example, the owners and occupiers of a house were traced back to when the first surviving manor court book began in 1717.

It is useful to have an idea of how the manor court worked and understand some of the terminology used in order to use the records effectively. Each manor governed local communities until well into the Tudor period, dealing with routine legal matters such as theft, illegitimacy and assaults. In the manor court rolls for Bramford in Suffolk, for instance, an inquest into the suicide of a young woman in the 1580s is entered on the same page as land transactions and cases of trespass.

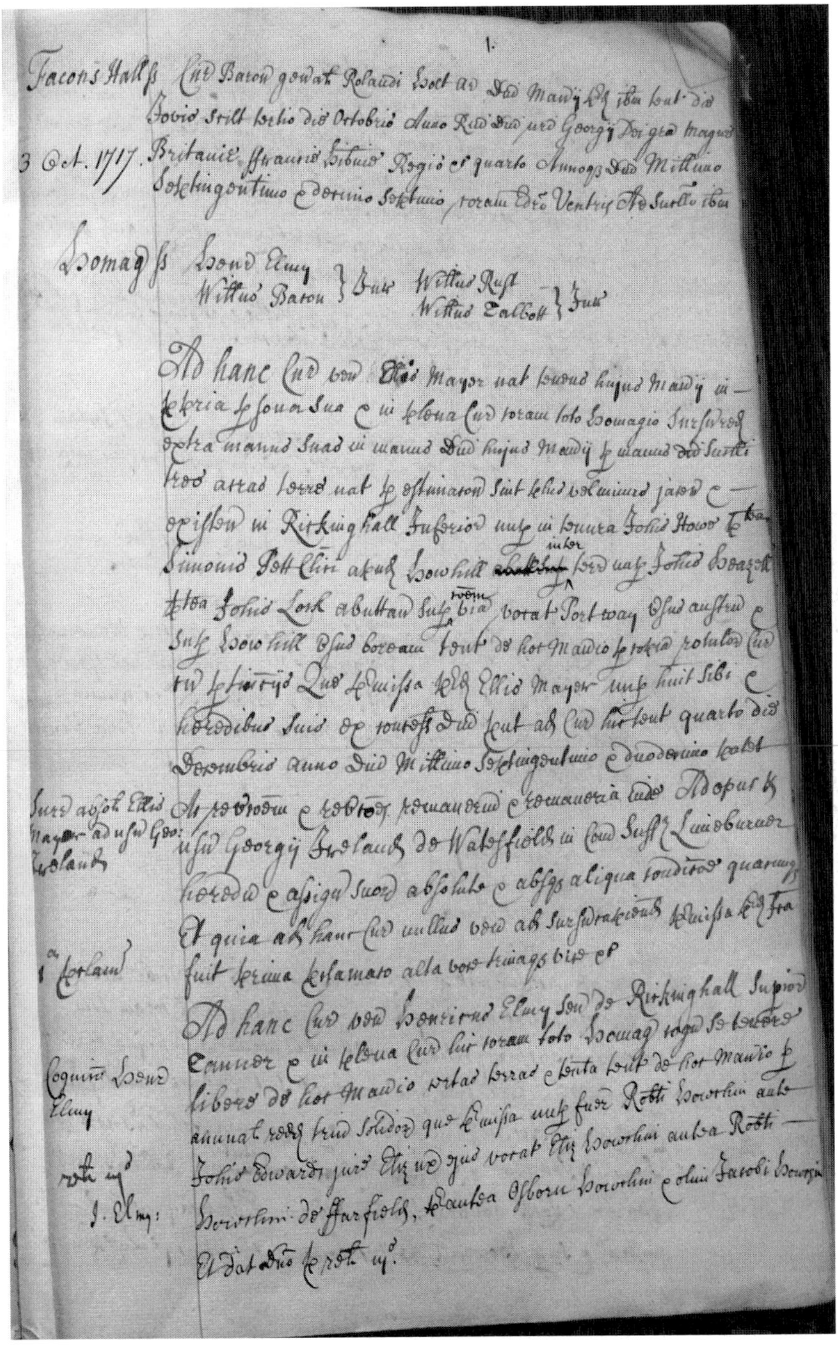
Facons Hall ss. Cur Baron general Rolandi Holt ar Dni Manerij ibm tent die
Jovis tertio decimo die Octobris Anno Regni Dni nri Georgij Dei gra Magne
3 Oct. 1717. Britanie ffrancie Hibnie Regis et quarto Annoq Dni Millimo
Septingentimo decimo septimo, coram Edro Ventris Ard Senescallo ibm

Homag ss Henr Elmy
Willus Baron } Jur Willus Rust
Willus Talbott } Jur

(Pages 121 and 122) Rickinghall Facons Manor Court Book, 1717–1804. (SRO Bury St. Edmunds: HB 502/2753/11/9)

D
Facons Hall
Beginning 3rd Oct 1717
Ending 21st May 1864

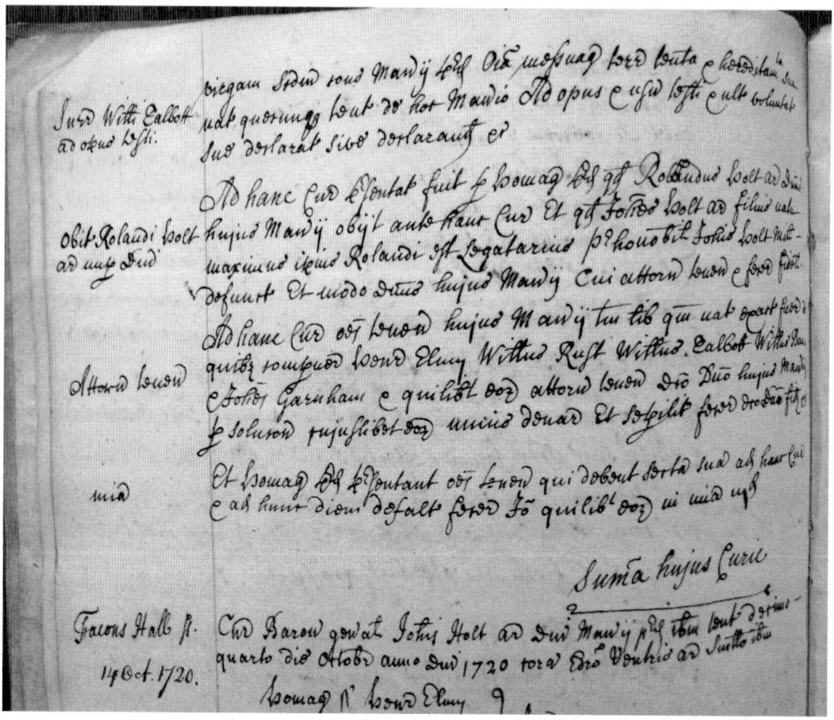
Suma hujus Curie
Facons Hall
14 Oct. 1720.

The manorial system was adopted by the Normans after the Conquest, when they superimposed their own system over the Saxon system of land ownership. Manors were geographical areas outside towns and boroughs granted by the Crown. It is important to remember that many areas we now think of as being part of a city or borough were not in the past. For example, Heigham, which is now part of Norwich, was once a separate hamlet with the manor owned by the Bishops of Norwich. Few, if any, manorial records exist for adjacent parishes such as St Benedict's, which fall within the original city boundaries. Another important point is that there might be several manors in one parish, and a manor might have land in several parishes.

The lords (and ladies) of a manor offered protection to people living within their manor in return for certain duties, such as working on the lord's land for a certain number of days each year. The lord had the legal right to decide what happened to the majority of land and property within the manor. The phrase 'tenure' commonly refers to the way in which a person came to hold land or property (i.e. having the right to use it). For the house historian most information can be found in the records relating to those who held land by customary tenure, traditionally in return for labouring on the lord's own land, which was known as the demesne. The descent of these holdings was governed by the custom (accepted rules) of the manor in question. In some places there were differences in who inherited a tenancy, with the youngest son inheriting under a system called 'Borough English'.

A court baron, later more commonly called a general court leet or customary court, met every three or four weeks. This was the court of the chief tenants and was responsible for regulating local affairs within the manor. The court baron appointed a reeve, who was responsible for managing the day-to-day affairs, such as managing livestock and representing tenants. The homage was a jury, made up of tenants, who served on the court baron.

The court baron also dealt with the transfer of copyhold land. Other court business included the reporting of tenants' deaths (both freehold and customary tenants) and the payment to the lord of the corresponding feudal due, called a 'heriot'. Occasionally, there were payments for the marriages of daughters of customary tenants (merchets) or records of the remarriage of widows. Many tenants are named in the court books as officials or jurors, noted as absent, or fined (amerced) for a minor offence.

The court leet appointed local office-bearers such as the constable and dealt with local petty offences such as theft, bigamy, adultery and illegitimacy and was responsible for the maintenance of highways and ditches. For instance, in the court books for the manor of Naseby in Northamptonshire, held at Northamptonshire Record Office, the court books for 19 April 1804 include a number of orders such as: 'no people to go gleaning until seven o'clock in the morning nor remain after 7 in the evening'. In the same book a presentment stated that a William Ward was fined for ploughing up 'balks and hades and thereby trespassed on the other Tenants'. The fine was to be reduced if he laid down the ploughed land with 'good and sufficient grass seeds'.

'Waste' was land not used for any specific purpose, usually adjoining the highway or manor boundaries. These were often granted for grazing at manor courts, although much was lost under the Enclosure Acts of the nineteenth century.

Most people look at manorial records because they discover their property once stood on copyhold land. Copyhold land (also known as customary tenure) was the commonest way in which to hold land until 1922, particularly outside boroughs and cities. It is usually described as falling somewhere between a leasehold and freehold and was so called because each tenant was given a copy of the entry recording their succession in the manor court roll.

The copyhold system was not a straightforward system of ownership or tenancy. The right to own or lease such land was granted under a system that dated back to feudal times, when the lords of the manor expected certain dues in return for granting such rights and protection.

Because tenants held land at 'the will' (permission) of the lord or lady of the manor their tenancy rights were set out in a copy of an entry in the court rolls (later in books) of that manor. This followed a ceremony of admission, which took place either at a full sitting of the court held in the manor house or local pub, or privately in a solicitor's office. Some admissions were for life, whilst others were for a set period of time. If the tenant outlived that term, they were entitled to be readmitted for a similar term on payment of a fine (a fee). Manors' traditional role in administering local affairs gradually declined from the eighteenth century onwards and they became almost solely concerned with dealing with copyhold land until it was abolished under the Law of Property Act of 1922.

Manorial records for Kenninghall in Norfolk illustrate the types of information to be found. After the death of Francis Burlingham in Kenninghall in 1814 his son James of the nearby parish of Fersfield attended the court to claim the lands left to him in his father's will. The court book records this as having been three acres, two roods and thirty-three perches of land and part of the park common which had been enclosed in 1801 under a Parliamentary Award. Its boundaries are described in detail including neighbours' names and the fact that there was a private road running alongside the northern and eastern boundaries. The western boundary adjoined a public road leading to Banham and three messuages 'lately occupied by Francis Burlingham and his tenants', and more of the park common had also been allotted to Francis under the enclosure act.

Further details of what happened to the property can be found in later entries. James Burlingham went on to 'surrender by the rod' (a symbolic handover) his messuages and cottages in Kenninghall to a James Wake in 1816 for £400. After James's death in 1850 his nephew John Wick claimed the remaining copyhold estate as left to him in his uncle's will and promptly sold it to George Gunns, a farmer of Banham (reference: NRO: Comtesse de Tourdonnet 4/6/86, Q193B).

The ownership of a cottage in Stanhoe is another example of how manorial records can be used. The name of the owner was initially established through the 1910–15 Valuation Survey as being an Isaac Seaman of the Strand in Middlesex. Isaac never lived at the property, but electoral registers recorded him as having voting rights in the parish based on its ownership. It was unknown how Isaac came to own it until the manor court records for the Manor of Easthall, Bokenhams and Shernbournes in Stanhoe were searched (reference NRO: MS 19810 Z 2 C).

The manor court books show that Isaac Seaman inherited the property in 1880 from the family of his deceased first wife, Mary Ann Matsell. The court books quote the will of his father-in-law, John Matsell, in which he left the property to the use of John's wife during her lifetime, then to Isaac. Interestingly, he still left it outright to Isaac, even though his daughter had died before he wrote his will. Further entries take the ownership back to John Matsell's father, also called John, in July 1842. Although no earlier manorial records survive for this court, this entry tells us that John Matsell senior had in turn been admitted to the properties in April 1824.

In contrast, freehold land was held primarily in return for a fixed rent, and its descent was not governed (or recorded) by the manor. There was no unified system for recording freehold or leasehold land. Nevertheless, it is still possible to find information about freehold and leasehold properties in manor court rentals and surveys. It is also possible to find records of the process of converting copyhold land to freehold, known as 'enfranchisement', which began in the 1880s and became universal after the copyhold system was abolished.

Freeholders can appear in the court books as jurors and in disputes over maintaining hedges and roads and so on. It is sometimes possible to use manor court records to trace freehold property if the neighbouring property was copyhold. In the case of a house in Burnham Westgate in Norfolk, for instance, every time the neighbouring copyhold property was sold, leased or inherited it included the details of owners and occupiers of the freehold property on its boundary in order to identify its location and boundaries. As a result, it is possible to identify the freehold property in relation to its copyhold neighbour back to 1740 (reference NRO: MC 1813/47–49 & NRS pre–1955 Blomefield). It is worth noting, however, that these records only mention the land, not the house. This does not mean there was no house standing on this site at this time, but simply that the records were only concerned with identifying boundaries.

Using Manorial Records and Terminology

It is not possible to provide comprehensive guidance on using manorial records in a book of this size. There are, however, some key records and terms that you will use. Because they can be difficult to interpret, this section includes a summary of some of the main terms you will come across. There can be variations between manors, but the main terms you will come across are as follows. The main records of use when researching a house are the manor court books and rolls, rentals and surveys.

Court proceedings were generally written on parchment rolls until well into the sixteenth century. The language used was generally Latin (often abbreviated) until 1733, when the requirement for legal documents to be in Latin was ended. The civil war period is an exception, with English used most of this time. However, with a bit of practice and understanding of what to expect it is still possible to use these records. This is because the format and terminology was often standardized. You may also be fortunate to find published transcripts of some manorial records and other manorial records such as rentals, surveys and lists of tenants are often in English.

The court records usually describe the type of court and date and give the name of the official presiding. Essoins (excuses) were normally listed first, followed by the names of the jury, and then any presentments. When details were entered into the manorial court books a copy was made for each person involved in the transaction. This was done by writing it out onto one document. So, if there were three people involved it was copied three times. These documents became known as 'indentures' as they were 'indented', or cut, with a wavy line between each copy. The wavy lines protected against fraud, as only these copies matched when put back together. Sometimes these copies are the only records surviving. Many can be found in other collections in archives such as house deeds, solicitors, business and estate records.

Yearly leases were common, and for each transaction a fine (fee) would be paid to the court. Those who held small amounts of land, either freehold or copyhold, often used them to raise money, and references to mortgages can be frequently found. This can confuse many researchers as a mortgage was simply a loan, and didn't mean the property was being sold each time.

There is a great deal of help available in how to use and interpret manorial records, from books to websites, such as this online tutorial. **www.nationalarchives.gov.uk/palaeography**

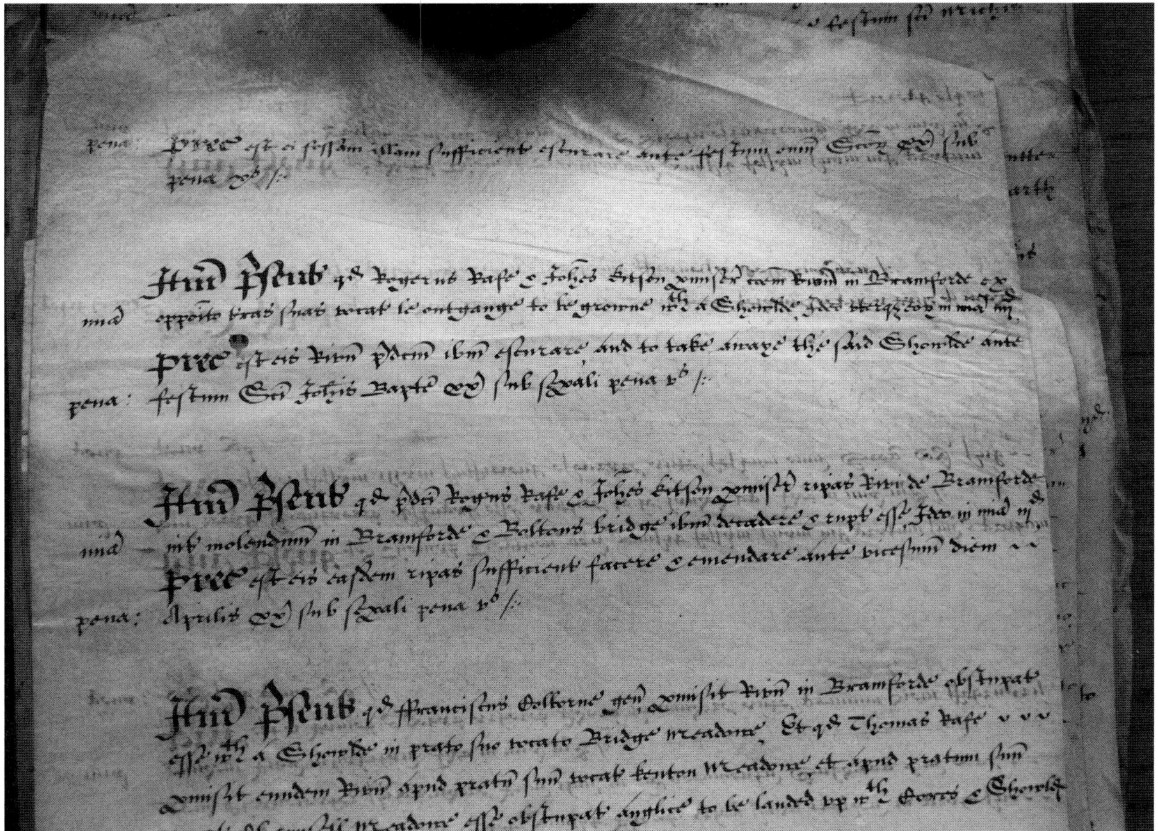

(Pages 127 and 128) Manor Court Roll of Bramford Hall. (SRO: Ipswich HB 8/670)

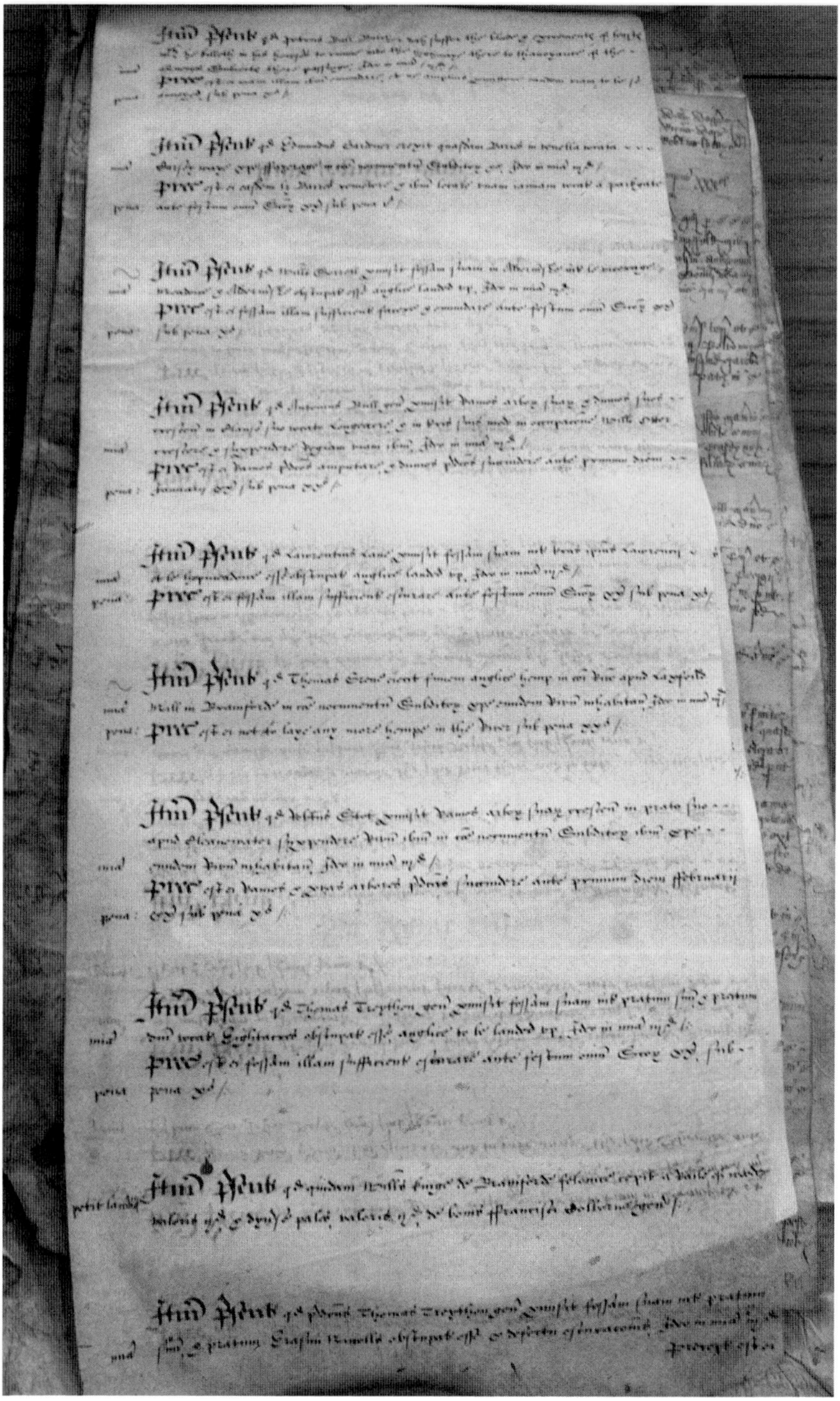

The National Archives also has various useful links describing manorial records and a glossary of terms used. **www.nationalarchives.gov.uk/mdr/aboutapps/mdr/about.htm**

An invaluable guide to the terminology in manorial records is *The Local Historian's Encyclopaedia.*

The University of Lancaster has developed a useful website which provides practical guidance on using and understanding manorial records. **www.lancs.ac.uk/fass/projects/manorialrecords/using/index.htm**

Some key terms you will come across are:

- A 'messuage' was a dwelling house with any adjacent buildings and lands used by a household. Entries in manor court books usually name neighbouring occupiers as a means of identifying boundaries.
- 'By the rod': the person giving up a tenancy or being admitted held the end of rod or stick carried by the steward as a symbol of the handover.
- Granting 'seizin', 'to the use', and 'to the use and behoof of', are used when someone was entitled to the income or another benefit from land. Sometimes this was the first stage in a process called 'lease and release', in which a piece of land could be transferred from one party to another without having to enrol a deed at court (see also the section on deeds).
- 'Fealty' meant the tenant took an oath that they would carry out the duties and services due to the lord, and be a faithful tenant. A 'quit rent' occurred when the tenant was 'quit' (discharged) from service to the lord of the manor.
- A 'fee certain' is the recording of a fixed amount set by custom, such as a peppercorn rent. These arrangements are often mentioned in wills and title deeds. For example, Thomas Browne, a merchant of Burnham Westgate, instructed his executor to allow Browne's nephew to occupy his house for four years in exchange for a peppercorn rent payable at the feast of St Michael the Archangel (NRO: NCC Will. 1729. 535 Rudd).
- 'Surrendering to the use of his or her will' describes when the heir of a customary tenant gave up the property to someone else after succeeding to it.
- A 'conditional surrender' was a gift subject to the fulfilment of a condition. In practice this was a means of mortgaging copyhold land. If the loan was not repaid the lender could only take

possession of the property if the Lord of the Manor accepted them as a tenant. In contrast an 'absolute surrender' meant there were no restrictions on a gift or bequest.

- A 'satisfaction' acknowledges that an agreement has finished under the terms agreed. It usually declared a mortgage had been repaid, and thus extinguished (ended) a conditional surrender.
- An 'expectant revision' granted certain rights over lands or properties. Such contracts and clauses were used to get round the fact that a married woman's property became her husband's until the nineteenth century. Wives were questioned separately in order to make sure they were not being coerced. For example, when Sarah Vincent, wife of Samuel, appeared at the Westfield manor court in 1765, she was admitted to various lands as the new tenant. The court record makes it clear that the land had been given to her for her 'sole use' by her father in his will, as a means of allowing her to retain some control over it. Nevertheless, any subsequent sale would have occurred under her husband's name, with Sarah being questioned as to whether she agreed.

Other related records are close and fine rolls, held at The National Archives. Close rolls date from the thirteenth to the fifteenth centuries. As they dealt with every branch of public administration they include many deeds. Fine rolls date from the thirteenth century until 1642. They include inquisitions post mortem (IPMs) which were introduced in around 1216. These were held when someone died holding lands granted by the Crown, in order to establish whether the king had any rights to it. In the case of land in Tackley in Oxfordshire, for instance, details about ownership are recorded in the inquisitions as early as the 1300s.

Finding Manorial Records

Some manorial records are still in private hands. Large collections can be found at The National Archives (TNA), local record offices and Cambridge and Oxford universities. County record offices often have details of relevant material held elsewhere.

Because of their legal significance, there is an official list of all known manorial records called the Manorial Documents Register (MDR), maintained by the Historical Manuscripts Commission (HMC) at The National Archives. An online version can be searched by manor name, parish, date and document type, but does not yet include all counties. **www.nationalarchives.gov.uk/mdr**

Many of the early close rolls, fine rolls and inquisitions post mortem have been published. These are available at The National Archives, the Society of Genealogists and some local record offices and local studies libraries.

Lists of manorial records can also be found via the ARCHON and Access to Archives (AA) websites.

Some manorial records have been transcribed and published. Check the British Record Society series and local history libraries.

Trade directories list lords of the manor for every parish.

Maps and Plans

Maps let you time travel via visual glimpses of areas at various points in the past. Maps and their associated records can confirm ownership and occupancy of lands and buildings; what some people did for a living; how many people lived in a property and whether it was surrounded by fields or in a slum area. Understanding the geography of a place can provide information on why and how a building was built in a particular place and why builders used certain materials. Maps also tell us something about neighbours and add to our knowledge of local and national events by showing us the impact of developments such as canals and railways, the growth of new industries and decline of others. There are even maps charting sickness, poverty and social class.

For instance, the impact of events such as enclosure and industrialization on the landscape is demonstrated by the first large-scale map of Norfolk, which was published in 1797 by William Faden. Within fifteen years of publication the extensive commons, heaths and warrens had largely disappeared. The 1842 tithe map for Heigham and Ordnance Survey maps of 1883 and 1905 show that what was once a green field in a hamlet next to Norwich became a central part of the city.

There are some problems with using maps that it is important to be aware of. Firstly, the fact that they show a building where yours stands today does not mean it is the same one. The next problem is lack of accuracy and detail. Until the Ordnance Survey maps were introduced no map attempted to show every detail of the area, village, town or city. Rather they were created to show specific items for a landowner or organization. A map might show every street in a town, but not every house. Many are simply representative, giving an idea of landscape so any properties shown are not necessarily in the right location or to scale. This can be seen on Faden's 1797 map of Norfolk, where many buildings are shown close to where they stood rather than on the exact spot, whilst others known to have existed at the time are not shown at all. In the case of county maps they were often paid for by subscription so only the subscribers' properties were shown.

For an excellent overview of the history of map-making in Britain see

Andrew Macnair and Tom Williamson's book on William Faden and his 1797 map of Norfolk. The Building History website has a useful overview of the history of mapping in Britain specifically in relation to building history, with links to a range of online maps **www.buildinghistory.org/maps.shtml**.

The Society of Cartographers produces an annual journal containing articles and reviews **http://soc.org.uk**.

The Map History website has much on the history of map-making. **www.maphistory.info**

What follows in this section is a summary of the main types of maps used by house historians and how they can be used. Each type of map has its own 'finding' section. However, the main places to look are local record offices, the British Library, 96 Euston Road, London, NW1 2DB, which has the largest collection of maps in the UK **www.bl.uk/collections/maps/html**, The National Archives and the National Library of Wales **www.llgc.org.uk/index.php?id=collections02**.

Many local museums have their own collections of maps. These are often kept in storage and indexes to them are not always widely available. The ARCHON and Access to Archives websites can be very useful in identifying such resources, but do check with local museums separately.

An increasing number of digitized copies of maps can be accessed online (some for free). Below is a selection.

The London Topographical Society sells copies of historical maps, plans and views of the London area at: 17 The Avenue, Northwood, HA6 2NJ **www.topsoc.org**

Motco Enterprises at the Court House, Shamley Green, Guildford, Surrey, GU5 0UB has a database of topographical prints, maps and panoramas of London which can be accessed free for personal use. CDs of the major London maps are for sale **www.motco.com**.

Genmaps has lots of free historic maps **http://freepages.genealogy.rootsweb.ancestry.com/~genmaps/index.html**

Some historic maps can be found on Google Earth. One example is the David Rumsey collection at: **www.davidrumsey.com/view/google-maps**. You can also use the modern maps to get a close-up view of your locality and compare features against older maps. **http://earth.google.co.uk**.

You can access two sets of Ordnance Survey county series free at British History Online **www.british-history.ac.uk/map.aspx**.

Vision of Britain includes maps, gazetteers, statistical data and historical descriptions of places between 1801 and 2001. **www.visionofbritain.org.uk**.

Map Seeker is a commercial site with a large selection of reproduction historical maps, plans and surveys **www.mapseeker.co.uk**.

The Bodleian Library in Oxfordshire has a comprehensive collection from a wide area. Their website also contains lots of useful links **www.bodley.ox.ac.uk/guides/maps/**

There are also numerous regional sites with maps, plans, surveys and charts for particular areas.

Architectural and Engineering Drawings

Architectural and engineering drawings and plans are a vital part of 'reading' a building. It is only relatively recently that planning permission was needed to make structural changes to properties and to build new ones. This means that the majority of plans tend to date from the early 1900s onwards. Even if there is no drawing available for your home there may well be other plans or drawings of buildings from the same area and time period. Such plans give an insight into what older properties looked like when first built. They also reflect fashions and styles from different areas around the country. For example, when researching a Victorian terraced house in Rupert Street in Norwich I found plans for other houses in the area from various dates. The whole area had suffered significant bombing damage during the Second World War and redevelopment plans of the area on the other side of the street and adjacent roads included plans and photographs of houses being demolished and rebuilt.

An 1860 map for the development of land in Heigham (now part of Norwich) behind the Black Horse pub on Earlham Road was drawn up by a local architect. This includes details of the plots being sold and a new road to be built named Mill Hill Road (reference NRO: Estate of Richard Reeve, D.S. 256 [3]). Early twentieth-century sales particulars for other properties on Mill Hill Road help build up a bigger picture of all the houses built on these plots.

Many plans can be found with sales particulars. For example, two sets of sales particulars for Stiffkey in Norfolk from 1848 and 1854 included maps and details of the properties being sold, including the names of tenants and adjacent landowners. A more recent sales particular for a 'period cottage' in Biddenden in Kent from 1979 included photographs, descriptions of the interior and plans of proposed alterations, with details of planning permission.

Finding Drawings and Plans

Again, local record offices and The National Archives are the main places to look. The National Archives holds a large collection of plans and building drawings for almost every kind of building constructed in the nineteenth and twentieth centuries. The Ministry of Housing and Local Government collection is particularly important as it includes plans for houses, hospitals, workhouses, libraries, town halls, public lodging

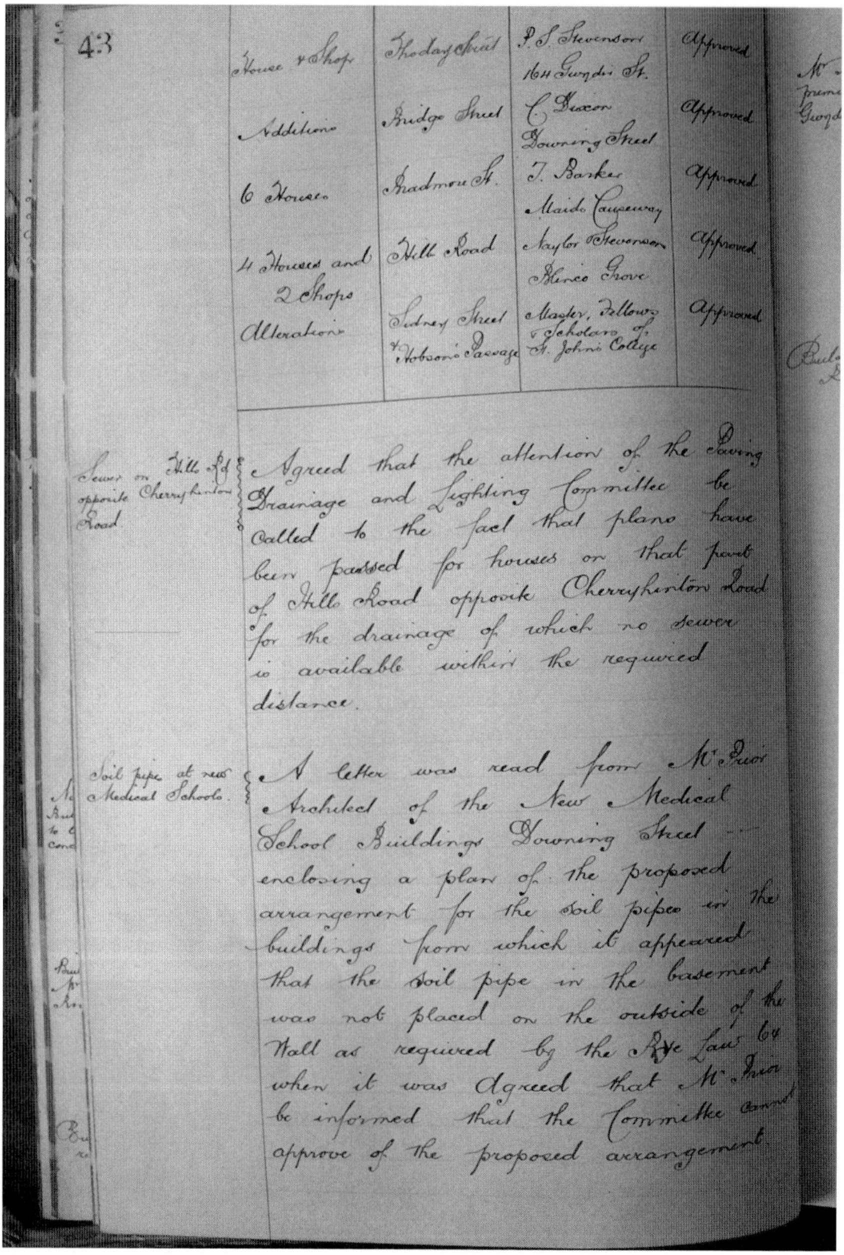

43

House & Shop	Thoday Street	P. J. Stevenson 164 Gwydir St.	Approved
Addition	Bridge Street	C. Dixon Downing Street	Approved
6 Houses	[illegible] St.	T. Barker Maids Causeway	Approved
4 Houses and 2 Shops	Hills Road	Naylor Stevenson Blinco Grove	Approved
Alteration	Sidney Street & Hobson's Passage	Master, Fellows & Scholars of St. John's College	Approved

Sewer on Hills Rd opposite Cherryhinton Road. — Agreed that the attention of the Paving Drainage and Lighting Committee be called to the fact that plans have been passed for houses on that part of Hills Road opposite Cherryhinton Road for the drainage of which no sewer is available within the required distance.

Soil pipe at new Medical Schools. — A letter was read from Mr Prior Architect of the New Medical School Buildings Downing Street enclosing a plan of the proposed arrangement for the soil pipes in the buildings from which it appeared that the soil pipe in the basement was not placed on the outside of the wall as required by the Bye Law 64 when it was agreed that Mr Prior be informed that the Committee cannot approve of the proposed arrangement.

(Pages 134 and 135) References in the Cambridge City Council Plans Minute Books in 1902 regarding new drainage needed for houses being built.
Application by Sidney French for a temporary building on Hills Road, 2 February 1920.
(Cambridge City Council Plans Minute Books, 1900–1919. Cambridgeshire Archives Service: A0013430)

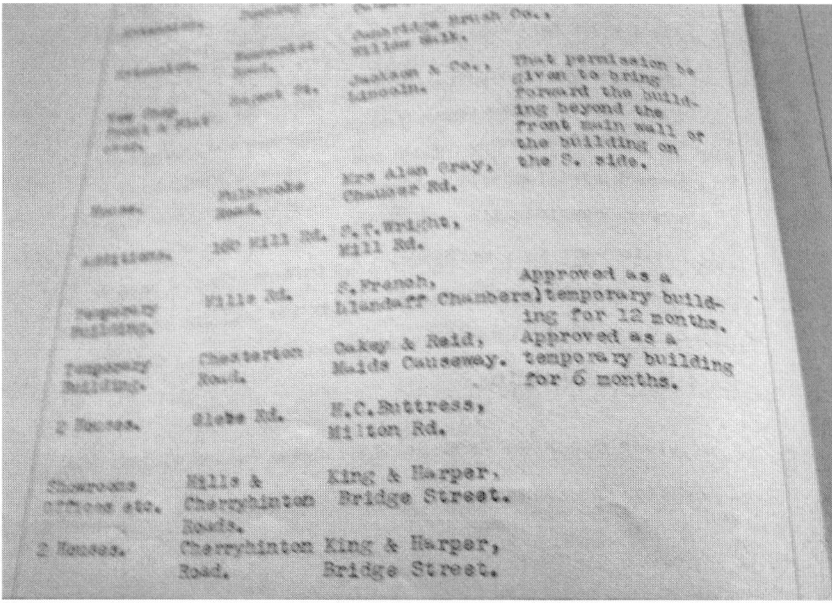

		Cambridge Brush Co., Willow Walk.	
		Jackson & Co., Lincoln.	That permission be given to bring forward the building beyond the front main wall of the building on the S. side.
		Mrs Alan Gray, Chaucer Rd.	
		C. T. Wright, Mill Rd.	
	Hills Rd.	S. French, Llandaff Chambers.	Approved as a temporary building for 12 months.
Temporary Building.	Chesterton Road.	Oakey & Reid, Maids Causeway.	Approved as a temporary building for 6 months.
2 Houses.	Glebe Rd.	H. C. Buttress, Milton Rd.	
Showrooms offices etc.	Hills & Cherryhinton Roads.	King & Harper, Bridge Street.	
2 Houses.	Cherryhinton Road.	King & Harper, Bridge Street.	

houses, museums and other public buildings. Other interesting collections relating to public works and institutions include churches, bridges, railway stations, asylums and air-raid shelters.

All new buildings and major alterations to existing buildings have been subject to local authority approval since the late nineteenth century. Building control plans, planning applications and supporting papers can therefore be found amongst local council records, although their survival before the mid-twentieth century can be variable. When new houses were being built in the Hills Road area of Cherry Hinton, the Cambridge City Council minute books for January 1902 reported on the need for new drainage. Other references detail local developer Sidney French applying to build two WCs at a house at 104 Hills Road in 1909 and a temporary building elsewhere on the same road in 1920.

Survey of London is part of the English Heritage Archive and carries out detailed architectural studies of London, which are published. These include contemporary and historical maps and plans, notes and drawings. **www.english-heritage.org.uk**. These are also available online via British History Online **www.british-history.ac.uk**.

County Maps, Town Plans and Parish Maps

Although county maps do not give as much detail as parish, town or city maps, they do provide a backdrop to your home in which it is possible to compare geographical features. The earliest English county maps date from the sixteenth century and may show the houses of the local gentry. Many show views of important buildings, illustrations of local industries such as rabbit warrens and ships and roads, rivers and other features.

The first county maps compiled by Christopher Saxton in the 1570s were based on simple surveys by people on foot. Their accuracy varies quite considerably and they only show locations in a very general way. The originals were usually in black and white with colouring added later. Over fifty county maps on a scale of one inch (and occasionally two inches) to the mile were published between 1700 and 1820.

A series of large-scale maps followed Gascoyne's 1669 map of Cornwall, including Budgen's 1724 survey of Sussex and Bowen's 1729 map of south Wales. Henry Beighton's 1728 map of Warwickshire is considered an exceptional piece of work by cartographers for its accuracy in comparison to the others. It was only after the 1750s that maps became of a consistently high standard using the latest mathematical and astronomical knowledge. By 1775 nearly half the country had been surveyed again. Between 1765 and 1780 twenty-five English county maps were published, covering over 65 per cent of the whole country. Many of these have since been republished and it is easy to obtain copies. Essex record office, for instance, sells copies of the 1645 Essex county map produced by Joannes Blaeu.

The surge of map-making in the second half of the eighteenth century was propelled by the emergence of an integrated national economy, improved transport systems, military threats from abroad and the growth of eighteenth-century enlightenment ideas promoting an understanding of the world via science and observation. Many were funded by subscriptions from the county's elite. Subscribers' names were given prominence, with Warburton displaying their coats of arms as a decorative border on his maps. Different editions may include additional names or coats of arms, or even have some removed, presumably in relation to extra orders or lack of payment. Yates's Staffordshire map did not originally include the names of estate owners, but when the copperplate passed to fellow map-maker William Faden, 158 names were added for a new edition. The Royal Society for the Encouragement of Arts, Manufactures and Commerce (known as the Royal Society of Arts from 1847) promoted map-making through prizes.

Comparing early county and town maps with more recent Ordnance Survey maps illustrates the changing landscape in each area. Obvious features are the enormous increase in built-up areas and the disappearance of common lands. Even rural counties have seen huge growth. Leicestershire's population, for example, was only around 115,000 when John Prior's map of the county was published in 1777. Some maps had little topographical detail, and you would hardly know any buildings existed at the time by looking at them. Others, such as John Rocque's maps of Berkshire, Middlesex and Surrey, were two inches to the mile in scale and show many parks and estates.

There were some early attempts to portray land use, parish and field boundaries, although these are few and far between. Even those which include parks and gardens may not be all that they seem. Some well-known examples show alterations to parks and estates which were obviously planned, but had not been undertaken when the maps were drawn up. By the end of the nineteenth century parish boundaries were routinely included on commercial maps. Roads do tend to be more accurately portrayed. Turnpike roads and gates (and therefore the site of turnpike houses) were usually shown, as were windmills.

The period between 1815 and 1840 saw many privately-financed new county maps, mainly led by Christopher and John Greenwood and Andrew Bryant. They were surveying at the same time as the new Board of Ordnance, from whom trigonometrical data was made freely available. As a result the county maps produced from this period onwards tend to be more accurate and representative of the visual landscape, and are generally considered to be of a higher quality than those produced by the Ordnance Survey.

Most town plans were produced as a separate series, although some county maps do also include town plans. Very few town plans exist before 1612, when John Speed's *Theatre of the Empire of Great Britaine* was published, containing a standardized collection of more than fifty. Earlier plans only tend to show outlines of villages, with perhaps the church and other prominent buildings detailed. There are numerous plans for London as the map trade was well established there by the 1680s. The number of London maps increased enormously during industrialization.

Other towns and cities saw maps being produced mainly from the eighteenth century onwards. Town maps from the nineteenth century help us understand why people lived in certain areas – jobs, access to water, and so on. Those produced by the Ordnance Survey in 1884–86 are extremely detailed. The Ordnance Survey five-foot plan of London, for instance, shows the names of detached houses, the layout of gardens with trees, ponds, paths and greenhouses, the width of street pavements, what factories manufactured, the number of seats in churches and the position of lamp-posts, pillar boxes and drinking troughs for horses. Town plans produced in the early 1800s for King's Lynn in Norfolk are another example. The King's Lynn map shows the different electoral wards created under the 1834 Electoral Reform Act and lists each street within those wards.

Town maps from the twentieth century show the scale of modern development; reconstruction after wartime bombing; and attempts at social engineering in the creation of garden cities, new towns and council house

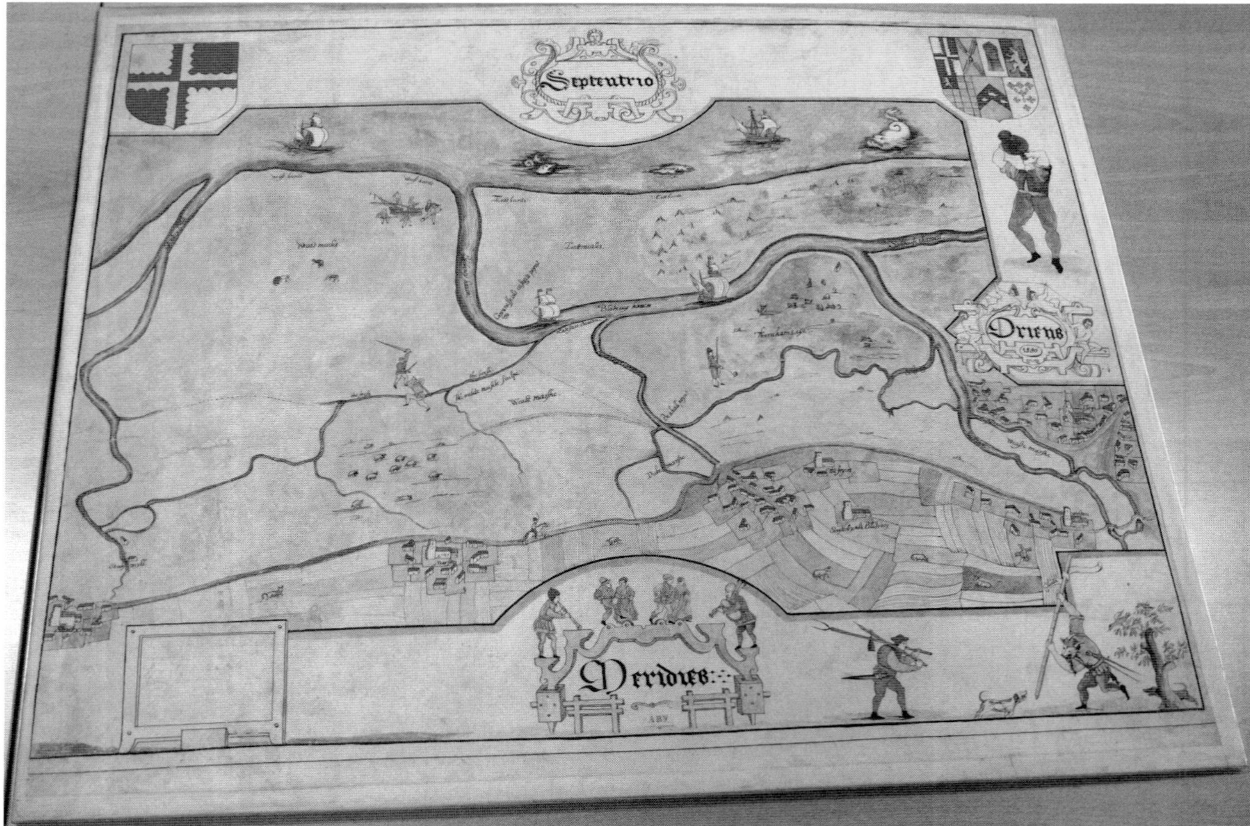

Nineteenth-century facsimile of map of Blakeney Haven and Port of Cley, 1586. (NRO: MC 2443/3)

estates. Crawley Museum in West Sussex has a series of maps showing the various stages of development planned for the new town, whilst Letchworth museum has copies of a plan for the first garden city in the UK.

Many parish maps exist, showing their boundaries and sometimes including details of who owned land. Many such maps belong with estate records, as they were drawn up for local landowners (see separate section on estate records). One rather lovely example is a copy made in the nineteenth century of a map first produced in 1586 of Blakeney Haven and Port of Cley. The maps form part of a collection deposited at the record office by a descendant of the Monement family.

One of the largest collections of parish maps was drawn up in around 1840 to assess Poor Law payments. Around 4,000 parishes had been valued by 1843, often with accompanying maps. These can be found with the Poor Law Commissioners' records at The National Archives, but copies do turn up locally.

Finding County, Town and Parish Maps

The British Library, The National Archives and local record offices and museums all have collections of county, town and parish maps.

Numerous reproductions exist. The London Topographical Society has, for example, published facsimiles of London maps. Copies of Faden's 1797 map of Norfolk were reproduced by the Norfolk Record Society in 1975 and Larks Press in 1989. A recent book on William Faden includes a copy of the original 1797 map for Norfolk and a digitized version on CD-ROM (see bibliography). A digital redrawing of this map can be explored at: **www.fadensmapofnorfolk.co.uk**. The same people have created digitized versions of Hodskinson's 1783 map of Suffolk **www.hodskinsonsmapofsuffolk.co.uk** and Faden's 1788 'The Country Twenty Five miles around London' map **www.fadensmapoflondon.co.uk**

Enclosure Maps and Awards

The process of enclosing open fields using the old strip farming method or common land by putting a hedge or fence around it has been going on for hundreds of years. Often referred to by the more traditional term 'inclosure', it was a means of increasing agricultural efficiency that began in the 1500s. Enclosure took place by agreement between landowners who took out private Acts of Parliament to do so.

A widespread enclosure movement during the eighteenth and early nineteenth centuries resulted in a massive redistribution of open fields, commons and 'waste' lands, especially once the process was made easier after the first General Enclosure Act of 1801. The majority of enclosures

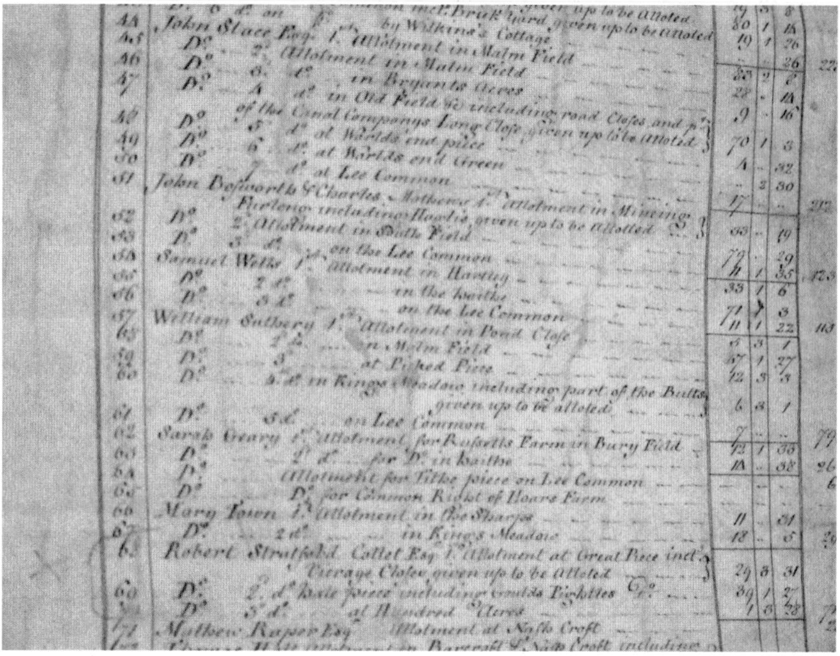
John Stace Esq. 1st Allotment ... by Wilkins's Cottage
Do 2d Allotment in Malm Field
John Bosworth & Charles Mathews 1st Allotment in Mimings Furlong
Samuel Wells 1st Allotment in Hawtry
William Suthery 1st Allotment in Pond Close
Sarah Geary 1st Allotment for Rufords Farm in Bury Field
Mary Town 1st Allotment in the Sharps
Robert Stratfield Collet Esq 1st Allotment at Great Piece
Mathew Raper Esq Allotment at Nash Croft

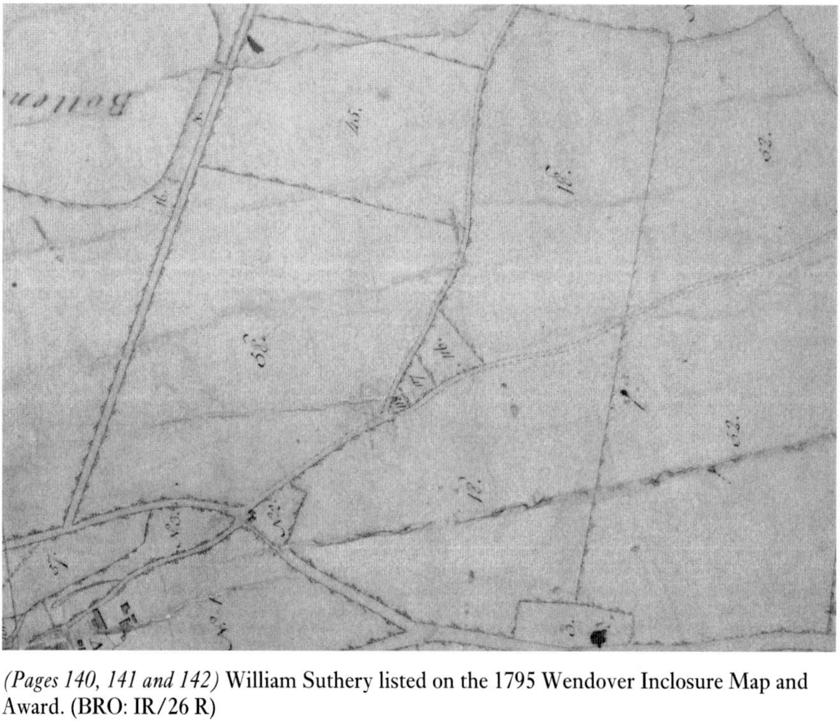

(Pages 140, 141 and 142) William Suthery listed on the 1795 Wendover Inclosure Map and Award. (BRO: IR/26 R)

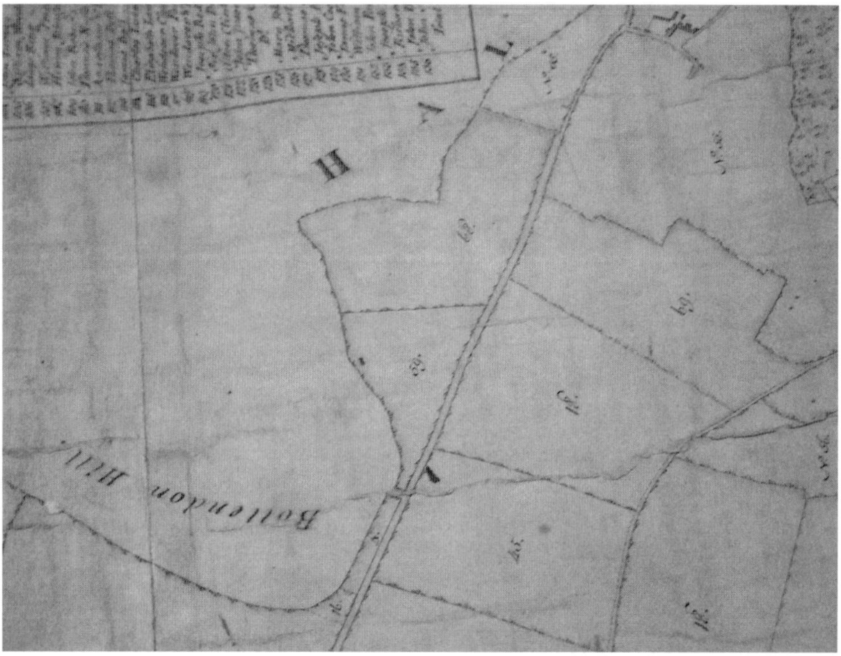

took place after this date, gradually petering out after the mid–1850s. One interesting aspect of this process is that the 'traditional' British landscape of fields surrounded by hedges often dates from this period, as hedgerows were planted to mark new boundaries around large fields.

Having a good understanding of the history of your area helps with interpreting what is and is not included on both the map and award. Enclosure maps are not as comprehensive as tithe maps and were not compiled for all parishes because fewer people were affected by the process of enclosure than had to pay tithes. This means there are often no maps and those that do exist may show only a very small part of the parish. For example, in Cambridgeshire land around the fens was allotted when they were drained.

The commissioners administering the process conducted a thorough survey, hearing the claims of those holding land in open fields or having rights of access to the common. This process could take several years before enclosure took place. Each landowner was then given one plot of land equal in size to the areas they formerly held as separate units. The common was divided and each landowner given an amount in relation to their total landholdings in the parish and access to the common. Any complaints about allotments were heard at the quarter sessions court. Exchanges of land were usually allowed if written consent was given, although the commissioners sometimes overturned these arrangements.

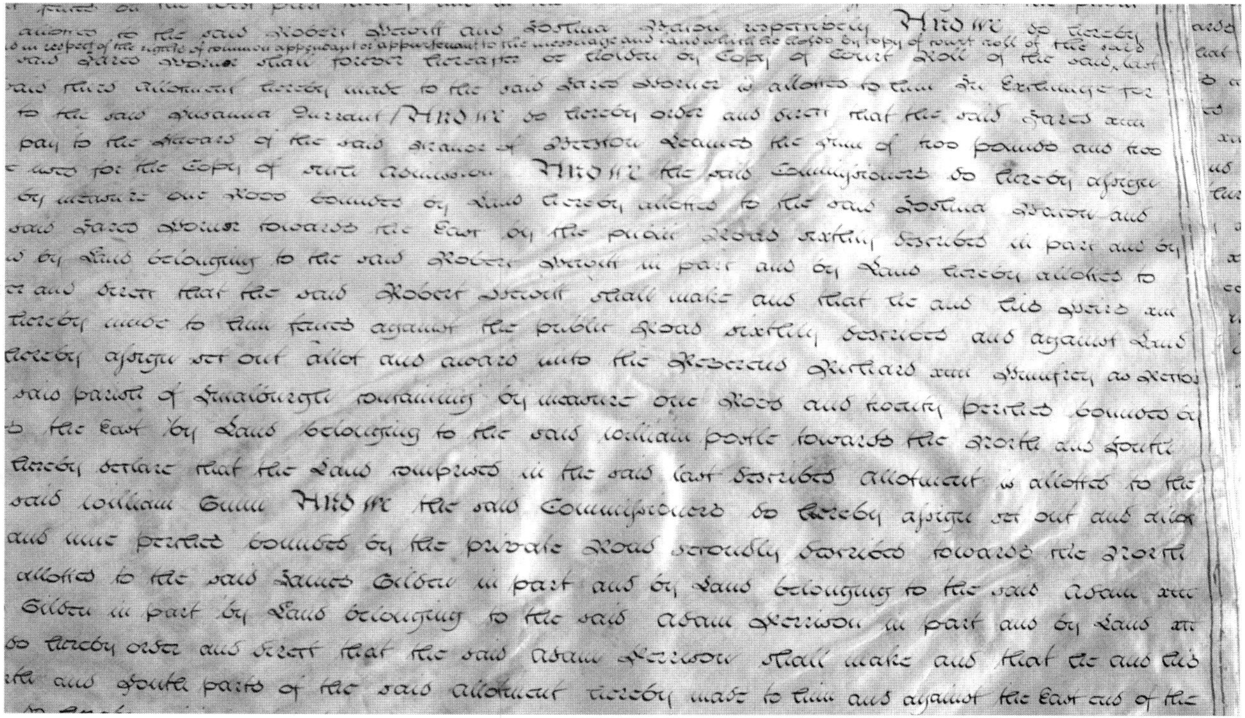

(Pages 143 and 144) Plot allocated to 'Rt. Hewett' adjacent to the sixth public road leading to the staithe on the Barton Turf Enclosure Map, 1810 and Award, 1809. (NRO: C/Sca 2/18)

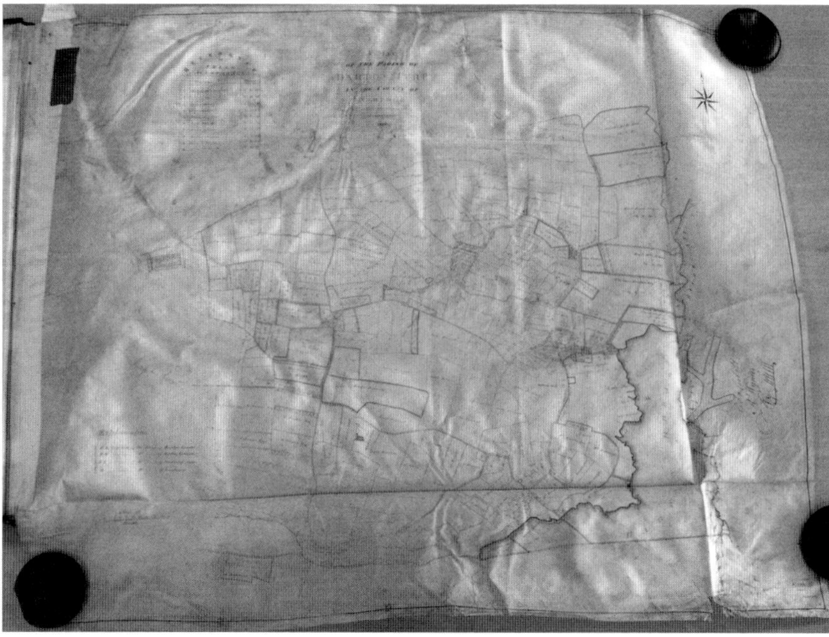

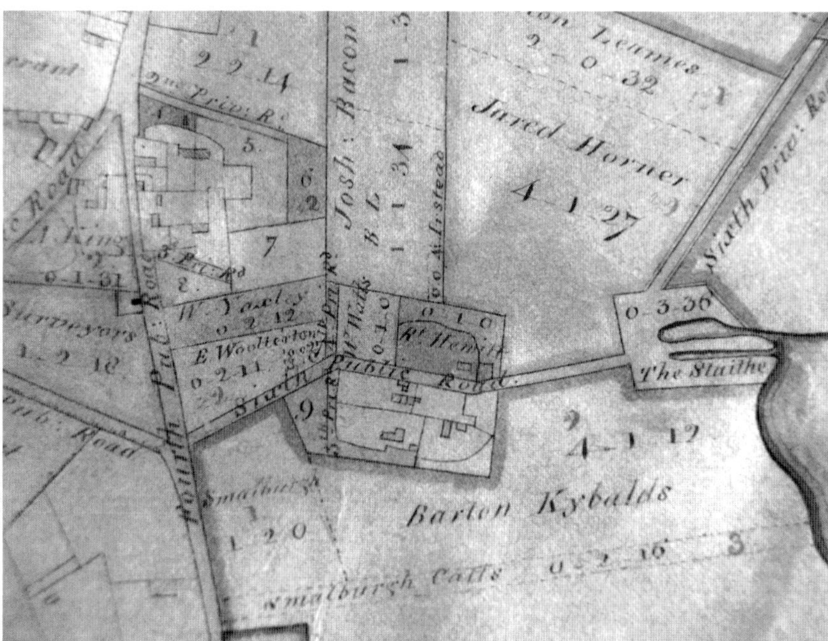
Jared Horner
4-1-27
Josh: Bacon
W. Yaxley
0-2-12
E. Woolterton
0-2-11
Public Road
0-3-36
The Staithe
Barton Kybalds
Staith Priv: Road

The expenses of enclosure were decided by the commissioners, and if necessary enforced by law.

Each enclosure map was accompanied by an award, the written list of everyone granted land under the scheme. This gives the landowner's name, the extent of the plot, and whether it was copyhold or freehold or another type of tenure. These list public bridleways and footpaths; watercourses; drains; public wells; field boundaries and adjoining roads plus whether these were public or private. The letter 'T' marked on the inside boundary of a plot indicates which owners were responsible for maintaining walls. The award also notes any common lands, open fields and charity land, the income from which was distributed amongst the poor. Some list quarries, gravel or sandpits granted to parish bodies. Although not every property was subject to enclosure, you may still find details of these as the awards describe adjoining properties as a means of identifying particular plots.

A 1795 enclosure map compiled for Wendover in Buckinghamshire after the passing of a private Act of Parliament proved very useful when researching properties in that area. An enclosure such as this could be agreed by the owners of two-thirds of land. In Wendover this meant just eight people, whilst the majority of tenant farmers had little say. Within a year of the Wendover Act being passed the large open fields were subdivided into rectangular fields and most of the commons enclosed, leaving only fifty acres on Bottendon (Boddington) Hill, which were finally enclosed in 1856.

The 1795 map includes specific details of both enclosed and non-enclosed lands. In the case of William Suthery, the accompanying enclosure award describes how he was granted five plots of common land, which comprised twelve acres, three rods and three perches valued at four pounds, two shillings and four pence. It also mentions that he was given one of these plots in exchange for Hill Piece, which had been enclosed at an earlier period. Suthery was to be responsible for making and maintaining the boundary fences on lands next to Boddington Hill.

Another example is the 1810 enclosure map for Barton Turf in Norfolk. This shows the names of people allotted land. The accompanying award, compiled in 1809, notes the names of the people allotted land in the margins. Other maps and awards are not so detailed, so be prepared to read through several pages of densely written detail.

Finding Enclosure Maps and Awards

Around seventy per cent of the original maps and awards survive. Most enclosure maps date from after 1801. Nevertheless, large numbers of earlier enclosure maps and associated other records detailing the ownership, tenancies, use and value of the land referred to do exist. These are mostly found amongst estate records or private collections. For more on the history of enclosure maps see *Maps and Plans in the Public Record Offices, c.1410–1860* (1967). For details of where to find enclosure maps see *The Enclosure Maps of England and Wales, 1595–1918* (2004) by R.J.P. Kain, J. Chapman and R.R. Oliver. An electronic catalogue listing enclosure maps across the country is maintained by UK Data Archive **http://hds.essex.ac.uk/em**

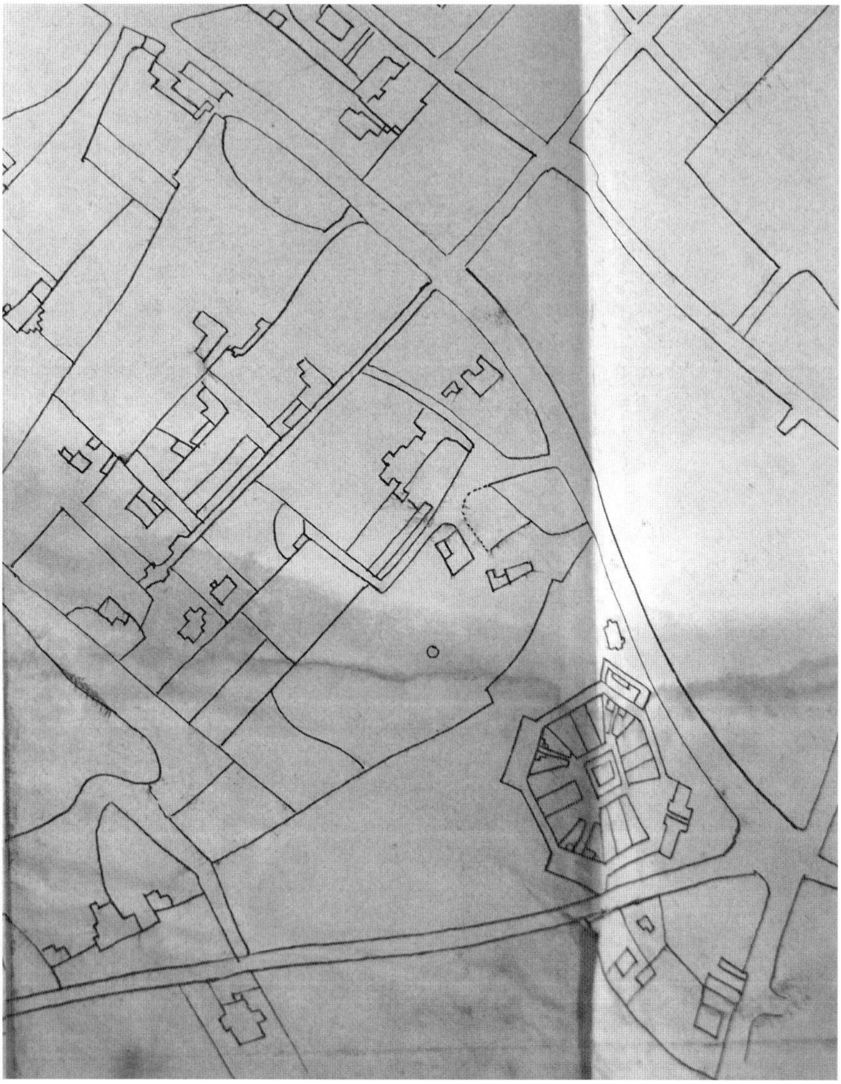

The area surrounding the former prison on the corner of Earlham Road in Norwich on undated sketches by the enclosure surveyor. (NRO: BR 90/57/39)

The most complete collection is at The National Archives, but they can be scattered amongst several different groups of records. The most common collections to find them in are the Court of the Common Pleas, the Court of Chancery; the Palatinates of Chester and Durham; the Duchy of Lancaster; the Land Revenue Record Office and the Ministry of Agriculture.

A large number of copies of enclosure maps are held in local record offices, and these are the easiest to locate.

Some background records relating to the survey process also survive in The National Archives and county record offices. One example is the sketches dating from 1809 to 1844 held at Norfolk Record Office in the collection of local surveyor F.W. Hornor. Those for places such as Heigham, which have no surviving enclosure map, are particularly useful. Whilst the sketches do not include plot numbers or names, many roads and well-known buildings such as the hospital, windmills and the prison on the corner of Earlham Road are identifiable, allowing comparisons to be made with later maps.

There are a growing number of enclosure maps online, usually associated with county record offices. The 'New Landscapes' website, for instance, contains all enclosure awards and maps for Berkshire from 1738 to 1883. **www.berkshireenclosure.org.uk**

Estate Maps and Plans

Estate maps have been drawn up for centuries to show the lands and other holdings of landowners, with the earliest dating from the Elizabethan period. Many estate plans have accompanying records which describe the lands in detail and list occupiers and tenants. Many include their immediate neighbours as it was important to show their boundaries.

The accuracy and amount of detail does vary enormously, especially before the eighteenth century. The best include some buildings, often the manor houses and churches. Some, such as the 1795 estate map for Caistor St Edmund in Norfolk, give the date when an owner's house was built. An early seventeenth-century map of Langley Green in Norfolk includes field names and who leased them as well as drawings of numerous houses at Langley Green, Church Green and Langmarsh Common.

Finding Estate Maps

Many estate plans and other estate records are held in local record offices, but The National Archives also has a large collection. These include those owned by the Crown; the Crown Estate Commissioners; the Forestry Commissioners; the Land Revenue Office and the Office of Works. There are a range of other collections nationally and locally which include maps from estates such as Greenwich Hospital, pre-nationalization railway and canal companies and the War Office.

Local record societies and the British Record Society have published copies of many historic maps.

The university colleges of Cambridge and Oxford have historically owned large amounts of land, and their archives include numerous estate maps.

Insurance Maps

Insurance companies needed detailed maps as part of their assessment process. Fire insurance plans are one of the main series of these types of map (see the section on fire insurance records). It is, however, possible to find other insurance-related maps in national and local archives.

Military Maps

Maps have been a crucial part of battles, campaigns and defensive measures for hundreds of years. The most relevant for researching property are those for battlefield training areas, assessing bomb damage and the rebuilding and redevelopment of bomb-damaged areas.

The period after the Second World War saw one of the biggest ever housing programmes. Bomb damage surveys were undertaken to chronicle the damage caused by air-raid bombing and the redevelopment of bomb-damaged areas. These often include maps as well as descriptions of the people and places affected.

Other related records are: air-raid precaution files, which include reports into unexploded bombs, shells and mines; bomb censuses and civil defence wardens' and police reports. The lists of exploded bombs, for instance, record the location, type of bomb, size of crater, numbers of injured and numbers and names of those killed. One police report on air raids for the Creeting St Peter area in Suffolk describes how nine bombs were dropped at Clamp Farm, Creeting St Peter, in the occupation of John Forrest, in April 1941 (SRO: Ipswich A1609/1-6).

A seven square foot bomb map held at Norfolk Record Office still has a large number of the original markers pinned to it, which denote where and when bombs fell as well as their size. This, combined with an annotated Ordnance Survey map from 1950 reveals the extensive damage some areas suffered. The accompanying Norwich City Engineer's records include reports of the streets in which property was damaged during the Blitz in 1942. Certain areas suffered more than most, including part of Rupert Street in Area E and F, where many of the Victorian terraces were subsequently demolished, being replaced by modern houses, flats and a park.

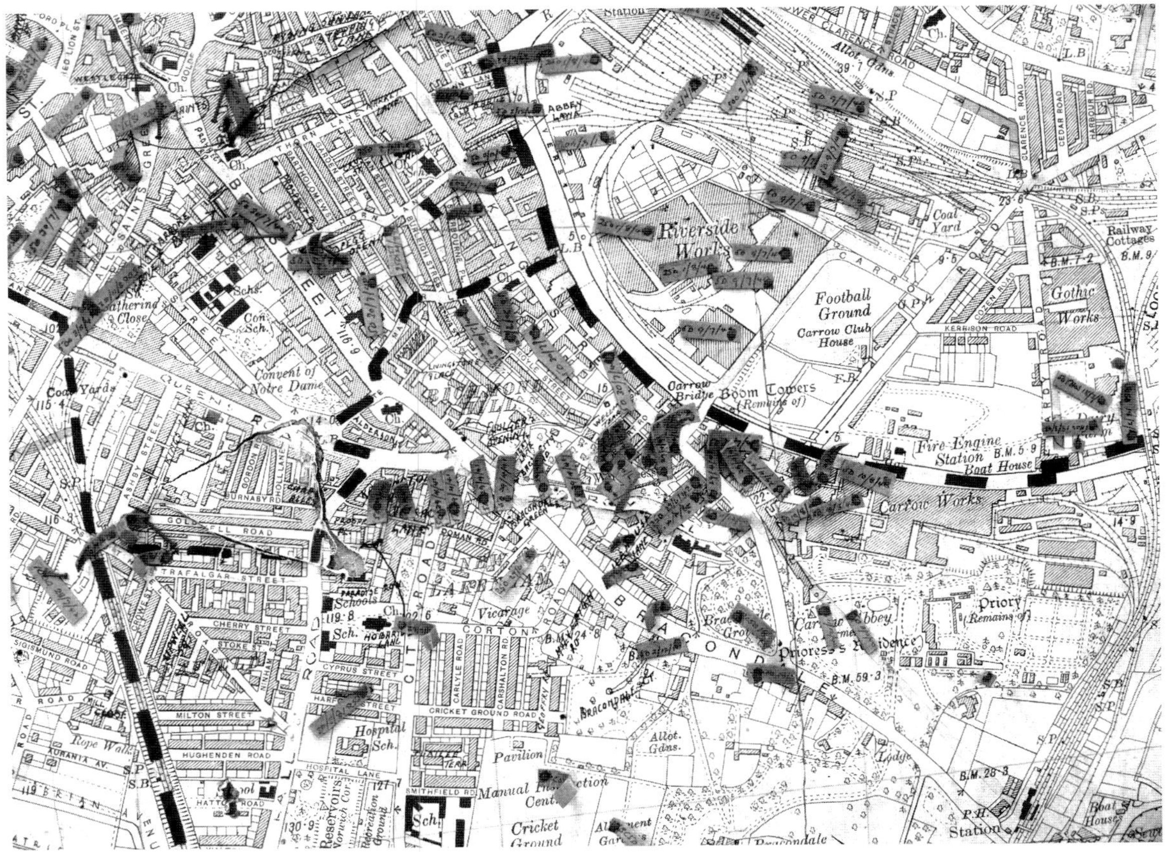

(Pages 149, 150 and 151) Norwich Bomb Map. (NRO: ACC 2007/195) Ordnance Survey Map of Norwich showing blitzed sites needing attention, c.1950. (NRO: N/EN 20/125)

Many former airforce and army bases are now used for residential housing. Their presence had a huge impact on local communities. Flight plans from those bases may not add much to your direct knowledge of your home, but will give you a better understanding of their history and the influence of the people based there. Such collections often include additional details and photographs of buildings or temporary quarters on the sites. One such for the Second World War USAAF Airbase at Hethel in Norfolk has photographs of some of the crew outside Nissen huts used as officers' quarters.

Finding Military Maps

The National Archives has maps relating to military and naval operations from the sixteenth to twentieth centuries.

Some military maps turn up locally, as in the case of the USAAF flight plans mentioned.

Survival of official surveys into bomb damage varies for each county.

The majority date from the Second World War and can generally be found amongst council records. Maps of unexploded ordnance across the region based on research in national and local archives can be found on the Zetica website **www.zetica.com**.

Ordnance Survey (OS) Maps

Ordnance Survey maps can show your home and its location at different points in time throughout the nineteenth, twentieth and twenty-first centuries. They also place your house in its wider geographical context by showing how it relates to other properties, roads, railways and public buildings.

The Ordnance Survey (OS) maps are probably the best known of all printed maps in the UK as they were the first standardized, detailed maps drawn to scale for the whole country. The Ordnance Survey emerged from concerns over potential threats of rebellion and invasion during the eighteenth century, which highlighted how important it was for the army to have accurate maps showing roads and rivers and other geographical features. As a result the Board of Ordnance was commissioned to start surveys in the mid–1740s.

Although Scotland was surveyed between 1745 and 1755, detailed map-making of England and Wales did not begin in the south of England and Wales until 1791, in response to concerns over invasion from France when the Board of Ordnance was set up. The Board was a supplier of munitions connected to the Royal Arsenal at the Tower of London and map production was just one part of its role. It began a survey of the southern counties in 1792. The first English map drawn up was for Kent and produced in 1801, followed by Essex in 1805. Originally called the Trigonometrical Survey, it very quickly became known as the Ordnance Survey and in 1841 the Ordnance Survey became an institution in its own right.

The first maps were on a scale of one inch to the mile and the original maps were updated at various points in time. Around a third of England and Wales was surveyed by the 1820s. From the 1830s surveys of England and Wales at the scale of six inches to the mile were produced. The first major change was the introduction of adjacent sheet numbering from 1837, so that maps for neighbouring areas were easily identifiable. The Ordnance Survey Act of 1841 meant all public boundaries had to be surveyed, although this was not completed until much later. This meant documenting any changes in parliamentary, local government, county or parish boundaries and it was soon realized that the six-inch scale was not detailed enough. Maps from 1847 onwards have the term 'printed from an electrotype' printed on them. From 1854, maps on a scale of 25 inches to the mile were produced, with Durham being the first in this series. Latitude and longitude were included from 1856. An 'electrotype' date was included from 1862.

Urbanization and the spread of the railways meant the early maps quickly became dated for some areas. In many cases changes such as railway lines were simply engraved onto the printing plates of existing maps rather than a new map being produced. In addition to this the whole country was not fully surveyed until the early 1870s. By this time the early maps were out of date, so a new survey was undertaken going from south to north. Maps showing railway insertions date from 1882. Dates of publication mainly appear from the late nineteenth century.

The one and six-inch maps are best for rural areas as they are not large enough to show much detail in urban areas. The lack of detail means they are most useful for getting a feel of the surroundings and landscape around the property you are researching. They can also be used for comparative purposes in conjunction with enclosure and tithe maps.

Ordnance Survey maps really become most useful to house historians from the mid–1870s, when the first large-scale survey of the country at a scale of 25 inches to the mile began. These were compiled between 1876 and 1887 and completed in 1888. A second series showing revisions was produced between 1891 and 1914, followed by a third between 1904 and 1939 and a rolling programme of revisions began in 1928. The second edition 25-inch scale was used as the basis for the 1910–11 tax on land values (see also the section on the Inland Revenue Valuation Survey). The OS maps are linked to the volumes containing details of owners, occupiers and rateable values by a series of keys which can be matched to the maps.

The 25-inch maps show the rough shape of buildings with roads to scale as well as trees and other details. Many of the original black and white maps were subsequently hand coloured. Some 25-inch maps had accompanying reference books up to 1886, published for HMSO and the Ordnance Survey Office. Known as *Parish Area Books* between 1855 and 1872, then as *Books of Reference,* these listed the size and use of each unit of land. Unfortunately, they do not exist for every county. The main areas covered are: Cheshire, Cumberland, Essex, Gloucestershire, the Isle of Man, Kent, Middlesex, Northumberland, Surrey, Westmoreland, Flint, Glamorgan, Monmouth and Pembroke.

The Ordnance Survey maps can be used to track changes in individual properties and the surrounding area. For instance, in Burnham Thorpe in Norfolk the 1889 Ordnance Survey map shows some small buildings to the west of the manor house which do not appear on the earlier tithe map. These can still be seen on the 1907 Ordnance Survey map, but not on later photographs, although the remains of the track that led to the cottages can still be seen.

One interesting aspect is the way in which Ordnance Survey maps can be used to identify some work-based properties. For instance, tollgate and turnpike houses are usually marked as 'TG' and 'TP'.

Although Ordnance Survey maps are generally highly accurate, there are still some omissions and errors. The first one inch to the mile map shows roads as wider than they really were, whilst the need to fit so much detail onto a small space resulted in some standardization of building shapes. Some maps may simply reproduce earlier works, without subsequent changes being shown. Some mapmakers put in proposed developments and changes so their maps would be up to date when published. If those plans never went ahead, or were changed radically, these maps will show buildings and alterations that never happened.

Such a discrepancy can be seen with a house in Burnham Market in Norfolk. Deeds, manorial records, sales particulars and other records confirm that this particular property was known as Westgate House by 1891. No name is shown for the property on the 1883 OS map, but there is another house called Westgate House to the left of the present one, on what is now called Church Close. This other Westgate House is still shown on the 1905 OS map, whilst the present house with that name is still unnamed. Whilst it is possible that two houses in Burnham Westgate had the same name at the same time, it is likely that the 1905 details were simply copied from the earlier version.

Finding Ordnance Survey Maps

The Ordnance Survey, Romsey Road, Southampton, Hampshire, SO16 4OU. Free online access to many of the Ordnance Survey maps is available at: **www.ordnancesurvey.co.uk**

The Ordnance Survey website contains a great deal of background history and information about the Ordnance Survey **www.ordnancesurvey.co.uk/oswebsite/aboutus/history**

Modern Ordnance Survey maps are covered by copyright laws. Although many records were destroyed during the Second World War, there is still an extensive collection at The National Archives and local archives, with some available online. Many record offices and local history libraries have copies of earlier ones which are no longer subject to copyright.

The Royal Geographic Society, 1 Kensington Gore, London, SW7 2AR, has a comprehensive collection **www.rgs.org**

The British Museum's map library has maps for the whole country and a growing number are being placed online. **www.britishmuseum.co.uk**

Some university libraries have collections of Ordnance Survey maps (and other maps), particularly if they have landscape history, geography and local history departments. Oxford and Cambridge universities both have extensive collections. **www.ox.ac.uk** and **www.cam.ac.uk**

Others with excellent collections include the University of East Anglia and Durham University. Durham has placed several of its Ordnance Survey maps online, including those for Newcastle and Gateshead from between 1833 and 1849. These can be accessed from the university website and via a link on the GENUKI page for Durham. The County Durham page on GENUKI also has links to several other maps, including an 1806 map of the county; a link to a website produced by Peter Dockerty showing maps of waggon ways and mines in County Durham and Ordnance Surveys from 1847–95 **www.nls.uk/digitallibrary/map**.

If the building you are investigating is or was on a parish or county boundary then the record books, boundary disputes, sketch plans and journals of inspection are all held at The National Archives. The HMSO and Ordnance Survey Office publications are described in Harley's *The Ordnance Survey and Land-Use Mapping*. Some local archives and studies centres have copies and they turn up in auctions and secondhand bookshops. Copies can also be found on the Old Maps website **www.old-maps.co.uk**. The 1885 maps showing boundary changes, produced by the Boundary Commission and covering the whole of England and Ireland and parts of Wales and Scotland, can also be found online at **www.londonancestor.com**

Old Maps sells an almost complete set of First Edition six-inch to the mile maps of England, Scotland and Wales. Other commercial companies selling copies of old Ordnance Survey maps include: Cassini Maps, Hillsprings, East Garston, Berkshire, RG17 7HW **www.cassinimaps.co.uk** Alan Godfrey Maps, Prospect Business Park, Consett, DH8 7PW **www.alangodfreymaps.co.uk** and MAPCO (Map and Plan Collections Online) **www.archivemaps.com**

Rail, Road and Canal Plans

Plans for new roads, alterations and diversions are nothing new. Many maps were produced to show proposed developments such as railway lines, new roads, canals and housing developments. Although these plans may never have gone ahead, or been radically altered, the maps still survive and show other features such as adjacent lands.

Turnpike roads were toll roads which people paid to use at various gates along their length. They took their name from an ancient practice whereby a pike acted as a barrier and was turned to allow access. Turnpike roads were administered by trusts set up in the eighteenth century to cope with a rapid increase in traffic that individual parishes or towns could no longer cope with. These trusts were authorized by private Acts of Parliament which allowed them to charge a toll (fee) towards upkeep of specific stretches of road. The first turnpike trust was established in 1663 on the Great North Road in Hertfordshire, but it was thirty years before others followed.

By 1750, most major routes in England had been turnpiked. By 1820, over 1,000 turnpike trusts controlled about 22,000 miles of British roads with over 7,000 gates. The final turnpike was created in Sussex in 1836. The private Acts which authorized turnpiking note where the toll bars and gates were to be erected, toll charges and any exemptions. Whilst maps of turnpike roads, only show a general stretch of road, they do list landowners and show some key landmarks. Combining these with surveyors' reports and the public notices issued in local newspapers can provide interesting background context for the history of your house. For

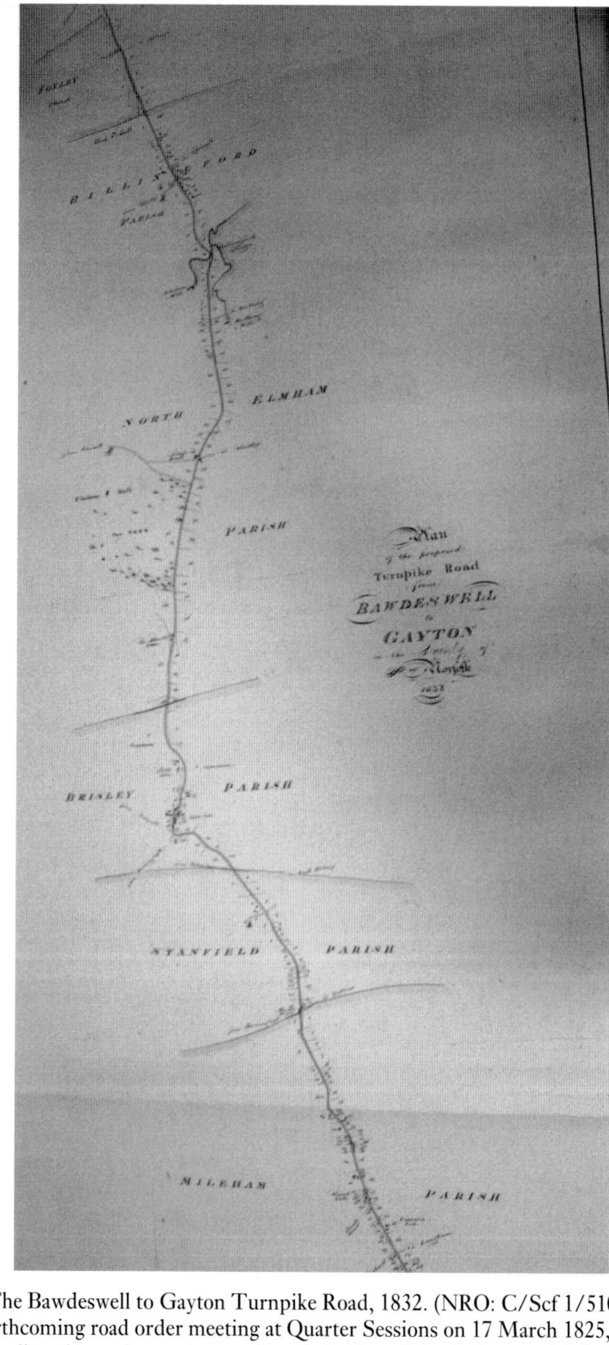

The Bawdeswell to Gayton Turnpike Road, 1832. (NRO: C/Scf 1/510)
Notice of forthcoming road order meeting at Quarter Sessions on 17 March 1825, Road Order Plans for the diversion and stopping up of roads in Great Massingham and Advertisement in the Norfolk Chronicle Newspaper regarding the same, 1825. (NRO: C/Sce 2/11/8)
Road Order Plan for Great Massingham in Norfolk, 1825. (NRO: Road Order Box 11, No.8)

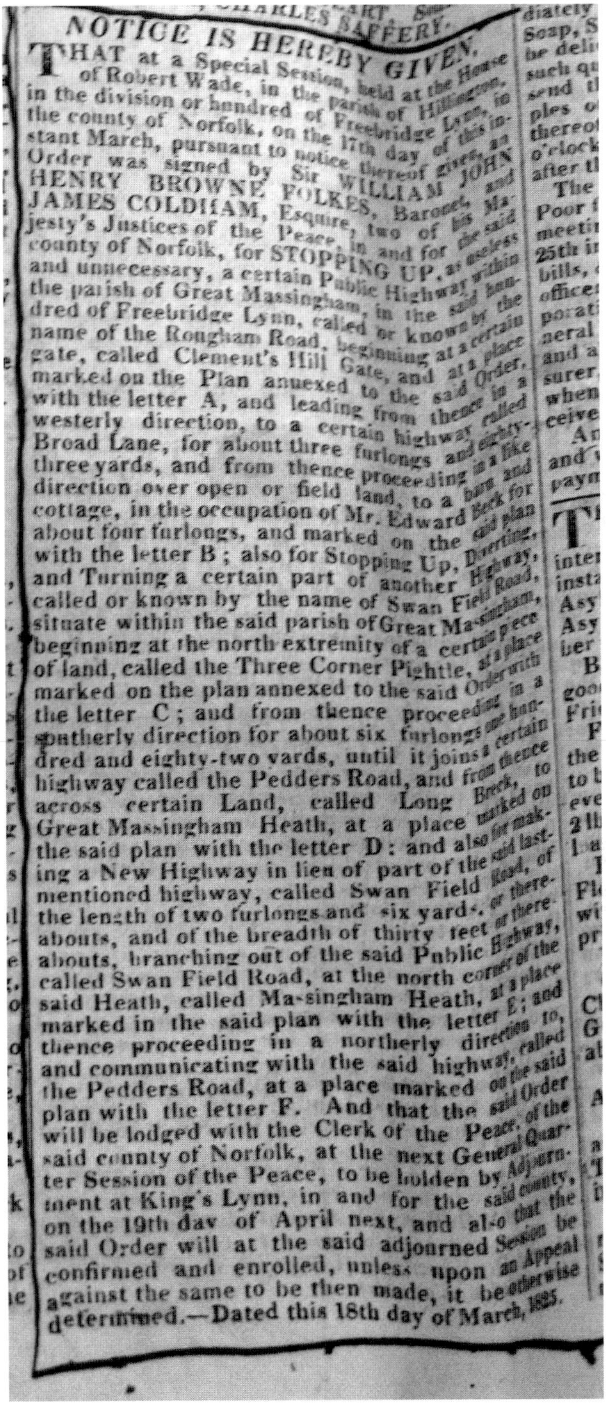

NOTICE IS HEREBY GIVEN,

THAT at a Special Session, held at the House of Robert Wade, in the parish of Hillington, in the division or hundred of Freebridge Lynn, in the county of Norfolk, on the 17th day of this instant March, pursuant to notice thereof given, an Order was signed by Sir WILLIAM JOHN HENRY BROWNE FOLKES, Baronet, and JAMES COLDHAM, Esquire, two of his Majesty's Justices of the Peace, in and for the said county of Norfolk, for STOPPING UP, as useless and unnecessary, a certain Public Highway within the parish of Great Massingham, in the said hundred of Freebridge Lynn, called or known by the name of the Rougham Road, beginning at a certain gate, called Clement's Hill Gate, and at a place marked on the Plan annexed to the said Order, with the letter A, and leading from thence in a westerly direction, to a certain highway called Broad Lane, for about three furlongs and eighty-three yards, and from thence proceeding in a like direction over open or field land, to a barn and cottage, in the occupation of Mr. Edward Beck for about four furlongs, and marked on the said plan with the letter B; also for Stopping Up, Diverting, and Turning a certain part of another Highway, called or known by the name of Swan Field Road, situate within the said parish of Great Massingham, beginning at the north extremity of a certain piece of land, called the Three Corner Pightle, at a place marked on the plan annexed to the said Order with the letter C; and from thence proceeding in a southerly direction for about six furlongs one hundred and eighty-two yards, until it joins a certain highway called the Pedders Road, and from thence across certain Land, called Long Breck, to Great Massingham Heath, at a place marked on the said plan with the letter D: and also for making a New Highway in lieu of part of the said last-mentioned highway, called Swan Field Road, of the length of two furlongs and six yards, or thereabouts, and of the breadth of thirty feet or thereabouts, branching out of the said Public Highway, called Swan Field Road, at the north corner of the said Heath, called Massingham Heath, at a place marked in the said plan with the letter E; and thence proceeding in a northerly direction to, and communicating with the said highway, called the Pedders Road, at a place marked on the said plan with the letter F. And that the said Order will be lodged with the Clerk of the Peace, of the said county of Norfolk, at the next General Quarter Session of the Peace, to be holden by Adjournment at King's Lynn, in and for the said county, on the 19th day of April next, and also that the said Order will at the said adjourned Session be confirmed and enrolled, unless upon an Appeal against the same to be then made, it be otherwise determined.—Dated this 18th day of March, 1825.

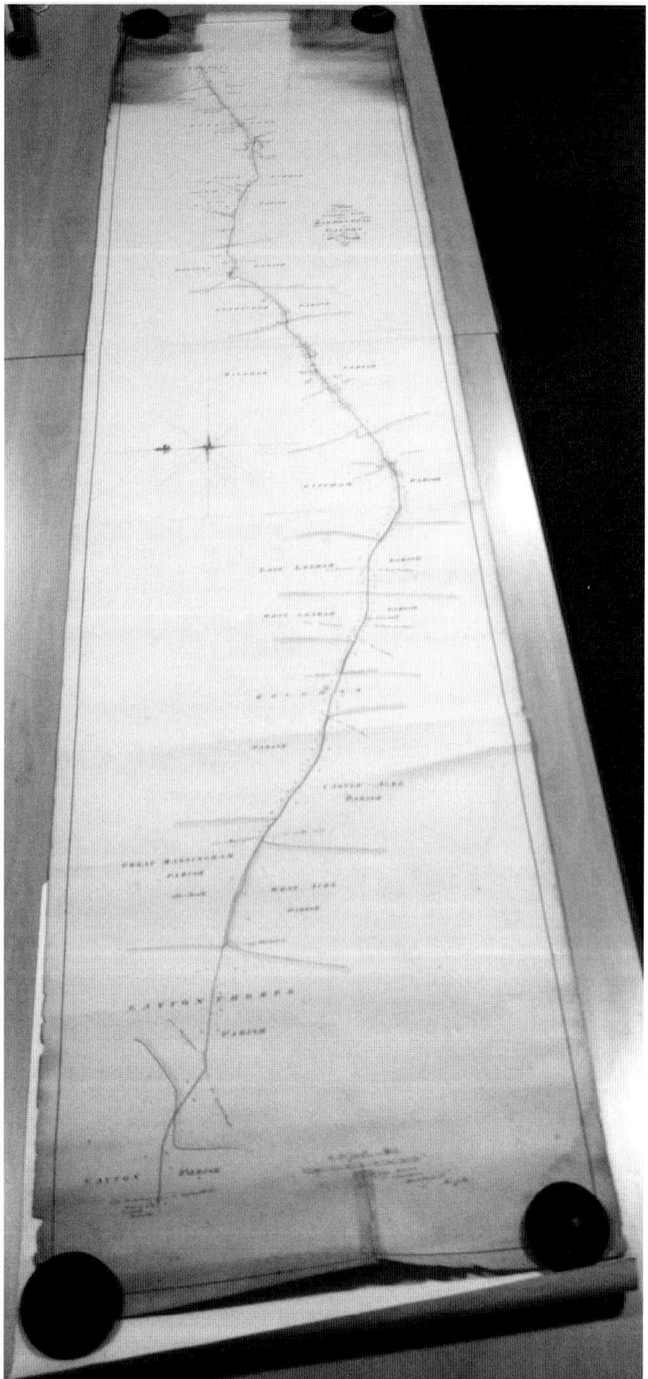

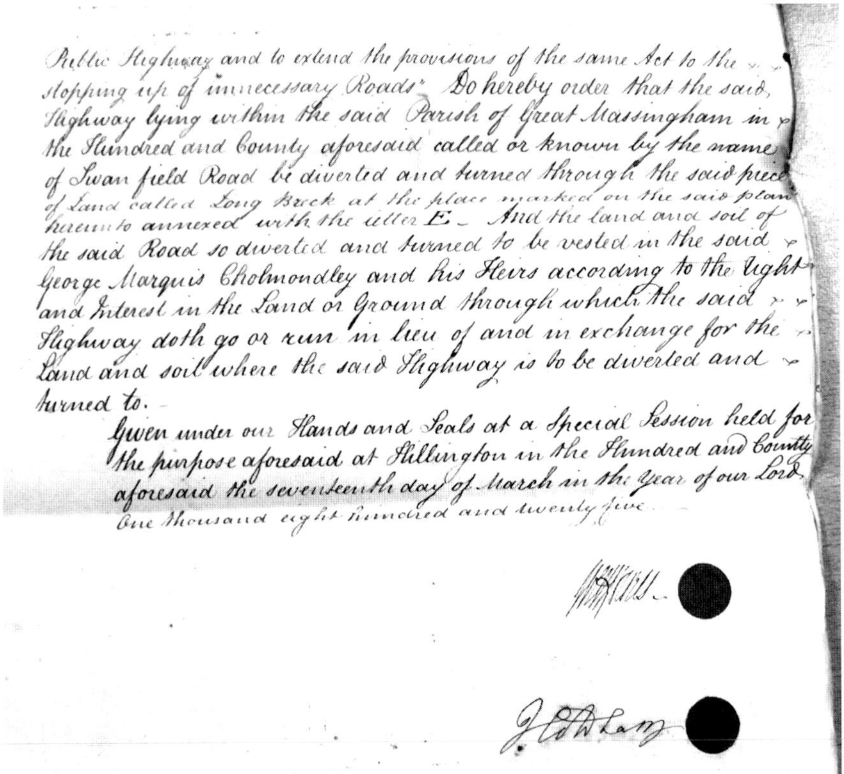

Public Highway and to extend the provisions of the same Act to the stopping up of unnecessary Roads" Do hereby order that the said Highway lying within the said Parish of Great Massingham in the Hundred and County aforesaid called or known by the name of Swan field Road be diverted and turned through the said piece of Land called Long Breck at the place marked on the said plan hereunto annexed with the letter E. And the land and soil of the said Road so diverted and turned to be vested in the said George Marquis Cholmondley and his Heirs according to the right and Interest in the Land or Ground through which the said Highway doth go or run in lieu of and in exchange for the Land and soil where the said Highway is to be diverted and turned to.

Given under our Hands and Seals at a Special Session held for the purpose aforesaid at Hillington in the Hundred and County aforesaid the seventeenth day of March in the Year of our Lord One thousand eight hundred and twenty five

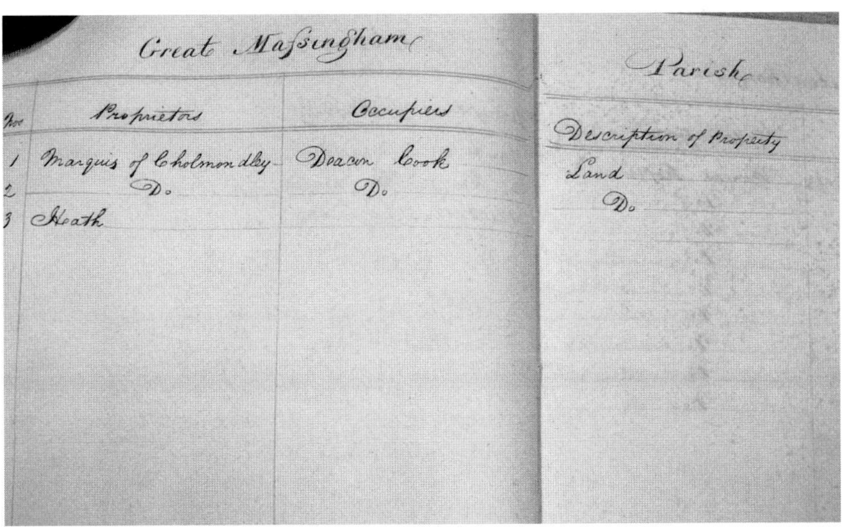

Great Massingham Parish

No	Proprietors	Occupiers	Description of Property
1	Marquis of Cholmondley	Deacon Cook	Land
2	Do	Do	Do
3	Heath		

example, the site of a property on Castle Acre Road in Great Massingham is shown on a new road plan drawn up in 1832 for the Bawdeswell to Gayton turnpike road. The Marquis of Cholmondeley was named as the main landowner. Other records in the same collection include notices of meetings and newspaper cuttings about proposed diversions and closing of roads in 1825.

During the late seventeenth and early eighteenth century many schemes to improve navigation along major rivers were authorized by private Acts of Parliament. Some of these involved digging 'cuts'. This expanded into the construction of artificial canals which linked different areas, with the first major canal completed in 1761, taking coals from mines in Worsley in Lancashire to Manchester. By the early 1800s all Britain's industrial districts were connected by a system of canals. Each route had maps and plans drawn up showing owners of land affected. Other records include the Acts themselves, public notices and letters of objection.

If your house was near a railway or tram line then it may appear on a public utility plan, which would have been deposited with the Clerk of the Peace when the project was proposed. Plans were accompanied by reference books, which give the owners' and occupiers' names. Parliament first required maps of proposed railway developments to be submitted in 1837. Copies of these maps (known as 'deposited plans') were filed with the local quarter sessions.

Much general development was triggered in the nineteenth century by the arrival of the railway and railway stations. This can be seen in the Hills Road area of Cambridge. R.G. Baker's 1830 map of the area shows Hills Road marked out, but, apart from the odd farmhouse, there were no buildings between the city centre and the village of Cherry Hinton. The Great Eastern line from London to Cambridge was constructed in 1845 and most of this area was developed in the late 1800s.

Finding Rail, Road and Canal Maps and Associated Records

Road and canal building Private Acts of Parliament, with supporting records, are held at the House of Lords Record Office, Palace of Westminster, London, SW1A 0PW. **www.parliament.uk**

County records offices have numerous records of proposals, plans, surveyors' reports and objections filed with quarter sessions court records.

Further records relating to railway building can be found in the British Transport section at The National Archives. These include maps and plans, private acts for railways and railway buildings and associated photographs.

Special Purpose Maps

A large number of maps come under the category 'special purpose' because they were drawn up for medical or sociological purposes, such as areas of poverty, social status, housing conditions and crime. For example, *Fowler's Cholera Plan of Leeds* of 1833 shows the districts affected. One of the best known is *Inquiry into Life and Labour in London (1886–1903)* by Charles Booth. Booth recorded the conditions of workers in a series of maps. People in black-shaded streets were 'Class A', the lowest, possibly criminal element. Class H was upper class, servant keepers, and shaded yellow.

The twelve volumes of maps include a street-by-street record of social class and income in London in the late nineteenth century. The City of London was not included as it didn't have enough residents. Accompanying the maps are notes made by the social investigators and policemen who escorted them. When Shoreditch in London was surveyed, for example, its character was described as: 'the whole locality is working class. Poverty is everywhere, with a considerable admixture of the very poor and vicious'.

Other fascinating social survey maps include those drawn up by Henry Mayhew in 1857 showing the statistical distribution of crimes such as rape, bigamy, prostitution and back-street abortion. Campaigning organizations such as the National Temperance League created maps in support of their campaigns or to gather information, which provide fascinating insights into different areas. Maps were also created by the authorities supplying sewerage, water and gas (see the section on public health records).

Finding Special Purpose Maps

Booth's poverty maps can be viewed by appointment at the London School of Economics (LSE) Archives Division, Archives and Rare Books, 10 Portugal Street, London, WC2A 2HD. They have been published by the London Topographical Society and can be viewed online at the London School of Economics archives at: **http://booth.lse.ac.uk**

Other special purpose maps can be found at the British Library and The National Archives.

Tithe Maps and Apportionments

Tithe maps and their accompanying written records provide information about property owners and their lands, houses, gardens and tenants from 1836. Tithe maps were created at a key point in British history as the effects of industrialization were beginning to have a major impact. As a

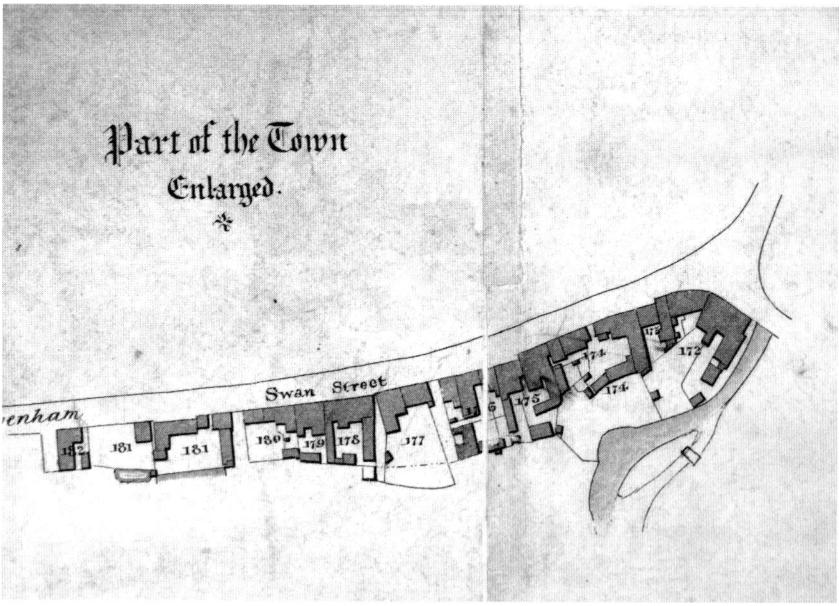

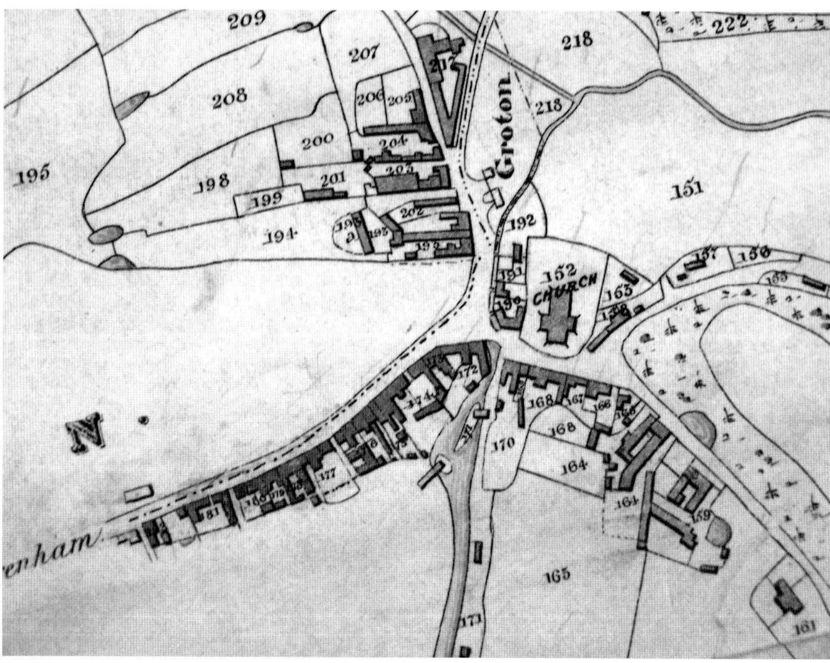

(Pages 162, 163 and 164) Tithe Map and Apportionment for Boxford, Suffolk. Close-ups of the apportionment entry and plot occupied by John Hubert (Herbert on 1851 census) and the enlarged section of Swan Street shown in the corner of the map. (SRO Bury St Edmunds FB 77/C1/1)

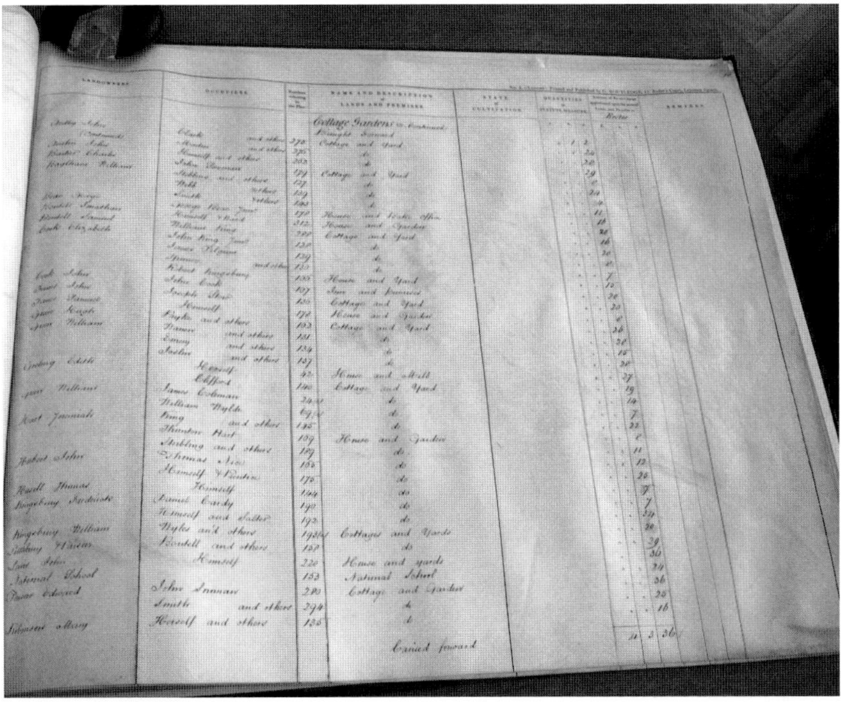

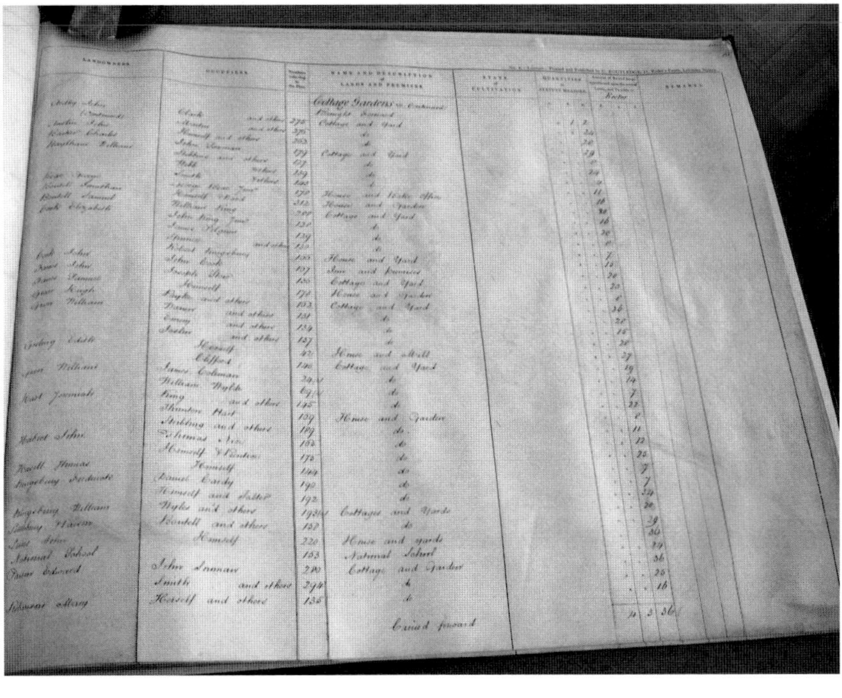

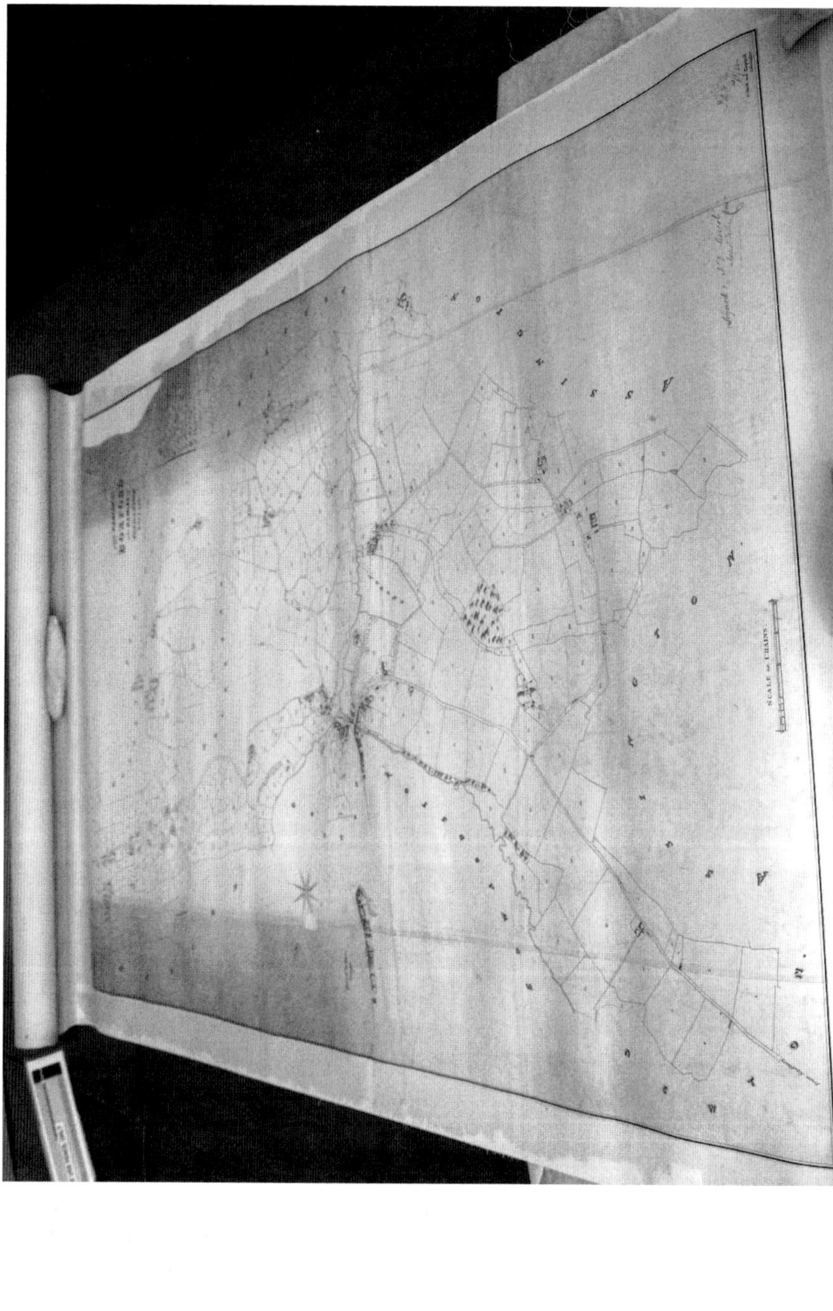

result they can provide a snapshot of rural life which has long since disappeared.

Tithes were a type of tax paid by parishioners to support their parish church and clergy. In theory, payments were meant to be payments given in kind; so that a tenth was given from every bushel of wheat, fleece of wool, crops, milk and so on. Land on which tithes were due formed the majority of land outside cities and boroughs. By the early nineteenth century tithes had become unpopular. The system penalized farmers, as manufactured goods were not subject to tithes. Many people believed it discouraged agricultural improvement as increased production meant an increased share being paid to the church. Nonconformists particularly resented it because they were supporting a church to which they did not belong.

Payment in kind was replaced (commuted) by a money payment in 1836 under the Tithe Commutation Act. A survey had to be made of each parish to evaluate the amount to be paid to the owners of the tithe to make sure they were properly compensated. The tithe survey comes in two parts: a map and an accompanying apportionment schedule. They were mostly drawn up between 1836 and 1850, although many later amended copies exist.

The apportionment recorded owners and occupiers of land subject to paying tithes, the acreage, how the land was used and its tithe valuation. The accompanying maps were often completed two or three years before the final award or agreement was finalized. The people listed on the apportionment can be compared with the census returns and land ownership with earlier records.

These maps divide each parish into numbered plots called 'tithe areas' and show every field or section of land, houses, cottages, barns and outbuildings. Dwellings are coloured differently from other buildings and some farmhouses and large houses are named. Each map shows the boundaries of woods, fields, roads and waterways. Those people exempt from paying tithes, such as the vicar and lord of the manor, do not have plot numbers allocated, although separate lists of exemptions are often included. As a result tithe records provide a fairly complete picture of a community and its land use.

By locating the site of a property on the map you can use the number given to it to find the corresponding entry in the apportionment. Alternatively, if you want to find where someone lived, then you can search for their name in the list of owners and occupiers then find the corresponding plot number on the map. It is worth noting who the neighbours were as records relating to them, such as wills, may prove helpful in your search. I did this to locate the exact places some of my ancestors lived in Yorkshire, Lincolnshire and County Durham. Although none of the buildings they lived in still exist, others that were nearby in the 1830s and 1840s do.

Tithe maps do vary in scale, accuracy and size, with some only showing field boundaries or buildings as blocks. In 1837, it was stipulated that the map was not evidence of accuracy unless it was sealed as well as signed. Approximately one sixth were sealed and only these (known as first-class maps) can be accepted as accurate.

There may be no tithe map for your area. In many cases the links between church and tithes ended with the Reformation. You may also find that your parish was one of the many that used an Enclosure Act to substitute monetary payments for payments in kind (see also the section on enclosure maps). Refusals to pay towards costs and a shortage of trained surveyors meant the survey could take a long time to complete. Nevertheless, most districts were mapped by 1850, although a minority were not completed until the 1860s and 1870s. The last tithe apportionment and map to be made was in 1883 for part of the parish of Hemingstone in Suffolk.

Where land ownership changed over time, these changes were recorded in a series of altered apportionments and maps. There were minor adjustments to the system during the nineteenth century and the Tithe Commissioner's roles passed to other bodies. By the twentieth century there was even more antagonism to the tithe system than before. The Tithe Act of 1936 began the end of the system, by replacing rent charge with redemption annuities payable for sixty years. The high cost of administering these finally brought an end to the whole system in 1977.

Finding Tithe Maps and Apportionments

An excellent overview of the tithe system and how to use the records can be found in *Maps for Family and Local History* by Geraldine Beech and Rose Mitchell (TNA, 2003).

A complete series can be found at The National Archives. Technically, a tithe map and apportionment constitute a single document, but those stored at The National Archives were separated before they were deposited. Local copies tend to still have the two sections together. The apportionment is usually rolled inside the map, or occasionally in a separate folder.

Three copies were made: one each for the tithe commissioners, diocese and parish, so many copies can be found locally. Many local record offices have film copies of those for their county held at TNA, but these are often very poor quality. They also have large collections of the parish and diocesan copies. Copies can exist in other forms, with Suffolk record offices, for example, having large-scale reproductions of those held at TNA in their map cabinets.

The commissioners opened a file for each district even if no tithes were payable. This means that their working papers may still survive at The National Archives, even where there is no map and apportionment.

There are a range of publications and projects featuring maps both in print and online, such as the Surrey Tithe Projects, where volunteers transcribe tithe apportionments. References to the payment of tithes can turn up in other sources, particularly parish records. An increasing number of parish records are being digitized. For example, the tithes paid in Little Leighs in Essex were written in the back of a parish register and can be seen via the record office catalogue. **http://seax.essexcc.gov.uk**

National Farm Survey, 1941–1943

The National Farm Survey is helpful to anyone who lives in a farm building. It was taken between 1941 and 1943 during the Second World War as part of the drive for self-sufficiency. A survey of around 300,000 farms and other agricultural holdings was initially taken in 1940. This rated productivity on a scale of A to C, but only the statistics from this survive. In 1941–43, a much more detailed survey was taken. All agricultural plots measuring five acres or more were assessed. Plans were drawn up of the land and its boundaries. Assessments were made of the condition of the land; who owned and occupied the farm; how many people worked on it; how well it was managed; what equipment was being used; how many animals it had and what food was being produced.

Four forms were filled in for each farm. Three were completed by the farmer and noted the amount and nature of vegetables, fruit, bulbs, flowers, hay and straw. The second form listed land use, the number of acres, animals and workers. The third form gave details of rent paid; the number of years the farmer had been there; machinery and working horses and any additional labour used. The fourth form was filled in by an inspector and either confirmed or corrected the first three forms. The inspectors also made comments on vermin infestations and how the farm was being run.

A survey of a farm in Alresford in Essex describes the owner's one hundred and thirty four acres being worth £115 in rents. He grew barley and oats and the farm had fifteen tons of hay and twelve tons of straw. It goes on to list the number of heifers in milk and cows in calf; petrol or oil engines; fowl and geese and turnips. The number of workers is noted as well as how many of them were over or under the age of twenty-one.

Although it is not an exact like-for-like comparison, the National Farm Survey can be used in conjunction with the Inland Revenue Survey of 1910–20 to provide insights into any changes that might have occurred within farming communities in this thirty-year period. In the case of the farm in Alresford its land and house was assessed in 1912 as a 'house,

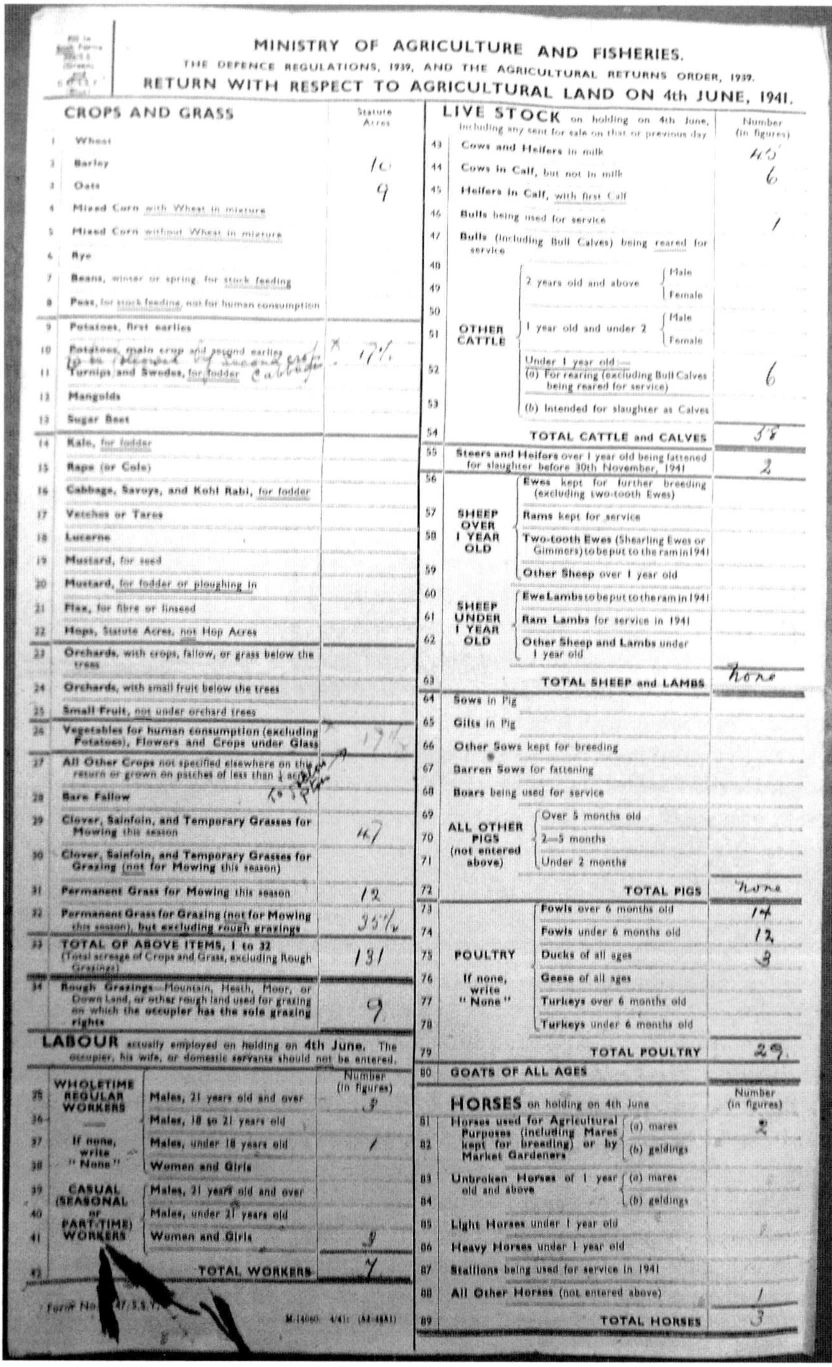

MINISTRY OF AGRICULTURE AND FISHERIES.

THE DEFENCE REGULATIONS, 1939, AND THE AGRICULTURAL RETURNS ORDER, 1939.

RETURN WITH RESPECT TO AGRICULTURAL LAND ON 4th JUNE, 1941.

	CROPS AND GRASS	Statute Acres
1	Wheat	
2	Barley	10
3	Oats	9
4	Mixed Corn with Wheat in mixture	
5	Mixed Corn without Wheat in mixture	
6	Rye	
7	Beans, winter or spring, for stock feeding	
8	Peas, for stock feeding, not for human consumption	
9	Potatoes, first earlies	
10	Potatoes, main crop and second earlies	17½
11	Turnips and Swedes, for fodder	
12	Mangolds	
13	Sugar Beet	
14	Kale, for fodder	
15	Rape (or Cole)	
16	Cabbage, Savoys, and Kohl Rabi, for fodder	
17	Vetches or Tares	
18	Lucerne	
19	Mustard, for seed	
20	Mustard, for fodder or ploughing in	
21	Flax, for fibre or linseed	
22	Hops, Statute Acres, not Hop Acres	
23	Orchards, with crops, fallow, or grass below the trees	
24	Orchards, with small fruit below the trees	
25	Small Fruit, not under orchard trees	
26	Vegetables for human consumption (excluding Potatoes), Flowers and Crops under Glass	17½
27	All Other Crops not specified elsewhere on this return or grown on patches of less than ¼ acre	
28	Bare Fallow	
29	Clover, Sainfoin, and Temporary Grasses for Mowing this season	47
30	Clover, Sainfoin, and Temporary Grasses for Grazing (not for Mowing this season)	
31	Permanent Grass for Mowing this season	12
32	Permanent Grass for Grazing (not for Mowing this season), but excluding rough grazings	35½
33	TOTAL OF ABOVE ITEMS, 1 to 32 (Total acreage of Crops and Grass, excluding Rough Grazings)	131
34	Rough Grazings—Mountain, Heath, Moor, or Down Land, or other rough land used for grazing on which the occupier has the sole grazing rights	9

LABOUR actually employed on holding on 4th June. The occupier, his wife, or domestic servants should not be entered.

			Number (in figures)
35	WHOLETIME REGULAR WORKERS	Males, 21 years old and over	3
36		Males, 18 to 21 years old	
37	If none, write "None"	Males, under 18 years old	1
38		Women and Girls	
39	CASUAL (SEASONAL OR PART-TIME) WORKERS	Males, 21 years old and over	
40		Males, under 21 years old	
41		Women and Girls	3
42		TOTAL WORKERS	7

Form No. ...47/S.S.7.　M.14060. 4/41. (S2-4881)

	LIVE STOCK on holding on 4th June, including any sent for sale on that or previous day		Number (in figures)
43	Cows and Heifers in milk		45
44	Cows in Calf, but not in milk		6
45	Heifers in Calf, with first Calf		
46	Bulls being used for service		1
47	Bulls (including Bull Calves) being reared for service		
48	OTHER CATTLE	2 years old and above: Male	
49		2 years old and above: Female	
50		1 year old and under 2: Male	
51		1 year old and under 2: Female	
52		Under 1 year old:— (a) For rearing (excluding Bull Calves being reared for service)	6
53		(b) Intended for slaughter as Calves	
54		TOTAL CATTLE and CALVES	58
55	Steers and Heifers over 1 year old being fattened for slaughter before 30th November, 1941		2
56	SHEEP OVER 1 YEAR OLD	Ewes kept for further breeding (excluding two-tooth Ewes)	
57		Rams kept for service	
58		Two-tooth Ewes (Shearling Ewes or Gimmers) to be put to the ram in 1941	
59		Other Sheep over 1 year old	
60	SHEEP UNDER 1 YEAR OLD	Ewe Lambs to be put to the ram in 1941	
61		Ram Lambs for service in 1941	
62		Other Sheep and Lambs under 1 year old	
63		TOTAL SHEEP and LAMBS	none
64	Sows in Pig		
65	Gilts in Pig		
66	Other Sows kept for breeding		
67	Barren Sows for fattening		
68	Boars being used for service		
69	ALL OTHER PIGS (not entered above)	Over 5 months old	
70		2—5 months	
71		Under 2 months	
72		TOTAL PIGS	none
73	POULTRY If none, write "None"	Fowls over 6 months old	14
74		Fowls under 6 months old	12
75		Ducks of all ages	3
76		Geese of all ages	
77		Turkeys over 6 months old	
78		Turkeys under 6 months old	
79		TOTAL POULTRY	29
80	GOATS OF ALL AGES		

	HORSES on holding on 4th June		Number (in figures)
81	Horses used for Agricultural Purposes (including Mares kept for breeding) or by Market Gardeners	(a) mares	2
82		(b) geldings	
83	Unbroken Horses of 1 year old and above	(a) mares	
84		(b) geldings	
85	Light Horses under 1 year old		
86	Heavy Horses under 1 year old		
87	Stallions being used for service in 1941		
88	All Other Horses (not entered above)		1
89		TOTAL HORSES	3

Alresford on the National Farm Survey, 1941. (TNA: MAF 32/828/305)

stable & buildings, garden, arable, pasture and saltings' covering 165 acres and 19 perches. The gross and rateable values are also given.

Finding the National Farm Survey

All copies of the survey can be found at The National Archives.

Newspapers

Newspapers often include details on specific buildings, housing projects, road building and local affairs. Local newspapers from the eighteenth century onwards have always included notices of house sales and tenancies to let at auction. For example, the Ipswich Journal for 31 July 1784 advertised the estates of Giles Borrett in Stradbrook for sale. Descriptions were given of the farm, houses, barn, stables and outhouses occupied by Mrs Mary Borrett. Also included were details of lands of various kinds and another farm 'late in the occupation of Mr. John Munby, and now his widow, tenant at will'.

Newspapers are also a vital source of information about events relating to the people who lived in your house such as birth, marriage and death notices and obituaries. If your home was used for trade or business in some way then there may be advertisements or notices of work appointments. If it was on manorial land you will find notices about when and where the manor courts met. Court cases often mention where someone lived, whilst reports into major projects such as redevelopments and slum clearance programmes describe the living conditions of people.

Finding Newspapers

The national newspaper library in London has collections from all over the UK. There are also comprehensive collections of local papers in the record offices and local history libraries across the country.

There are many indexes and published extracts from local newspapers, many of which are only available locally. In the Cambridgeshire Collection held at the Central Library, for example, I found articles on how particular roads in Cherry Hinton developed, including details of campaigns against particular projects.

Online access to indexes, extracts from reports and digitized copies is growing rapidly. Several county pages on the GENUKI website have links to extracts from local newspapers compiled by volunteers. Some county record offices and local history libraries are involved in projects to put indexes and/or images online. One example is the Lincolnshire 'Lincs to the Past' website, which includes a subject index to over 23,000 newspaper articles. **www.lincstothepast.com/help/about-lincs-to-the-past**

Printed indexes to *The Times* newspaper from 1785 to 1985 have been available for many years at record offices and local studies centres. In most areas these have been superseded by a licence agreement allowing free access using your library card to digitized copies and online indexes at *The Times Digital Archives, 1785–1985*. Ask your local library for details. Many of those which subscribe also enable remote access to library card holders.

The *Illustrated London News* was the first fully illustrated weekly newspaper. Its Historical Archive 1842–2003 has been digitised by Gale Cengage Learning. **http://gale.cengage.co.uk/iln** This can also be accessed via some UK public libraries and educational organisations.

The British Newspaper Archive is a commercial site which allows subscribers to access digitized copies of local newspapers held at the British Library. You can see a certain number of articles free. **www.britishnewspaperarchive.co.uk**

The British Library's own eighteenth and nineteenth-century newspapers website is also available through libraries and to subscribers at home. If your local library subscribes to this service you can use it free with your library card. Ask your local library for details. I used this to follow up on a reference to Roman remains found in the grounds of a house in Essex in 1884 and found a contemporary newspaper report in *The Essex Standard, West Suffolk Gazette, and Eastern Counties' Advertiser*. This stated:

> The utmost courtesy and attention was rendered by the occupier of the farm, Mr. H. Barton, who generously granted permission to make the explorations, and whose substantial aid by himself and his labourers was highly appreciated, as was his kindness in hospitably providing a friendly lunch.

The *London Gazette* reported legal cases and therefore includes many references to people and property. You can search and see archive copies free under the section for 'Historians'. **www.london-gazette.co.uk** An example is the report on 1 December 1818, which carried a notice that the property of John Dawson, a bankrupt of Foulsham in Norfolk, was to be sold at the Ship Inn to pay his debts:

> A messuage or dwelling-house, now in three tenements, situate in Foulsham aforesaid, and now in the several occupations of Thomas Fox, Elizabeth Hubbard, and Dawson, as tenants from year to year, with the yards and appurtenances thereto belonging; and also a piece of garden, ground lying opposite to, and near, the said premises, and now in the occupation of the said Dawson. For further particulars enquire of Mr. Decker, Solicitor Walsingham Norfolk.

INTERESTING EXCAVATION OF A ROMAN VILLA & ROMAN REMAINS AT ALRESFORD.

An intimation having been made that Roman remains had been discovered in the neighbourhood of Wyvenhoe, a party of zealous antiquarians proceeded thither on Monday, Nov. 24th. Notwithstanding that a keen, crisp hoar-frost in the early morning covered the surroundings with a robe of whiteness above the verdure of autumnal green, the sun soon dispelled the apparently wintry aspect, and upon arriving at the spot there was a fairly numerous muster, including Mr. Harwood, of Church Hall, Alresford; Rev. C. Hewson, of Fingringhoe; Mr. J. D. Ward, Elmstead; Mr. M. H. Barton, Alresford Lodge; Mr. A. Stannard, of Greenstead Hall; Mr. C. Golding, Colchester; and various others, together with labourers, villagers, mariners from vessels alongside the creek, yachtsmen of Brightlingsea and elsewhere. The party at once set zealously to work in digging and uncovering the ground, and it became evident they were standing upon the remains of an extensive villa residence, apparently of some former Roman occupier of considerable importance. Proceeding with the search, various floors, inlaid with tesselated pavements, of considerable size—formerly separate apartments—were uncovered, extending in parallelogram form over a considerable distance of more than 300 feet, and a suggestion was made by Mr. Golding, who superintended the excavations, that other sites in the field should be opened. This resulted in the successful discoveries of numerous cinerary and other urns and pottery. In some of them, especially those of the black and light grey ware, ashes of burnt substances, apparently of human remains, were come upon, and the whole spot appears to be imbued with remnants of ashes, bones, and urns. Remains of deer and ox bones were unearthed, and burnt ashes, charcoal, oyster and other shells, remain throughout the field. The painted colouring, chiefly red, but occasionally interspersed with green, black, and yellow, were clearly discernible, although when exposed to the air after the damp earth they gradually crumbled into decay. Specimens were, however, preserved, and the "Samian" ware, with pieces of glazed black pottery with red devices of flowers and other figures, green glass, and tiles, &c., fully repaid the searchers. The site, being upon an eminence, commands an extensive view of the creek and port of Brightlingsea, and upon critical enquiries, although it is now known from its size as the Eight-acre Field, it formerly bore the appellation of "Near-Ford" Field, a name suggestive in itself that a ford across the creek was formely passable here, and even until a late time it seems that one has been used by the villagers. The whole district would probably prove that the Romans very extensively occupied and resided on the banks. The utmost courtesy and attention was rendered, by the occupier of the farm, Mr. M. H. Barton, who generously granted the permission to make the explorations, and whose substantial aid by himself and his labourers was highly appreciated, as was his kindness in hospitably providing a friendly lunch—very welcome after the biting sharp wind upon the open expanse. The proceedings of the day concluded with a repast given by Mr. C. Harwood, of Church Hall. Most of the coloured fragments are apparently portions of the painted walls of rooms.

The Essex Standard, West Suffolk Gazette, and Eastern Counties' Advertiser, 29 November 1884.

Parish Records

The parish was the main unit of local government until the nineteenth century. As a result it was responsible for both civil and ecclesiastical (church) administration. Parish records (also called 'parish chest' records) are those documents produced through the day-to-day running of the parish. From the late 1500s each church was obliged to keep these records safely in a locked chest, thereby giving them their name. Because the Church of England played such an important part in local affairs there is a phenomenal range of records that come under this heading, which can provide essential information about the people who lived and worked in your home and how they interacted with their neighbours.

Those parish records of most use to the house historian relate to the administration of parish affairs and collection of rates by churchwardens and overseers. You may therefore be able to find out whether the people who lived in your home owned or rented property of enough value to qualify them to pay poor rates; if they disputed what they had to pay; whether they were prosecuted for non payment or received poor relief. If you live in a parish almshouse, workhouse or on church lands, then parish records can give you interesting insights into their role within the local community. Some of these resources, such as glebe, are dealt with separately in this book. What follows here are other parish records of use in researching a house.

Parish Registers

Parish registers of baptisms, marriages and burials are the most well known and commonly used of all parish records. From 1538 every parish was obliged to record every baptism, marriage and burial conducted by the Church of England. Over time, the amount of information given in church registers has increased. However, these records tend to be most useful when you already know who was living in your property, as most do not give precise addresses before the mid-nineteenth century, and those in small rural areas often don't for much longer. Nevertheless, some do give addresses or identifiable locations, such as the registers for Whaplode in Lincolnshire. The baptismal entries for 1818, for instance, describe where various people lived. Thomas and Susanna Harrison were noted as living in a 'double-roofed house Spalding Road', whilst Thomas and Elisabeth Watson resided at 'Stocks Hill'.

Not every parish register has survived or been kept as well as it should and you may not find baptisms, marriages or burials of people where they lived. Nevertheless, it should be possible to find some genealogical information about the people who inhabited your home. Parish registers can also include information on buildings and land. As mentioned in glebe records, many lists of parish properties are entered in registers. One example is a register for West Tofts with Buckenham Tofts on the Norfolk and Suffolk border. This includes a note dated 1863 which describes how the old hall at nearby Lyndford was pulled down:

> This house was built by Mr Nelthorpe in the year 1720 but had undergone alterations since that period having been greatly added to at various times, the whole of which additions were most ingeniously concealed by an outer casing of white brick.

Helpfully, a drawing of the hall accompanies this note.

Parish Rates

Land and property have been taxed in one form or another for hundreds of years. Until the mid to late nineteenth century the majority were administered locally in the form of rates and assessed on the value of a property a person owned or rented. Even the few national taxation schemes such as land tax were administered locally. Rates were collected by parish officials for a variety of purposes, with the most common being to maintain the poor and church, and contribute to highway maintenance. As a result they can provide much information about owners and occupiers of property and details such as its size and rateable value.

The rateable value of properties in Kenninghall in Norfolk, for example, can be found in the parish poor rates books. Those for property owned by James Burlingham in 1835 state he was the owner of a town house and land on Park Common. The house and land was assessed at £42, with the poor rate to be collected at the rate of two shillings in the pound, meaning that James paid £4 and 4 shillings. James is also recorded separately as owning an uninhabited cottage and another piece of land, also on Park Common.

The Highways Act of 1555 obliged parishioners to provide labour and elect a surveyor to take charge of the work needed for the upkeep of roads, bridges, embankments and causeways within a parish. This position continued until the Highways Act of 1835. Parish records can therefore include payments for labour and maintenance, and the names of people involved.

Many disputes arose over highway maintenance between parish officials and their parishioners, as well as with neighbouring parishes. Such disputes frequently ended up in court. For example, in 1795 the Norfolk county quarter sessions held at Swaffham on 20 July heard a grand jury presentment that: 'The road leading from Swaffham to King's Lynn through West Bilney, lying in Pentney is obstructed by gates built across

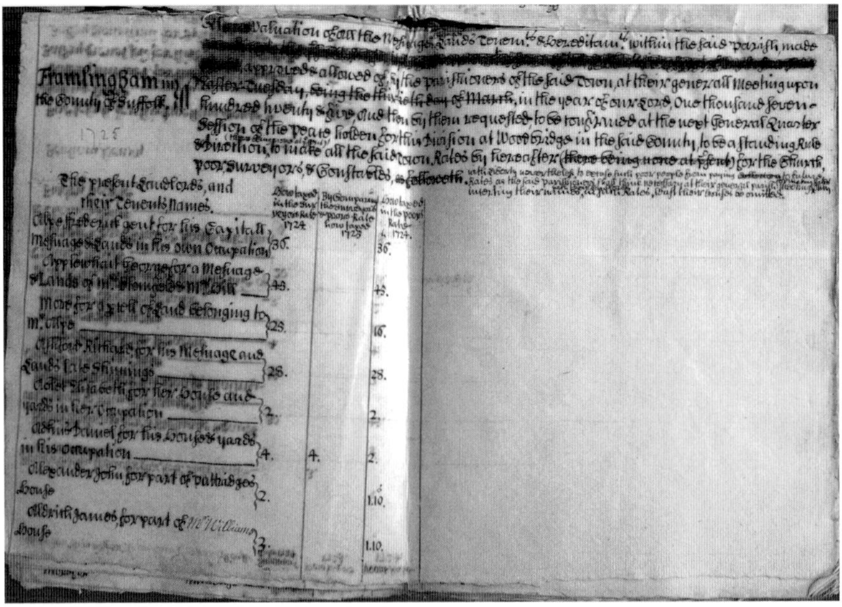

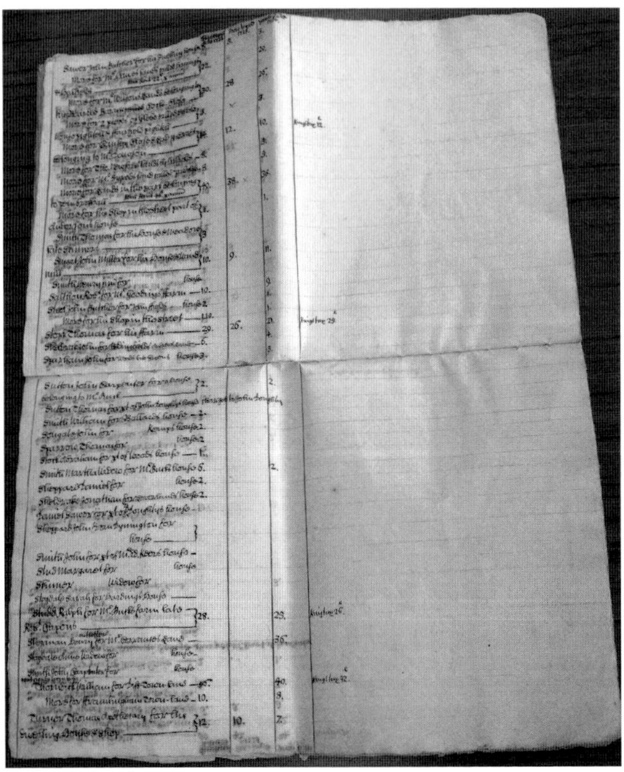

Valuation of lands for rateable value in Framlingham in Suffolk, 1725. (SRO Ipswich: FC 101/F1/1–4)

it by inhabitants of Pentney.' The parish of Pentney was found guilty. (NRO: QS Papers Box 63).

Once the parish took over all responsibility for the poor in the 1600s, taxes had to be raised to pay for their care. Where these survive they act as a census of the heads of rate-paying households. A poor rate was set every Easter based on a percentage of the value of property (both owned and leased) and was usually recorded in the churchwardens' account books. These include information on who paid rates, and if well kept can provide an annual listing of all ratepayers, along with how much they paid. If a parish needed more money to support its poor it could increase the number of times in a year the poor rate was collected.

It was also important to record how such monies were distributed and to check that they were being used efficiently and effectively. This means that payments towards the upkeep of parish buildings such as the workhouse, repairs of fences, roads and bridges appear, along with the names of those undertaking the work. Such changes in the amounts local taxpayers had to pay can give a good indication of economic fluctuations locally and nationally.

Other Parish Records

Vestry minutes and agreements are another useful source of information on properties. The 'vestry' was a decision-making body of parish officials that took its name from the room in which it met. It made decisions on almost any subject remotely connected with the running of the church itself. The vestry council selected the parish constable, parish surveyor and parish constable. In the vestry minute books of Salle in Norfolk for 1873, for example, there is an account of rents and crops 'derived from the Church Property', including people's names and the value of the land they inhabited. They also dealt with disputes over tithe or poor rates, with references to these often appearing in their account books. If the vestry could not resolve an issue then they could take the matter to the Justice of the Peace, so more detail may be found in court records.

Urban areas may have additional rates for facilities such as sewerage. Whilst it might seem tedious to work through a list of payments, changes in the amount being paid may signify structural changes, whilst the list of occupiers will assist in tracking when a property changed hands.

A number of other records, such as deeds and leases relating to land and properties, can be found in the parish chest records. The parish records for Bottisham in Cambridgeshire include papers relating to building of a new parsonage between 1838 and 1843, including specifications of work to be done.

A bundle of these for the period 1704–05 from Rickinghall Superior in Suffolk, for example, describe several plots of land and buildings in the

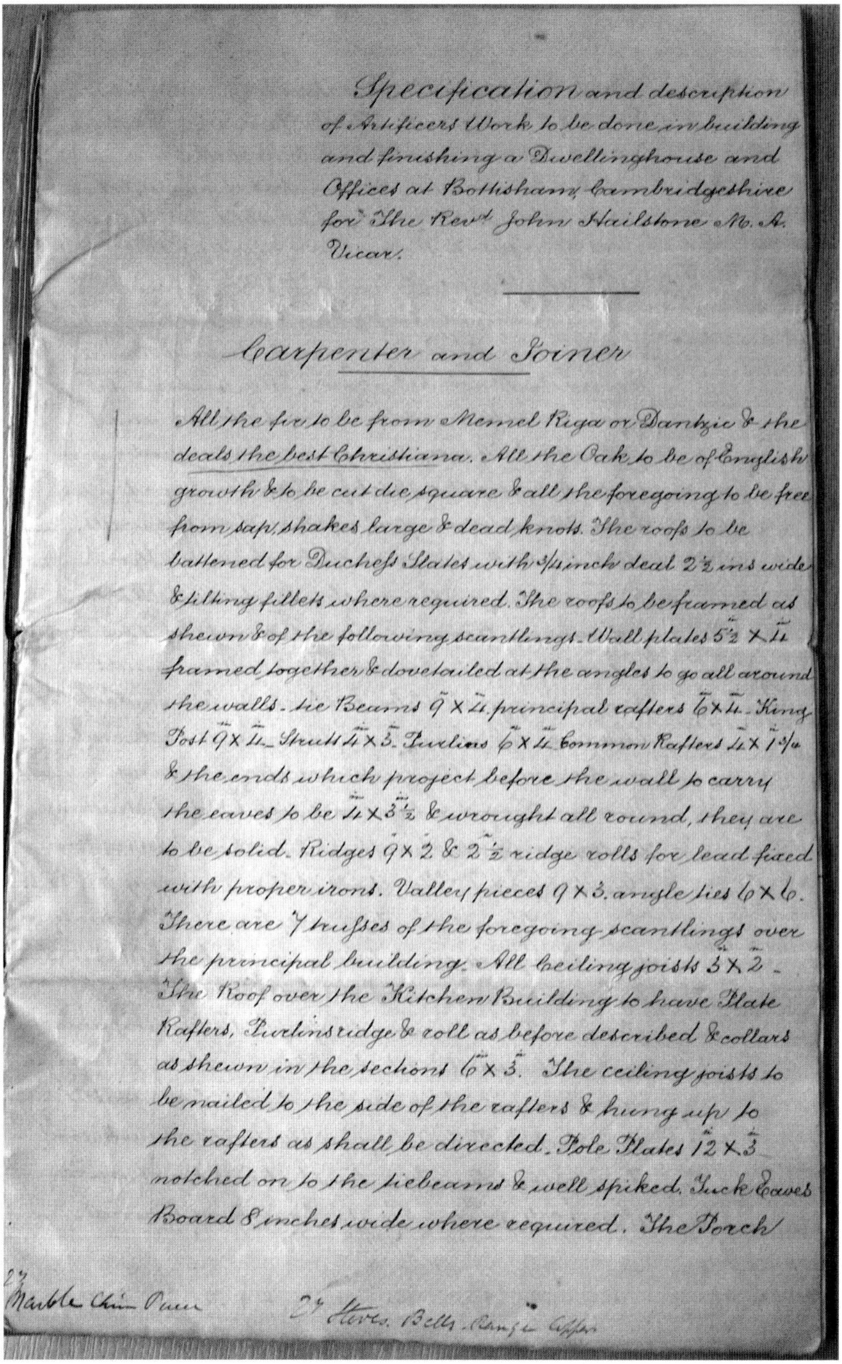

Specification and description of Artificers Work to be done in building and finishing a Dwellinghouse and Offices at Bottisham Cambridgeshire for The Revd John Hailstone M.A. Vicar.

Carpenter and Joiner

All the fir to be from Memel Riga or Dantzic & the deals the best Christiana. All the Oak to be of English growth & to be cut die square & all the foregoing to be free from sap, shakes large & dead knots. The roofs to be battened for Duchess Slates with 3/4 inch deal 2½ ins wide & tilting fillets where required. The roofs to be framed as shewn & of the following scantlings. Wall plates 5½ × 4 framed together & dovetailed at the angles to go all around the walls - tie Beams 9 × 4 principal rafters 6 × 4 - King Post 9 × 4 - Strutts 4 × 3 - Purlins 6 × 4 Common Rafters 4 × 1¾ & the ends which project before the wall to carry the eaves to be 4 × 3½ & wrought all round, they are to be solid. Ridges 9 × 2 & 2½ ridge rolls for lead fixed with proper irons. Valley pieces 9 × 3. angle ties 6 × 6. There are 7 trusses of the foregoing scantlings over the principal building. All Ceiling joists 3 × 2 - The Roof over the Kitchen Building to have Plate Rafters, Purlins ridge & roll as before described & collars as shewn in the sections 6 × 3. The ceiling joists to be nailed to the side of the rafters & hung up to the rafters as shall be directed. Pole Plates 12 × 3 notched on to the tiebeams & well spiked. Tuck Eaves Board 8 inches wide where required. The Porch

27 Marble Chim Piece 27 Stoves. Bells Range in Offices

Bottisham, Cambridgeshire Parish Registers. (Cambridgeshire Archives Service: P13/3/3)

village, such as this lease naming the owner and tenant of a farm belonging to the parish. Other records which may be found in parish records refer to compensation for damages to property through war, riots or damage. Also from Rickinghall is an 1823 order compensating William Turner under an Act of Parliament for his barn and other buildings having been burned down.

An interesting example of what can turn up is the declaration by Edward Lant of Upwood, Huntingdonshire, labourer, 'as to the lands owned by Pooley in 1848' (reference: Fellowes family, Lords de Ramsey of Abbots Ripton CRO: Huntingdon R13/1/106). This began with Edward giving his age, residence and occupation, and stating that he had lived in Upwood all his life and always worked for Mary Pooley, widow of Thomas. Edward was obviously being asked to corroborate the details of an estate in Upwood bought by Mary Pooley about sixty years before of Pavatt Hangar who 'lived at or near Norwich'. Before describing other properties nearby and stating who inherited Mary's tenements after her death, Edward described the Pooley property as:

> Three Commonable Messuages (namely) of a Commonable Messuage occupied by Henry Johnson and afterwards by the said Mary Pooley to the time of her decease. Also of another commonable Messuage now divided into two tenements which Messuage was formerly in the occupation of Philip Reignall afterwards of Everett Barnes (with whom I then lived) and part thereof in the occupation of Hannah Hall and the remainder unoccupied And also of another Commonable Messuage formerly occupied by William Kay and by my Grandfather and now in the occupation of Samuel Vass. And I do further declare that the occupiers of the aforesaid commonable Messuages annually stocked the Commons belonging to the said parish of Upwood . . .

Finding Parish Records

The essential guide to understanding and using parish records is W.E. Tate's *The Parish Chest* (Phillimore, 1983).

The majority of parish records are kept in local record offices. Copies on film for many parishes can be seen at the Society of Genealogists or via LDS family history centres. Some record offices are placing digitized copies online, often in partnership with commercial organizations such as Ancestry and Find my Past (see, for example, those from London Metropolitan Archives on Ancestry). Others such as Kent Archives have their own schemes **http://cityark.medway.gov.uk** Some are free whilst others are pay-to-view.

Local record offices and family history societies and the Society of Genealogists all have extensive collections of transcripts and indexes to parish registers, and occasionally other parish records. The main free websites are Family Search **www.familysearch.org** and FreeREG **www.freereg.co.uk**. The Family Search website also has a growing collection of digitized images of parish records available free.

Rate books also occur among records of borough and district councils, the former Poor Law Unions, quarter sessions and civil and ecclesiastical parish records. These are generally deposited at local record offices.

Online Parish Clerks is a volunteer project encouraging the transcription of local records. For more information on what is available see **www.onlineparishclerks.org.uk**

Quarter Sessions Records

Quarter sessions courts were the equivalent of a magistrate's court today, hearing less serious crimes. Serious cases were tried by visiting assize judges (equivalent to the Crown Court today) and these records are held at The National Archives. A significant number of cases and records relating to properties and land can be found in quarter sessions records. For instance, a presentment was made at King's Lynn quarter sessions in 1795 against Philip Green, a shopkeeper of West Bradenham in Norfolk, for failing to 'scour the rivulet adjacent to land he occupies next to Church way in West Bradenham, that rivulet is obstructed and has damaged wall of Rev. James Bentham'. In another case at the same court Henry Mason was accused of having: 'forcibly expelled John Carlton of Great Cressingham, yeoman from the barn which Carlton leased for a term of four years' (reference NRO: C/S3/66 Bundle One).

Quarter Sessions records can be particularly helpful if you live in a former public house, asylum, Nonconformist church or chapel, or near a railway line or major road. This is because JPs were responsible at various points in time for checking parish surveyors kept the highways in good repair, licenced alehouses, Dissenting ministers and private lunatic asylums, and plans of all intended railways and canals had to be deposited with the Clerk of the Peace (see also the section on maps and plans). References to disputes over buildings on common land can also occasionally be found amongst quarter sessions court records.

Finding Quarter Sessions Records

Quarter sessions records were kept by the Clerk of the Peace until their abolition in 1971, when their records were transferred to county record offices. Many background papers such as recognizances and statements have been indexed, but few of the minute books. The court books are in

Latin before 1733 except for much of the civil war period in the mid–1600s. However, the supporting documentation, such as recognizances, statements and bonds, is usually in English.

Returns of the Owners of Land, 1873–76

The Returns of the Owners of Land were a one-off listing of anyone who owned more than one acre of land in the United Kingdom, except in London. In 1872 Local Government Boards were instructed to make a list of owners using rating records. The Returns for England and Wales were prepared for 1873. Those for Scotland were prepared for 1874 and Ireland in 1876.

The returns are arranged alphabetically by county and include the name of the owner, the place they lived, how much they owned in that county and its gross estimated rental value. For example, when Caistor St Edmund in Norfolk was surveyed it showed Harriet Dashwood as the owner of Caistor Hall. The amount of land she owned was 1,371 acres and 15 perches and the estimated gross rental value was £2,190 and 16 shillings.

Finding Returns of Owners

Many copies have been produced in book or on CD format, such as those for the West Riding of Yorkshire by Back to Roots.

Those for Wales can be searched free at: **www.cefnpennar.com/1873index.htm**

UK Genealogy Archives hosts a free online database for eleven counties at: **www.uk-genealogy.org.uk/cgi-bin/DB/search.cgi?action=loadDB&DB=1**

Commercial companies hosting copies online include Ancestry **www.ancestry.co.uk** and The Genealogist **www.thegenealogist.co.uk**

Sales Particulars

Advertising the sale or tenancies of houses, lands and other properties in newspapers, on broadsheets and elsewhere has long been popular. Sales particulars have been produced by auctioneers and solicitors since at least the early 1800s. They describe properties being sold and can include plans and maps. Many are deposited in record offices by estate agents, whilst others can be found amongst estate, family and business records such as the Pardle collection at the Lincolnshire Archives.

A set of sale particulars from 1902 for the Hills Road area of Cherry Hinton in Cambridgeshire is a good example. These describe the building plots being sold, accompanied by a map, whilst one for

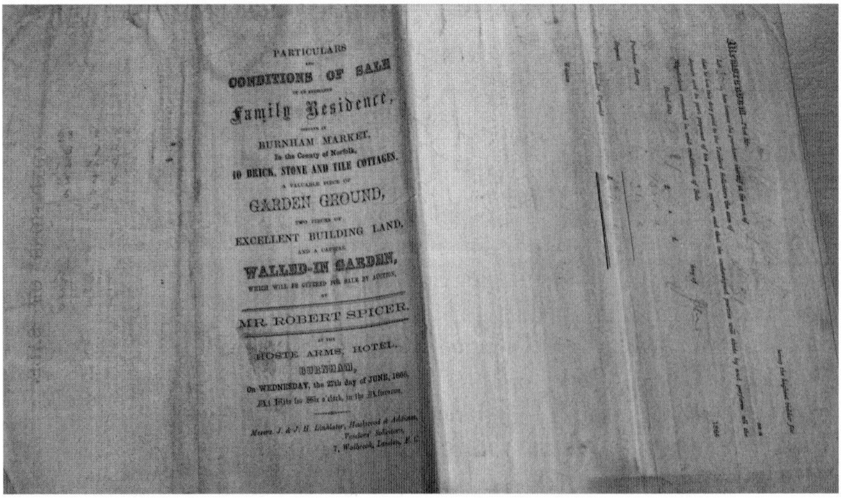

PARTICULARS

CONDITIONS OF SALE

Family Residence,

BURNHAM MARKET,

In the County of Norfolk,

10 BRICK, STONE AND TILE COTTAGES,

GARDEN GROUND,

EXCELLENT BUILDING LAND,

WALLED-IN GARDEN,

MR. ROBERT SPICER,

HOSTE ARMS, HOTEL,

BURNHAM,

On WEDNESDAY, the 27th day of JUNE, 1866,

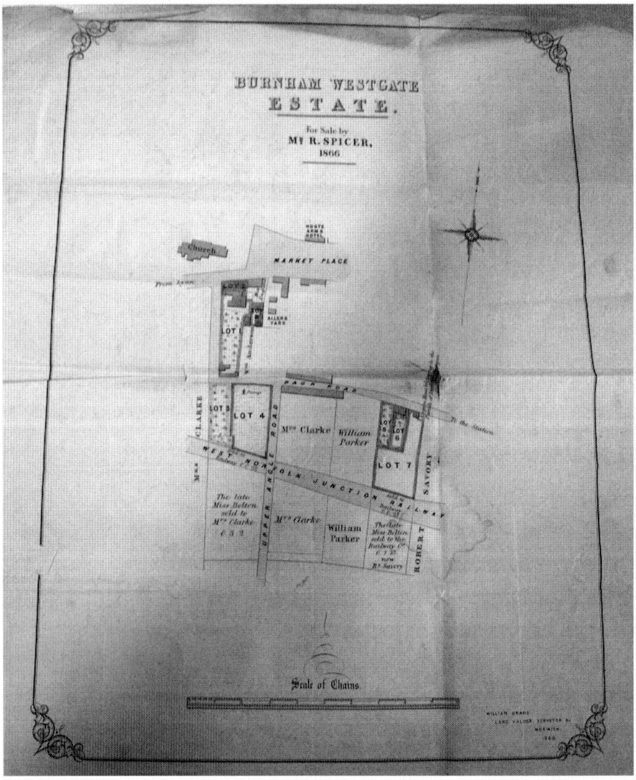

(Pages 180–183) Bidwell & Sons Sales Particulars, 1902, of Hills Road area, Cherry Hinton. (Cambridgeshire Archives Service: 515/SP183)

Sales Particular for Burnham Westgate, 1866. (Norfolk Heritage Centre)

HILLS ROAD

AND

CHERRYHINTON ROAD,

Within Two Miles of St. Mary's Church, and about One Mile from the important Railway Centre of the University Town of Cambridge.

Particulars & Conditions of Sale

OF

VALUABLE FREEHOLD

BUILDING LAND,

To be Sold by Auction, by direction of the Rev. A. H. Samman, with the consent of the Board of Agriculture, by

MESSRS.

GRAIN, MOYES & WISBEY,

AT THE

"LION" HOTEL, PETTY CURY, CAMBRIDGE,

On Tuesday, April 8th, 1902,

AT SIX O'CLOCK IN THE EVENING PRECISELY.

TEN PLOTS OF FREEHOLD LAND

Situate on the Hills and Cherryhinton Roads, with frontages thereto of from 130 to 160 feet, and each Plot containing an area of One Acre.

The Land abuts on Main Roads in a healthy and favourite locality, and while situate close to the Town, escapes the Borough Rates.

Particulars, Plans, and Conditions of Sale, of ALGERNON J. LYON, Esq., Solicitor, 22, St. Andrew's Street; or of Messrs. GRAIN, MOYES & WISBEY, Land Agents, &c., 66, St. Andrew's Street, Cambridge.

"EXPRESS" PRINTING WORKS, KING STREET, CAMBRIDGE.

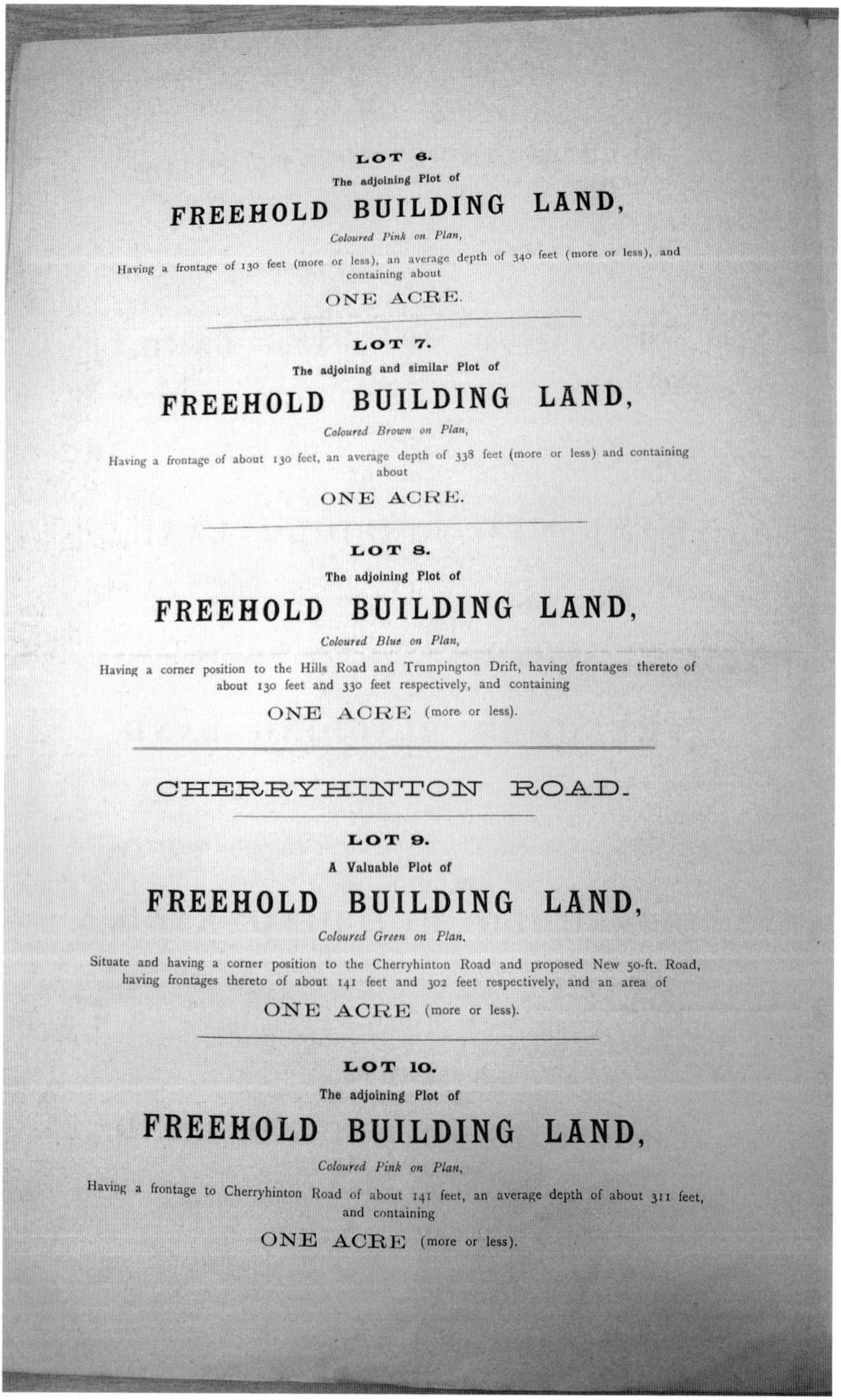

LOT 6.

The adjoining Plot of

FREEHOLD BUILDING LAND,

Coloured Pink on Plan,

Having a frontage of 130 feet (more or less), an average depth of 340 feet (more or less), and containing about

ONE ACRE.

LOT 7.

The adjoining and similar Plot of

FREEHOLD BUILDING LAND,

Coloured Brown on Plan,

Having a frontage of about 130 feet, an average depth of 338 feet (more or less) and containing about

ONE ACRE.

LOT 8.

The adjoining Plot of

FREEHOLD BUILDING LAND,

Coloured Blue on Plan,

Having a corner position to the Hills Road and Trumpington Drift, having frontages thereto of about 130 feet and 330 feet respectively, and containing

ONE ACRE (more or less).

CHERRYHINTON ROAD.

LOT 9.

A Valuable Plot of

FREEHOLD BUILDING LAND,

Coloured Green on Plan.

Situate and having a corner position to the Cherryhinton Road and proposed New 50-ft. Road, having frontages thereto of about 141 feet and 302 feet respectively, and an area of

ONE ACRE (more or less).

LOT 10.

The adjoining Plot of

FREEHOLD BUILDING LAND,

Coloured Pink on Plan.

Having a frontage to Cherryhinton Road of about 141 feet, an average depth of about 311 feet, and containing

ONE ACRE (more or less).

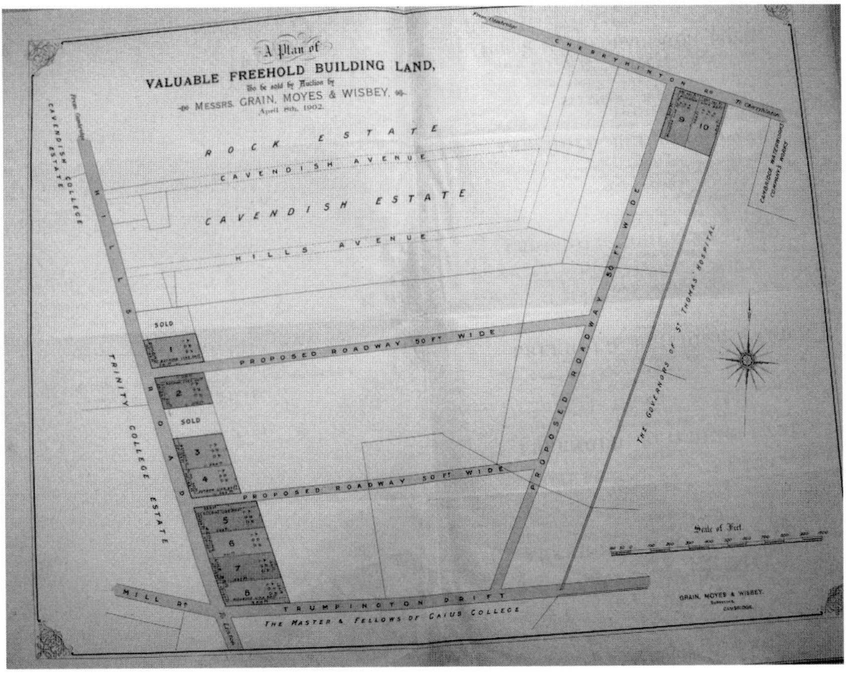

Burnham Westgate in 1866 shows adjacent plots with the names of their occupants.

Sales particulars often give detailed descriptions of larger properties by room and include plans, whilst large estates may include the names of tenants and details of leases. This was the case with the Caistor Hall estate in south Norfolk in 1944. A booklet includes a description of the house and contents, with photographs, as well as farms and lands on the estate, including occupiers. The hall was described as: 'of considerable archaeological interest and abutting upon the ancient Roman town', and comprising: 'a substantial brick and tile Residence of Georgian character, well planned and of pleasing appearance'.

Even if you cannot locate a sales particular for your home it can be helpful to check for any for other properties in the same street or area, especially those built at the same time or in a similar style. In the case of a former grocer's and carpenter's shop in Stiffkey in Norfolk I was unable to find any specific reference to a sales particular for it. However, when checking an 1848 sales particular with accompanying plan for various pubs, cottages and land in the same village, I found it included this shop. Confirmation it was the same shop came from comparing this plan with the tithe map and apportionment of 1840. These tithe records also revealed that the man who left it in his will when he died in 1894 was listed as a tenant in 1840. It would therefore appear that he bought the shop in 1848 when this sales particular was compiled.

Finding Sales Particulars

The majority of sales particulars can be found in county record offices, mainly amongst estate agents' and solicitors' collections. Accompanying maps and plans will also turn up in map catalogues. You may also find them amongst parish, business and estate records, so I would always recommend checking any placename listings.

Some local history libraries and museums have their own collections. They also turn up for sale at auction, in secondhand bookshops and online, particularly on sites that sell old maps and deeds.

Valuation Office Survey, 1910–20 (also known as the 'Lloyd George Domesday')

Under the 1910 Finance Act a valuation survey was made of all properties in England and Wales. This survey was nicknamed the 'Lloyd George Domesday', after the Chancellor of the Exchequer (later Prime Minister) who approved it, and because it was the first comprehensive national survey of all land and property ownership since the Domesday survey of 1086. This 'New Domesday' was organized by the Board of Inland Revenue's Valuation Office in order to establish the rateable values of all property as they stood on 30 April 1909, to tax them more efficiently. The survey was conducted over the next year. As a result it provides an account of all buildings standing just before the First World War. The survey was discontinued in 1920 as it cost more than was raised in increased taxes.

The books give a brief description of each property, the names of owners and occupiers and a note of its value, with properties shown on large-scale Ordnance Survey maps. Each property (called 'hereditaments') appears in three records – two maps and a field book. The maps provide a numerical reference to the entry in the field books. These list the names of owners and occupiers; whether a property was freehold or leasehold; if it was subject to tithes; details of insurance; who paid for repairs; gross values; rights of way; amenities such as gas, electricity and running water; how the building was constructed; how many rooms it had; what the windows were like; what condition it was in and furnishing and fittings. Some include details of plans and a date of construction.

Finding the Valuation Survey

The original field books and finished maps are held at The National Archives. However, those for most Crown land; Basildon; Birkenhead;

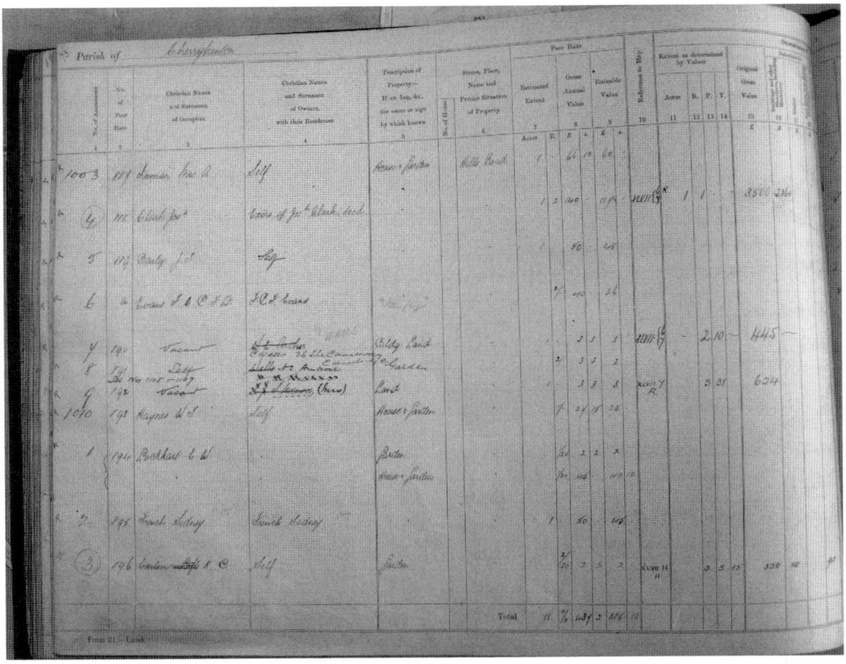

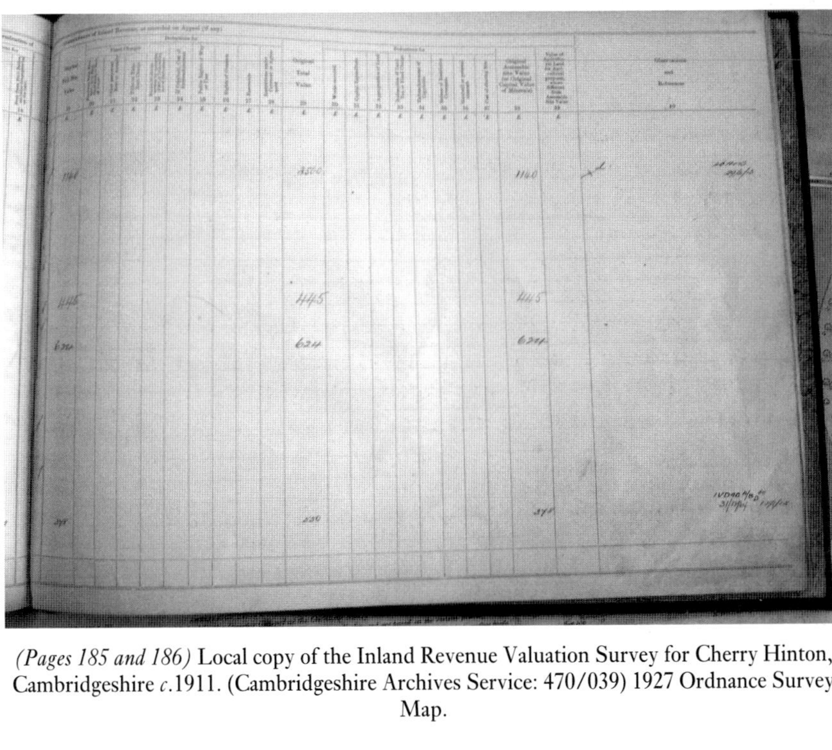

(Pages 185 and 186) Local copy of the Inland Revenue Valuation Survey for Cherry Hinton, Cambridgeshire *c.*1911. (Cambridgeshire Archives Service: 470/039) 1927 Ordnance Survey Map.

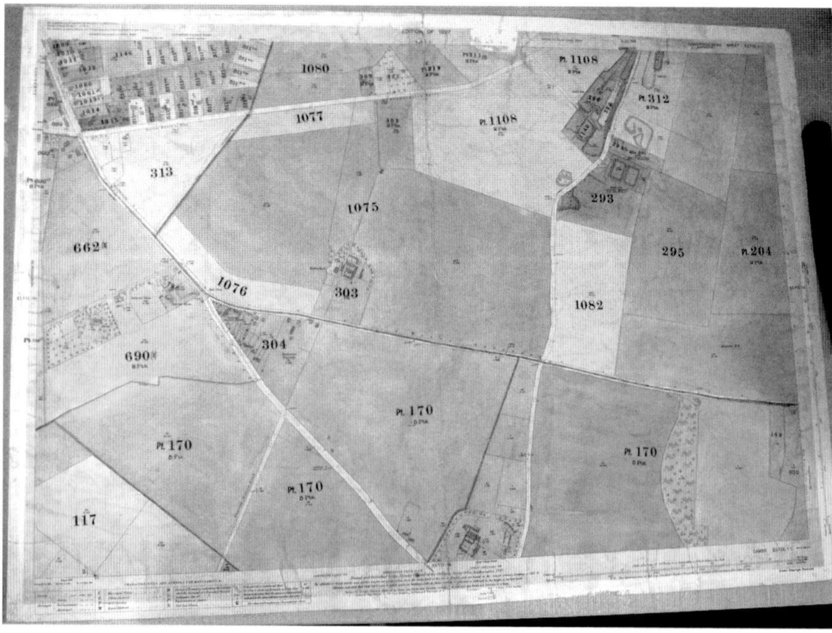
1080
1077
Pt 1108
Pt 312
313
1075
293
662
295
Pt 204
1076
303
1082
304
690
Pt 170
Pt 170
Pt 170
Pt 170
117

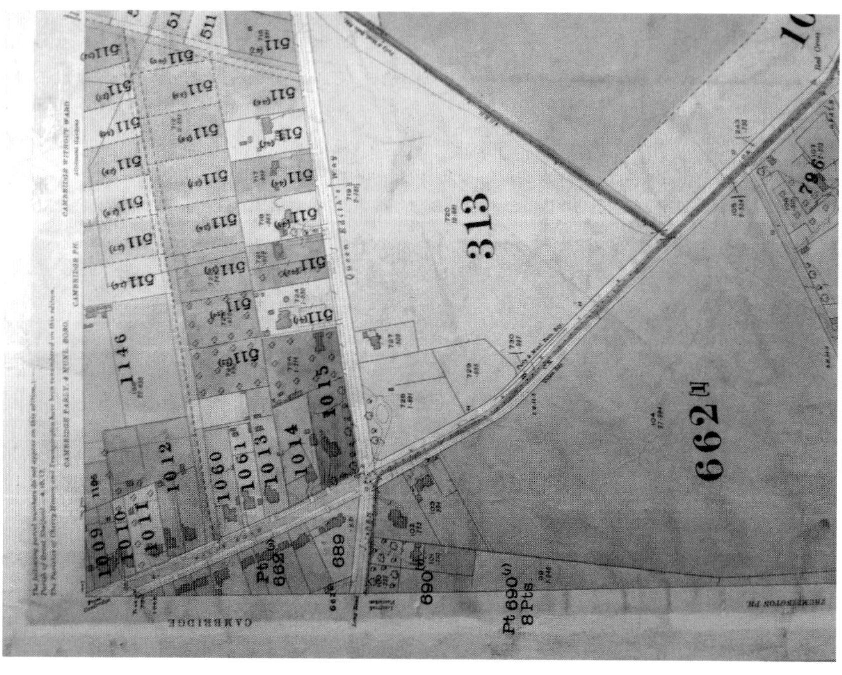
313
662
1146
1012
1060
1061
1013
1014
1015
1009
1010
1011
689
Pt 662
690
Pt 690
8 Pts.
CAMBRIDGE

Chelsmsford; Coventry; the Isle of Wight; Liverpool; Portsmouth; Southampton; Winchester, most of the Wirral and Chichester are missing. The National Archives Labs site can be used to identify and order Valuation Office Survey Maps in advance of a visit. **www.nationalarchives.gov.uk/maps/maps-family-local-history.htm**

Copies of the field books and the working maps can often be found in county record offices. This proved to be the case in Buckinghamshire where I found a copy of the Wendover survey and accompanying map and Cambridgeshire for a property in Cherry Hinton.

Some county record offices, such as Oxfordshire, are placing digitized copies online. **www.oxfordshire.gov.uk/oro**

Wills, Administrations and Inventories

Wills, administrations and inventories for the people who owned, lived or worked in your home or the land it stands on are another hugely important resource. This is because they may tell you what property a person owned or leased, who lived in it, what size it was, who owned it before and whether it was copyhold of a manor or freehold. Probate records can also tell us more about the people themselves, confirming and expanding on their relationships, revealing scandals, attitudes and beliefs.

The 1896 will of Benjamin Henry Habberton, proved at the Norwich probate registry, is one such example. House deeds, census returns, trade directories and electoral registers had established he owned the house being investigated in Burnham Market in Norfolk. However, his will revealed more information about him, his relationships and other properties he owned. Two houses with outbuildings and a well were described as previously belonging to an Arthur Coleman, whilst two acres of marsh had been bought from the Bradford Banking Company and another two from a Richard Cowburn. Benjamin went on to name the tenants of three other cottages in the village and provide details of previous owners to several more, including the fact that two cottages and a blacksmith's shop had belonged to his first wife.

The 1908 will of Alice Worton of Berners Street, Oxford Street in Middlesex demonstrates how it can be worthwhile checking wills for occupants of buildings listed on census returns, electoral registers and in trade directories. In it, she states that:

> I declare that the flat at Berners Street in which I now reside though taken for the sake of convenience in the name of the said William James Cook is really mine and I have always paid the rent for it and any liability for rent repairs or otherwise in respect thereof is to be borne by my estate in exoneration of the said William James Cook.

In some cases it is the deeds which lead to relevant wills and administrations as they specifically refer to bequests made. Wills can also lead us to other sources of information such as business records and trade directories. In the case of James Buckingham of 91 Fairfax Road, South Hampstead, in London, he mentions his freehold and leasehold property and specifically mentions his dairyman's business 'carried on there and the goodwill thereof along with all fixtures furniture plate print.' Further bequests include a third share of a hotel at Malvern carried on in partnership with the Misses Brown under the style of Brown and Buckingham.

The 1894 will of John Carter of Stiffkey in Norfolk led to manorial records and the wills of other relatives. In it John describes how he became the administrator of the estate of his daughter-in-law, Caroline Carter, after her death in 1879 and guardian of his grandchildren by her and his son William. John Carter goes on to make bequests to his family of property which he bought in 1865, which were part freehold and part copyhold of the manor of Stiffkey.

Administrations were usually granted where someone died without making a will. These are generally of most use in providing some genealogical detail, such as the names and occupations of the administrator, their bondsman and the deceased.

Inventories can really bring the interior of your home to life. Until 1782, a 'true and perfect inventory of the goods and chattels' of the deceased had to be supplied, although they do not always appear to have been issued with wills. They were usually issued with administrations because there was no other record of what the deceased owned. Even after 1782 many administrations still include inventories for this reason.

Inventories value the furniture and fittings and other belongings inside a building and its outhouses room by room. Inventories can be used to reconstruct how buildings and the rooms in them would have appeared when a person died. *Village Records* by John West (Phillimore, 1997) includes practical examples of how this can be done, accompanied by drawings.

The Archdeaconry of Suffolk inventory of 1667 for John Burlingham of Wattisfield in Suffolk is an example of how such documents can help build up a picture of the family's day to day life. This inventory lists three chairs, three stools, one warming pan, one 'fyre' pan, a pair of tongs, three pieces of pewter, one dripping pan and other goods worth a total of twelve pounds in the hall. In the chamber were one old bed, two old hutches, one old flock bed, one 'shred covlett' and two pairs of sheets worth a total of fifteen pounds. The inventory goes on to describe goods in the buttery and various outhouses.

Legacy duty, or death duty as it is more commonly known, was introduced in 1796. Payments of this tax were entered into estate duty office registers, more commonly known as death duty registers. These registers form part of the collection of Inland Revenue records held at The National Archives.

The information in the death duty registers shows what happened to a person's estate after his or her death and what the estate was really worth, excluding debts and expenses. As a result, death duty registers can include information on both the deceased and beneficiaries such as the names of next-of-kin, even when this detail is missing from a will or administration. Other information given includes details of estates and annuities; where and when probate was granted; family relationships and personal details of beneficiaries; how much each beneficiary was to receive; the conditions of each gift and when and what duty was paid.

However, it is really only from 1815 that the death duty registers begin to contain anything approaching a full record of all grants of probate, as that is when duty had to be paid by everyone except a spouse on any legacies or residue worth over £20. From 1881, all personal property was taxed and from 1894 all property was taxed when estate duty replaced probate duty.

Finding Probate Records

Finding probate records is divided into two time periods, before and after 1858. Before 1858, wills and administrations were generally proved by church courts, of which there were over 250 in England and Wales. However, county boundaries do not necessarily match ecclesiastical ones. For example, some parishes in Suffolk come under the jurisdiction of the Norwich consistory court. In these cases a will may have been proved either there or in a Suffolk archdeaconry court.

As the majority of wills and administrations were granted by local church courts the best place to start looking is in the nearest county record office. They will guide you through the local court system and advise you if records are likely to be found in another area.

You can check which court was most likely to have proved a will in *Probate Jurisdictions: Where To Look For Wills* by Jeremy Gibson & Else Churchill (FFHS, 2002). The LDS 'England Jurisdictions 1851' map can also be used to identify which courts were responsible for particular areas. **http://maps.familysearch.org**

The Prerogative Court of Canterbury (PCC) was the most important of all the church courts as it had overriding jurisdiction over the whole of England and Wales. The PCC records are held at The National Archives, where it is possible to access them in person. The wills have been digitized and can be downloaded for £3.50 each from The National Archives website. Their administrations are not yet online. Many local record offices and family history societies also have copies of the PCC indexes, although some may only refer to people from their areas. **www.nationalarchives.gov.uk**

It is possible to view Welsh wills up to 1858 free online via the National Library of Wales. **www.llgc.org.uk/index.php?id=2**

The Prerogative Court of York (PCY) covered the counties of York, Durham, Northumberland, Westmoreland, Cumberland, Lancashire, Cheshire, Nottinghamshire and the Isle of Man. These are held at the Borthwick Institute of Historical Research, University of York, Heslington, York, YO10 5DD **www.york.ac.uk/inst/bihr**. Indexes to some years can also be found on the Origins Network site **www.origins.net**

As many wills and indexes are on film, you may also be able to order a relevant film through a Latter Day Saints (LDS) Family History Centre. The Society of Genealogists (SoG) has a range of probate indexes and indexes for the whole country. The SoG has also collaborated with the Origins Network to supply many of their indexes and transcripts online for a fee.

A large number of indexes to probate records are widely available through record offices, family history societies, and in some cases on sale, or online. To find a society check the Federation of Family History Societies (FFHS) at **www.ffhs.org.uk**.

An increasing number of organizations are putting digitized images of wills and administrations online. Some are pay-to-view, whilst others are free. These include Find my Past **www.findmypast.co.uk**, Ancestry **www.ancestry.co.uk** and The Genealogist **www.thegenealogist.co.uk**.

Locating probate records from 1858 is very straightforward as a centralized system came into force on 11 January that year. Under the new system the country was divided into areas, each served by a District Registry. Applications for grants of probate could be made either at the Principal Probate Registry (PPR) in London or a district registry office. The PPR holds copies of the original wills from 1858 to the present day for the whole of England and Wales.

Because copies of the locally proved wills were sent to London, a complete set of wills for the whole country, with accompanying indexes from 1858 to within the last six months, are held at the Principal Probate Registry, First Avenue House, High Holborn, London, WC1V 6NP, where you can order copies in person for £6. Copies of the indexes can be also found at many local record offices to at least the 1920s, and online from 1858 to 1966 on Ancestry **www.ancestry.co.uk**.

You can order copies by post, including a four-year search for £6 from the Postal Searches and Copies Department at Leeds District Probate Registry, York House, York Place, Leeds, LS1 2BA. Payment should be made in sterling to 'HMCS'.

The LDS church has film copies of all wills from 1858 to 1925. These can be viewed at the Salt Lake City Library or the London Hyde Park Centre.

You can also order copies of the relevant films to view at an LDS family history centre near you.

If a will or administration was granted locally you may be able to view copies up to the early or mid–1900s free at your local record office. Some include indexes to locally proved wills on their online catalogues.

The National Library of Wales holds indexed copies of Welsh wills from 1858 to 1940. **www.llgc.org.uk**

All death duty registers from 1796 to 1903 are held at The National Archives, Kew. Unfortunately, many of the registers for the 1890s were destroyed by fire and there are no records available after 1903. This is because from that date all death duty records were (and still are) kept for thirty years in case of queries or disputes. Once thirty years have passed, the file is considered closed and is destroyed. Copies of some of the indexes and registers can be found at LDS centres and online at The National Archives and Find my Past website. Further information on using death duty registers can be found in The National Archives research guides on wills. **www.nationalarchives.gov.uk/visit**

Chapter 6

PRESENTATION AND WRITING YOUR HOUSE HISTORY

Once you have finished your research you will want to present it to others. You may have started your research with an idea in mind of what you want to do with the information you gather. However, many people simply start off by wanting to know more about the history of their home, then once they have completed their research or got as far as they feel able or want to, start to ask either how they are going to share that with others, or present it in an interesting manner. There will also come a point for many people at which they decide to stop researching, even though it is possible that more could be found. The beauty of researching the past is that it doesn't go away and you can always pick up your research and start again.

Although this section comes at the end of this book, there is an argument for writing up what you find as you go along, or at least stopping after certain stages to do so. Doing this often helps with identifying gaps in your knowledge or contradictions. It can also assist with deciding how much further you want to go and whether that might be possible.

Whilst it is crucial that you record all your findings, a list which simply details what you did and found (or not) is not likely to be of great interest to those not involved in the research process. Even then it doesn't really bring the story of your home to life, engage others or create that 'ooh, that's interesting' reaction in others. The most popular options are to write a presentation piece in a folder, a written book or booklet, create a photo story montage or a poster, or put the information on a website.

Most people tend to start their presentation of what they have uncovered by putting everything in. I personally start this way so I know I have all the crucial information. I then start to edit and summarize so that it becomes a story rather than just a list of facts.

If you plan to create an in-depth written history you will probably want to tell the story of your house from the past coming forwards. If you want to describe how you went about your research then your writing is more likely to start from the present and move back in time. A short introduction which summarizes the history will set the scene and help others keep track of main events and characters. This is also where you can describe your research process, mention any problems encountered or anomalies and state whether or not you have exhausted all possible sources, or if more research might be possible. I personally like to include a separate list of all sources used in whatever type of presentation I create.

Whilst writing a book is often what people hope to achieve, it can be laborious and time-consuming. A series of snapshots which stand alone will allow you to feel you have achieved a finished piece of work. These can be strung together into one large piece as times goes on.

If you want others to read and take interest in what you produce then it must be interesting. A good history will provide an interesting historical biography of your ancestors that will entertain and inform. Many of the house histories I have seen are dull because they simply concentrate on recording names and dates from documents in a list format linked by sentences. Others are so vague you are left searching for factual details, and wondering where the information came from.

Telling the story of your house should, like a good family history, biography or autobiography, aim to answer the journalist's basic questions: Who? What? When? Where? Why and How? Every story has a beginning, middle and end. Decide what yours are going to be. This will give you a structure to work to, but be prepared to change it as the 'story' takes on a life of its own.

Examine the geographical area. Use maps to determine exactly where they lived. Was it mountainous, near the sea, crossed by rivers and canals? The separate section on building up knowledge of your local area has lots of tips on where to find out more about the geography and history of an area. As well as helping you discover more about your property, adding in the local and national events that will have affected the people who lived in your home helps bring its story to life.

National and local newspapers will tell you what was happening nationally and internationally, as well as providing an insight into the prevailing social and political attitudes. Use sources such as trade directories, newspapers, village histories and fiction from the time period you are writing about (Dickens, Austen, the Brontë sisters, Thackeray and so on). Keep a critical eye to make sure your information is from authoritative sources, i.e. an established historian or someone who provides a list of sources and bibliography that gives you confidence in their research.

One of my favourite techniques is to use a timeline, or a series of short timelines, as in the example below. Another is to use existing material from other sources. I also like to use quotes from contemporary sources, including fiction. For example, when writing a piece about the village of Mainsforth in County Durham I used a quote from the historian Robert

Surtees (1779–1834): 'God has placed me in paradise'. Or, when writing about five different houses in Burnham Market in Norfolk, I used the diaries and memoirs of Elizabeth Helsham, which have been reproduced online by one of her descendants. Not only do they mention some of the people who worked, owned and lived in some of the properties, but she also describes social gatherings, local scandals, day-to-day life and national events.

Caistor Hall Timeline

National and Local Events	Dates	Caistor Hall and Caistor St Edmund
	1795–97	Caistor Hall is built
	1795	Estate Map for Caistor St Edmund compiled. No building shown on the hall site
Edward Jenner develops smallpox vaccine	1796	Horatio Dashwood enters Pembroke College, Cambridge
Faden's Map of Norfolk published	1797	Faden's Map of Norfolk shows a building on the Caistor Hall site
	1798–1813	Jarrett Dashwood is rector of Caistor St Edmund
Income tax introduced	1799	Horatio Dashwood – future owner of Caistor Hall – graduates from Pembroke College, Cambridge
	1800	Birth of Harriet Louisa Warren in Caistor – future wife of Horatio Dashwood, lady of the manor and owner of Caistor Hall
Act of Union unites Britain	1801	
First national census taken	1802	First Dashwood entry in the Caistor St Edmund parish registers
		Horatio Dashwood is ordained as a deacon

Britain declares war on France	1803	Horatio Dashwood becomes a priest in Caistor St Edmund
Death of Norfolk diarist, Parson James Woodforde of Weston Longville		
Battle of Trafalgar – Norfolk-born Lord Admiral Nelson dies	1805	Enclosure Map drawn up for Caistor St Edmund. Buildings shown on the hall site

Quotes from fictional authors and poets who have written about the same town, village, area or county, or copies of paintings or drawings and sketches from artists can also add colour. Don't forget to use copies of documents you have gathered (copyright and reproduction rights permitting). When writing the story of a house in Needham Market in Suffolk I used copies of sketches of Suffolk by locally-born artist Samuel Read (1816–83) to illustrate it.

One wonderful example of a house history which combines all these elements is *A Commoner's Cottage*. Written by Frances Mountford in 1992 it is the history of her house in Surrey over four hundred years. It beautifully blends sketches, snippets of local history, details about clothing through the ages, life in the village, explanations of legal terms in documents and so on in an accessible and engaging manner. The people who lived in her home come to life.

Another very easy way to add background interest is to include summaries of the information you have gathered from local histories, trade and post office directories and gazetteers. These provide potted histories of parishes, towns, villages and histories across the UK.

There is no right or wrong style; only what works for you. However, you might want to consider the following. Who are you writing for? If you are writing for others, what they are expecting to learn from your book? Use plain English and avoid slang as it will date quickly.

At this point a certain amount of imaginative or creative writing might be needed. However, you need to be careful not to claim things happened unless you are sure they did. Using words such as 'probably', 'might', 'presumably' and 'possibly' are helpful here.

True creative writing about historical events and documentary evidence does not mean inventing something that didn't happen or rewriting history. Instead it allows you to breathe life into that piece of evidence or document. Visualize stages in the history of your home and the people who lived in it as a series of snapshots in time and space. You can use other visual aids such as postcards of the area, copies of paintings, old maps, copies of drawings from newspapers and history books.

I cannot tell you how to write or what to do if you get stuck. But, if inspiration is lacking, start with a simple list of key events for a time period, person or event. Focusing on an important episode allows you to look back at what happened before, and forward to what would happen next. You can then gradually build on these points by adding more detail such as where people lived and worked.

There are large numbers of guides on writing available to buy or online. However, I would suggest focussing on those aimed at the family history market and at historical biographies, as these address many of the issues you will experience when writing about a house. John Titford's various guides on writing and publishing your family history are extremely good. A writing group or course may also give you confidence and tips on how to approach it.

Remember that your aim is to create a written history of the home you have researched. This means that the most important steps are to start, carry on and finish.

Chapter 7

DIRECTORY OF RESOURCES

Organizations

Borthwick Institute of Historical Research

University of York, Heslington, York, YO10 5DD
www.york.ac.uk/inst/bihr

Blue Plaques Team

English Heritage, 23 Savile Row, London, W1S 2ET
www.english-heritage.org.uk/blueplaques
English Heritage Blue Plaque scheme

British Association for Local History

PO Box, Somersal Herbert, Ashbourne, Derbyshire, DE6 5WH
www.balh.co.uk

British Library

96 Euston Road, London, NW1 2DB
www.bl.uk
Range of records including maps and electoral registers

British Record Society

C/o James Henderson, Rosemount, Riggs Place, Cupar, KY15 5JA
www.britishrecordsociety.org

British Telecom Archives

Third Floor, Holborn Telephone Exchange, 268–270 High Holborn, London, WC1V 7EE
www.bt.com/archivesonline

Chiltern Open Air Museum

Newland Park, Gorelands Lane, Chalfont St Giles, Buckinghamshire, HP8 4AB
www.coam.org.uk
Re-erects historic buildings

Comisiwn Brenhinol Henebion Cymru – the Royal Commission on the Ancient and Historical Monuments of Wales

Plas Crug, Aberystwyth, Ceredigion, SY23 1NJ

Crawley New Town Museum

Goffs Park House, Old Horsham Road, Southgate, Crawley, West Sussex, RH11 8PE
www.crawleymuseums.org

General Registry Office

Postal Application Section, PO Box 2, Southport, Merseyside, PR8 27D
www.gro.gov.uk
Birth, Marriage and Death Certificates

Guildhall Library

Aldermanbury, London, EC2P 2EJ
www.cityoflondon.gov.uk/guildhalllibrary
Business; apprenticeship; guild; electoral registers; poll books; fire insurance and land tax records

House of Lords Record Office

Palace of Westminster, London, SW1A 0PW
www.parliament.uk

Hulton Getty Picture Collection

Unique House, 21–31 Woodfield Road, London, W9 2BA
Images dating from the 1800s

Institute of Historical Research

University of London
Senate House, Malet Street, London, WC1 7HU
Holds copies of poll books

Land Registry

Earle House, Portland Street, Hull, HU2 8JN
www.landreg.gov.uk

Letchworth Garden City Museum

296 Norton Way South, Letchworth, Hertfordshire, SG6 1SU
www.gardencitymuseum.org

London Metropolitan Archives

40 Northampton Road, London, EC1R 0HB
www.cityoflondon.gov.uk/lma

London School of Economics (LSE) Archives Division

Archives and Rare Books, 10 Portugal Street, London, WC2A 2HD
http://booth.lse.ac.uk
Booth's poverty maps

London Topographical Society

17 The Avenue, Northwood, London, HA6 2NJ
www.topsoc.org

Middlesex Registry of Deeds

London Metropolitan Archives, 40 Northampton Road, London, EC1R 0HB

Modern Records Centre

Warwick University, Coventry, CV4 7AL
Collections relating to motor manufacturing, trade unions and businesses

Museum of English Rural Life

University of Reading, PO BOX 229, Whiteknights, Reading, RG6 6AG
www.merl.org.uk
Holds records of farms, agricultural engineers and related businesses

Museum of Science and Industry

Liverpool Road, Manchester, M3 4JP
Includes records of many businesses in the North-West

Milton Keynes Living Archive

The Old Bath House, 205 Stratford Road, Wolverton, Milton Keynes, MK12 5RL
www.livingarchive.org.uk

National Library of Wales

Aberystwyth, Ceredigion, Wales, SY23 3BU
www.llgc.org.uk

National Monuments Record Centre (NMR)

Great Western Village, Kemble Drive, Swindon, SN2 2GZ
www.english-heritage.org.uk/professional/archives-and-collections/nmr
Archives and photographic collections, including Royal Commission on Historical Monuments (RCHME) and English Heritage archives.

National Maritime Museum

Manuscripts Section, London, SE10 9NF
www.nmm.ac.uk
Information on shipbuilding companies

Office for National Statistics

Segesworth Road, Titchfield, Fareham, Hampshire, PO15 5RR
www.statistics.gov.uk
Current electoral registers

Ordnance Survey

Romsey Road, Southampton, Hampshire, SO16 4OU
www.ordnancesurvey.co.uk
Free online access to many maps

Port Sunlight Museum & Garden Village

23 King George's Drive, Port Sunlight, CH62 5DX
www.portsunlightvillage.com

Principal Probate Registry

First Avenue House, High Holborn, London, WC1V 6NP

Public Record Office for Northern Ireland (PRONI)

2 Titanic Boulevard, Belfast, BT3 9HQ
www.proni.gov.uk

Royal Geographic Society

1 Kensington Gore, London, SW7 2AR
www.rgs.org
Ordnance Survey maps

Society of Genealogists

14 Charterhouse Buildings, Goswell Road, London, EC1M 7B
www.sog.org.uk
Range of Indexes, transcripts and records

The National Archives

Ruskin Avenue, Kew, Richmond, Surrey, TW9 4DU
www.nationalarchives.gov.uk

Tyne and Wear Archives

Blandford House, Blandford Square, Newcastle upon Tyne, NE1 4JA
www.tyneandweararchives.org.uk
Holds information on shipbuilding companies

Victoria and Albert Museum

Archive of Art and Design, 23 Blythe Road, London, W14 0QX
Holds archives of many manufacturing firms

Weald and Downland Open Air Museum

Chichester, West Sussex PO18 0EU
www.wealddown.co.uk
Over 45 historic buildings from the thirteenth century to Victorian

West Stow Anglo-Saxon Village

Ickingham Road, West Stow, Bury St Edmunds, Suffolk, IP28 6HG
www.weststow.org

Yorkshire Registry of Deeds

Wakefield, Newstead Road, Wakefield, Yorkshire, WF1 2DE
www.archives.wyjs.org.uk

Websites

www.nationalarchives.gov.uk/a2a Access to Archives (A2A). Database of catalogues contributed by record offices
www.alangodfreymaps.co.uk Alan Godfrey Maps
www.ancestry.co.uk Ancestry. Includes birth, marriage and death indexes; census returns; parish records; business records; directories; phone books
www.archivemaps.com Archive Maps
www.archiveswales.org.uk/index Archive Wales. Introductory guide to Welsh house history research
www.nationalarchives.gov.uk/archon ARCHON. Online directory of archive repositories
www.bbc.co.uk/history/trail BBC History
www.bbc.co.uk/history/society_culture/architecture_01.shtml BBC's Concise History of British Architecture
www.berkshireenclosure.org.uk Berkshire enclosure maps and awards
www.bodley.ox.ac.uk/guides/maps/link.frme Bodleian Library map collection
www.bricksandbrass.co.uk/house_dating_tool.php Bricks and Brass dating tool
www.british-history.ac.uk British History Online
www.britishmuseum.co.uk British Museum

www.britishnewspaperarchive.co.uk British Newspaper Archive
www.buildinghistory.org Building History
www.bucks.gov.uk/bcc/museum/ea_buckinghamshire_photos.page Centre for Buckinghamshire Studies photographic collection
www.buildinghistory.org/maps.shtml Building History. History of mapping
www.burkes-peerage.net Burke's Peerage and Burke's Landed Gentry
www.cam.ac.uk Cambridge University
www.cassinimaps.co.uk Cassini Maps
http://cityark.medway.gov.uk City Ark. Medway area in Kent archives
www.cyndislist.com Cyndi's List. Family and local history links
www.nationalarchives.gov.uk/domesday Domesday Book at The National Archives – searchable map at: **http://labs.nationalarchives.gov.uk/wordpress**
http://domesday.pase.ac.uk Domesday mapping project by Prosopography of Anglo-Saxon England (PASE)
www.english-heritage.org.uk/viewfinder English Heritage. Database of photographs and Survey of London
www.english-heritage.org.uk/professional/protection/process/national-heritage-list-for-england English Heritage and Royal Photographic Society. Photographs of listed buildings
www.eroll.co.uk/?engine=adwords!7308&keyword=Electoral+Roll&match_type Eroll. Last years electoral registers
www.exploringsurreyspast.org.uk Exploring Surrey's Past
www.fachrs.com Family and Community Research Society (FACHRS). Focussing on Victorian period
www.familysearch.org Family Search
www.fadensmapofnorfolk.co.uk Faden's 1797 map of Norfolk
www.fadensmapoflondon.co.uk Faden's 1788 25 miles around London map
www.genealogical.co.uk/index.html Family and Local History Handbook
www.fffhs.org.uk Federation of Family History Societies
www.findmypast.co.uk Includes birth, marriage and death indexes; business records; census returns; parish records; electoral registers
www.bl.uk/collections/map_fire_insurance.html Fire insurance maps at British Library
www.foxearth.org.uk Foxearth and District Local History Society
www.francisfrith.co.uk Francis Frith photographic archive
www.freebmd.org.uk FreeBMD. Free indexes to birth, marriage and death indexes
www.freecen.org.uk FreeCEN. Free indexes and transcripts to census returns
www.freereg.co.uk FreeREG

www.ukgenealogyarchives.com Genealogy Supplies – census, directories etc

www.genealogysupplies.com Genealogy Supplies – census, directories etc

http://freepages.genealogy.rootsweb.ancestry.com/~genmaps/index.html Genmaps

www.georgiangroup.org.uk Georgian Group. Information on Georgian buildings

www.gro.gov.uk/gro/content/certificates General Registry Office. Certificate Ordering Service

www.genuki.org.uk GENUKI. Family and local history umbrella site

www.port.ac.uk/research/ghhgis Great Britain Historical Geographical Information System (GIS). Details localities from historical sources

www.hearthtax.org.uk Hearth Tax indexes

www.hiddenhousehistory.co.uk Hidden House History. Timeline and list of resources

www.historicaldirectories.org Historical Directories. Free access to trade directories

www.historypin.com History Pin. Interactive website

www.hodskinsonsmapofsuffolk.co.uk Digitized redrawing of Hodskinson's 1783 map of Suffolk

www.hydeparkfhc.org Hyde Park Family History Centre

www.ideal-homes.org.uk Ideal Homes: History of South-West London suburbs

http://gale.cengage.co.uk/iln Illustrated London News

www.imagesofengland.org.uk Images of England. Lists all listed buildings

www.letchworthgardencity.net Letchworth Garden City. History of Letchworth

www.lincstothepast.com/help/about-lincs-to-the-past Lincs to the Past

www.lincolnshire.gov.uk/index Lincolnshire. Link to Local Studies Library catalogue and photographs

www.localhistories.org Local Histories. Lists local groups

www.londonancestor.com London Lives. Includes 1885 Boundary maps

www.london-gazette.co.uk London Gazette

www.londonlives.org London Lives. Free searchable collection of manuscripts from eight archives

www.lookingatbuildings.org Looking at Buildings. Architectural guides via Pevsner guides and Buildings Books Trust

www.nationalarchives.gov.uk/mdr Manorial Documents Register

www.nationalarchives.gov.uk/mdr/aboutapps/mdr/about.htm Guide to manorial records from The National Archives

www.lancs.ac.uk/fass/projects/manorialrecords/using/index.htm Manorial records guide from University of Lancaster

www.maphistory.info Map History
www.mapseeker.co.uk Map Seeker
www.fordham.edu/halsall/mod/modsbook20.html Modern History Sourcebook
www.motco.com Motco. Sells topographical prints and maps
www.multimap.com Multimap. Sells historical maps
http://homepage.ntlworld.com/geogdata/ngw/places.htm National Gazetteer of Wales
www.nationalarchives.gov.uk/nra National Register of Archives. Location of archives across the country
www.nationaltrust.org.uk National Trust. Information on different historical building styles **www.newlanark.org** New Lanark model village
www.old-maps.co.uk Old Maps
www.genuki.org.uk/indexes/OPC.html Online Parish Clerk schemes via GENUKI
www.british-history.ac.uk/map.aspx Ordnance Survey maps free at British History Online
www.nls.uk/digitallibrary/map Ordnance Surveys for County Durham, 1847-95
www.origins.net Orgins Network. Includes will indexes
www.ox.ac.uk Oxford University
www.parishchest.com Parish Chest. Publications for sale
www.nationalarchives.gov.uk/palaeography Paleography online tutorial
www.pastscape.org.uk PastScape. Information on archaeological and architectural records
www.pen-and-sword.co.uk Pen & Sword Books. Local history publisher
www.pepysdiary.com Pepys Diary
www.periodproperty.co.uk/information.shtml Period Property. Information on architectural features
www.phillimore.co.uk Phillimore. Local history publisher
www.genuki.org.uk/big/eng/RegOffice Local registry offices via GENUKI
www.cefnpennar.com/1873index.htm Welsh Returns of Owners of Land, 1873-76
www.uk-genealogy.org.uk/cgi-bin/DB/search.cgi?action=loadDB&DB=1 Eleven Counties of Returns of Owners of Land, 1873-76
http://seax.essexcc.gov.uk SEAX. Essex record office catalogue
www.origins.org.uk/genuki/NFK/places/s/sedgeford/census1829.shtml Sedgeford 1829 census transcript
http://soc.org.uk Society of Cartographers
www.spab.org.uk Society for the Protection of Ancient Buildings

www.suttonpublishing.co.uk Sutton Publishing. Local history publisher
www.bodley.ox.ac.uk.ilej *The Builder*, 1842–1966. First 10 volumes
www.thegenealogist.co.uk The Genealogist. Includes parish register transcripts, wills and Returns of Owners of Land
www.victoriacountyhistory.ac.uk Victoria County History series
www.visionofbritain.org.uk Vision of Britain. Historical information over 200-year period, including maps and gazetteers
maps of waggonways and mines Waggonways in County Durham
www.zetica.com Zetica. Maps of unexploded ordnance
http://maps.familysearch.org England Jurisdictions 1851
www.192.com Electoral registers

Select Bibliography

Anthony, Adolph, *Tracing your Home's History*, Collins, 2006
Alcock, Nat, *Old Title Deeds*, Phillimore, 2001
Barratt, Nick, *Guide to Your Ancestors' Lives*, Pen and Sword, 2010
Barratt, Nick, *Tracing The History of Your House*, 2nd Ed., The National Archives, 2006
Beech, Geraldine and Mitchell, Rose, *Maps for Family and Local Historians: The Records of the Tithe, Valuation Office and National Farm Surveys of England and Wales, 1836–1943*, 2nd Ed., The National Archives, 2004
Boog-Watson, E.J. and Caruthers, J.I., *Houses*, Oxford University Press, 1958
Breckton, Bill and Palmer, Jeffrey, *Tracing the History of Houses*, Countryside Books, 2nd Ed., 2000
Bristow, Joy, *The Local Historian's Glossary of Words and Terms*, 3rd Ed., Countryside Books, 2001
Chapman, Colin, *PRE–1841 Censuses and Population Listings*, Dursley, 1990
Clement, Eunice, *The Story of the New Towns*, Crawley Museum Society, 2008
Cobbold, Richard, *Biography of a Victorian Village, 1860*, Batsford, 1977
Darley, Gillian, *Villages of Vision*, Five Leaves Publications, 2007
Davidson Cragoe, Carol, *How To Read Buildings: A crash course in architecture*, Herbert Press, 2008
Dietsch, Deborah K., *Architecture for Dummies*, John Wiley & Sons, 2007
Gibson, J., *The Hearth Tax and other Stuart Tax Lists*, FFHS, 1996
Gibson, Jeremy and Churchill, Else, *Probate Jurisdictions: Where To Look For Wills*, 5th Ed., FFHS, 2002
Gibson, J. and Rogers, C., *Electoral Registers since 1832*, FFHS, 1989
Dowdy, Mac, Miller, Judith and Austin, David, *Be Your Own House History Detective*, BBC Books, 1997
Harris, Richard, *Discovering Timber-Framed Buildings*, 3rd Ed., Shire Publications, 2006

Hey, David, *The Oxford Companion to Family and Local History*, 2nd Ed., Oxford University Press, 2010
Kain, R.J.P. & Oliver, R.R., *The Tithe Maps of England and Wales*, Cambridge University Press, 1995
Kain, R.J.P. et al., *The Enclosure Maps of England and Wales, 1595–1918*, Cambridge University Press, 2004
Lloyd, David W., *The Making of English Towns. 2000 years of evolution*, Victor Gollancz Ltd., 1992
Mount, Harry, *Lust for Window Sills. A Lover's Guide to British Buildings from Portcullis to Pebble-Dash*, Little, Brown, 2009
Mountford, Frances, *A Commoner's Cottage*, Alan Sutton, 1995
Nicholson, Graham and Fawcett, Jane, *The Village in History*, Weidenfeld and Nicolson with the National Trust, 1988
Norfolk Historic Buildings Group Journals
Oliver, R., *Ordnance Survey Maps a Concise Guide for Historians*, Charles Close Society for the Study of Ordnance Survey Maps, 2005
Pevsner, Nikolaus. County architectural guides. See **www.pevsner.co.uk**
Richardson, John, *The Local Historian's Encyclopedia*, Historical Publications, 1974
Softley, Barbara, *Within the Bounds: Sidbury Parish Past and Present*, West Country Books, 1998
Style, Colin and O-lan, *House Histories for Beginners*, Phillimore, 2006
Stuart, Denis, *Latin for Local and Family Historians*, Phillimore, 1995
Tate, W.E. *The Parish Chest*, Phillimore, 1983
Titford, John *Writing up Your Family History*, Countryside Books, 2003 (Kindle version, 2011)
West, John *Village Records*, 3rd Ed., Phillimore, 1997
Yorke, Trevor, *British Architectural Styles: An Easy Reference Guide*, Countryside Books, 2008
Yorke, Trevor, *Tracing the History of Villages*, Countryside Books, 2001

INDEX